THE
OEDIPUS
COMPLEX

The Free Press of Glencoe

WILLIAM N. STEPHENS

THE
OEDIPUS
COMPLEX

CROSS-CULTURAL EVIDENCE

with a Chapter on Kin-Avoidances
in Collaboration with Roy G. D'Andrade

ACKNOWLEDGMENTS

THIS BOOK WAS MADE POSSIBLE BY a two-year post-doctoral fellowship granted by the Elizabeth McCormick Memorial Fund of Chicago, to which I am greatly indebted. I also must thank the William F. Milton Fund of Harvard, for paying the research expenses.

The research was tremendously facilitated by two great collections of ethnographies: The Human Relations Area Files and Harvard's Peabody Museum Library.

Of the many people who were of help to me, I must first acknowledge my debt to three of my professors at Harvard: Dr. Wesley Allinsmith, Dr. George W. Goethals, and Dr. John W. M. Whiting. Secondly, thanks are due to the authors of previous cross-cultural studies, whose ratings have been used in this work; their names are listed in Chapter 3. Third, I want to thank my diligent cross-cultural coders: Dr. Lindsey C. Churchill, Mrs. Roberta Churchill, Mrs. Diane D'Andrade, Mr. John K. Harley, Mrs. Cynthia Landauer, Mrs. Constance Pilz, Mrs. Judith W. Stephens, and Mrs. Katherine Wilson.

Three people made a special contribution to the design and presentation of these studies: Dr. Roy G. D'Andrade, coauthor of the chapter on kin-avoidances; Dr. Lindsey C. Churchill, statistical consultant on all studies; and Mr. Harry A. Scarr, the principal manuscript critic.

v

Finally, appreciation is due to the anthropologists who, risking life and health in strange and distant places, gathered the ethnographic data that are the factual foundation for all studies to be reported.

For permission to use quotations, thanks are due to the following: to Columbia University Press for permission to quote from "Experimentelle Traeume," by Karl Schroetter, which is translated into English in *Organization and Pathology of Thought*, by David Rapaport; to Yale University Press for permission to quote from *Smoke from Their Fires*, by Clellan S. Ford and from *The Cheyenne Indians*, by G. B. Grinnell; to the University of Minnesota Press for permission to quote from *The People of Alor* (copyright 1944) by Cora DuBois; to the University of Chicago Press for permission to quote from *The Tarahumara*, by W. C. Bennett and R. M. Zingg (copyright 1935 by the University of Chicago), from *Chiricahua and Mescalero Apache Texts*, by Harry Hoijer (copyright 1938 by the University of Chicago), and from *An Apache Life Way*, by Morris E. Opler (copyright 1941 by the University of Chicago); to The Macmillan Company for permission to quote from *The Golden Bough*, by Sir James G. Frazer, and from *When the Tree Flowered*, by John G. Neihardt; to Oxford University Press for permission to quote from *Both Sides of Buka Passage*, by Beatrice M. Blackwood, from *The Web of Kinship among the Tallensi*, by Meyer Fortes, and from "Nyakusa Kinship," by Monica Wilson, in A. R. Radcliffe-Brown and D. Forde, *African Systems of Kinship and Marriage;* to the University of Michigan Press for permission to quote from *Araucanian Culture in Transition*, by Mischa Titiev; to International Universities Press for permission to quote from "Some Aspects of Navaho Infancy and Childhood," by Clyde Kluckhohn, in Geza Roheim, *Psychoanalysis and the Social Sciences*, Vol. I; to Alfred A. Knopf for permission to quote from *Island of Bali*, by Miguel Covarrubias; to Jules Henry, The American Orthopsychiatric Association, and Alfred A. Knopf for permission to quote from *Doll Play of Pilaga Indian Children*, by Jules and Zunia Henry; to The Bernice P. Bishop Museum for permission to quote from *Southern Lau, Fiji: An Ethnography*, by Laura Thompson; to the University of California Press for permission to quote from *The Eastern Timbira*, by Curt Nimenaju; to Holt, Rinehart, and Winston for permission to quote from "The Function of Male Initiation Rites at Puberty," by John W. M. Whiting, Richard Kluckhohn, and Albert Anthony, in E. E. Maccoby, T. M. Newcomb, and E. L. Hartley, *Readings in Social Psychology*, Third Ed.; to the W. B. Saunders Company and The Institute for Sex Research for permission to quote from *Sexual Behavior in the Human Male*, by A. C. Kinsey, W. B. Pomeroy, and C. E. Martin; to The Hogarth Press for permission to quote from *Contributions to Psycho-Analysis: 1921–1945*, by Melanie Klein; to David Higham Associates for permission to quote from *Himalayan Village*, by Geoffrey Gorer; to Routledge and Kegan Paul and to W. W. Norton and Company for permission to quote from *Totem and Taboo*, by Sigmund Freud, and from *The Psychoanalytic Theory of Neurosis*, by Otto Fenichel.

CONTENTS

ACKNOWLEDGMENTS   v

1. Diluted Marriage   1
2. The Oedipus Complex Hypothesis   16
3. The Cross-Cultural Method   49
4. Sexual Problems   77
5. Menstrual Taboos   85
6. Kin-Avoidance   124
7. Initiations, Totemism, Sorcery, and Fear of Others   151
8. The Oedipus Complex Syndrome   172
9. Polygyny and Mother-Child Households   175
10. Conclusion   182

Appendixes

I. Independence of Cases   189
II. The Sex Anxiety Index   200

III.   Coding and Rating Menstrual Taboos   206
IV.   Coding and Rating Kin-Avoidance   213
V.   Coding the Variable "Breasts Not Sexual Stimuli"   227
VI.   Coding the Variables Related to Father's Role   230
VII.   Coding Folklore   234
VIII.   Ratings of Diluted Marriage Variables   244

Bibliographies

Ethnographic Bibliography   249
General Bibliography   262
INDEX   267

Then he had also killed this one who would not permit people to live. Then Child of the Water returned to his mother. "I have also killed the Bull who kills with his eyes," he said to her.

Then White Painted Woman, feeling very happy and saying, "That is good!" danced around and around.

—from *Chiricahua and Mescalero Apache Texts*, by Harry Hoijer

A long while ago before the hoop was broken and the people still were good, there was a right way and a wrong way to do everything, and something bad would happen if you did the wrong way. I have told you how a man could not speak to his daughter-in-law and she could not speak to him, even when they lived in the same tepee. If they had to say something to each other, they said it to the son's mother and she said it to the other one. Neither could the two eat together. It was the same way with a brother and sister when they were no longer little children. They respected each other so much that if they had to say something to each other they would say it to their mother and she would tell it. These ways were good for the people, but now there is nothing good at all. . . .

—from *When the Tree Flowered*, by John G. Neihardt

. . . Someone then strikes him from behind and when he turns his head to see who has struck him, his foreskin is seized and in two movements cut off by the Lion Man.

—from *The Function of Male Initiation Ceremonies at Puberty*, by John Whiting, Richard Kluckhohn, and Albert Anthony

". . . Wives are like our mothers. When we were small, our mothers fed us. When we are grown, our wives cook for us. If there is something good, they keep it in the pot until we come home. When we were small, we slept with our mothers. When we are grown, we sleep with our wives. Sometimes when we are grown, we wake in the night and call our wives 'mother.' . . ."

—from *The People of Alor*, by Cora DuBois

THE
OEDIPUS
COMPLEX

1

DILUTED MARRIAGE

Stas ?
where he got data? → validity → did't
do it honey
what if existing data is
faulty

THIS BOOK DOES TWO THINGS:
it describes a phenomenon, and it proposes a hypothesis to
account for the phenomenon.

The hypothesis is described in Chapter 2. It is based on a
Freudian concept: the Oedipus complex. The hypothesis is
not merely proposed; it is actually tested. That is, several
parts of the phenomenon were *predicted,* on the basis of the
Oedipus complex hypothesis, *before* the facts were known.
Essentially, this book is organized as a series of tests of the
Oedipus complex hypothesis.

In later chapters the hypothesis will be formulated and
then tested. I will devote the opening chapter to a general
view of the phenomenon itself—how it appears, what it is
composed of.

The phenomenon is a network of correlations between
cross-cultural variables. Each variable represents one or sev-

1

eral customs, found in some primitive societies. These customs appear to be of two types. On the one hand are conditions that seem to represent a "dilution" of the husband-wife relationship: the post partum sex taboo, polygyny, and mother-child households. The other variables, I feel, reflect Oedipal problems. They are: menstrual taboos, kin-avoidances, initiation ceremonies, totemism, sorcery, as well as a variety of fearful superstitions and restrictions pertaining to sex.

The three "diluted marriage variables" seem to represent a highly patterned "diluted marriage complex." That is, the three are very strongly associated with each other. Most societies (in my samples) that have a high proportion of polygynous marriages also have a large proportion of mother-child households, and observe the long post partum sex taboo. Monogamous societies (in my samples) rarely have a high proportion of mother-child households, and seldom observe the long post partum sex taboo. Individual scores on these three diluted marriage variables are given in Appendix VIII.

Throughout this book, the post partum sex taboo will be emphasized and the other two, polygyny and mother-child household, will be more-or-less ignored. I shall describe how the long post partum sex taboo is associated with menstrual taboos, kin-avoidances, etc., and I shall discuss these findings. To have a proper perspective on these findings, the fact should be kept in mind that the post partum sex taboo is only one of the variables in this tightly knit diluted marriage complex. Most statements about the post partum sex taboo (i.e., reporting correlational findings) could also be applied to the other two: frequency of polygyny, and frequency of mother-child households.

At this point we should examine further these diluted marriage variables.

The Post Partum Sex Taboo

The post partum sex taboo is a rule against a woman having sexual intercourse with anyone after she has given birth to a child. The "variable" measured here is the *duration* of the post partum sex taboo. In some primitive societies it is very long; a woman must remain sexually continent for several years after giving birth. In other societies the taboo is very short—lasting just a few weeks. In still others, the taboo is nonexistent.

A very long post partum sex taboo appears to be a common feature of primitive societies. It characterizes about half of the societies in my cross-cultural samples. Its geographic distribution is rather uneven. It seems to occur frequently in Negro Africa, Melanesia, and western North America; in Asia, it appears to be relatively rare.

The ratings of the duration of the post partum sex taboo were made (that is, conceived and supervised) by John W. M. Whiting and Richard Kluckhohn.[1] They rated the post par-

1. The ratings were originally made for a cross-cultural study of initiation ceremonies, done in collaboration with Albert Anthony (Whiting, Kluckhohn, and Anthony, 1958). The crucial discovery in this entire area was made by these three authors. They rated the duration of the post partum sex taboo, proposed a hypothesis as to its effect (the hypothesis was that the long post partum sex taboo intensifies the Oedipus complex), and then tested the hypothesis by correlating the duration of the post partum sex taboo with the presence of initiations for boys. My studies represent, in large part, a follow-through on their discovery. However, "my Oedipus complex hypothesis" is considerably different from "their Oedipus complex hypothesis"; I have a different conception of the Oedipus complex, and its causes and effects.

tum sex taboo as *long* when it lasted at least one year. On this basis, they divided their sample of primitive societies into two groups: societies with a *long* post partum sex taboo (in which, customarily, a woman remains sexually continent for at least a year after giving birth); and societies with a *short* post partum sex taboo (in which, customarily, the post partum sex taboo lasts less than one year). In making the cutting point one year, they capitalized on a measurement advantage of the post partum sex taboo: its distribution (as to duration) is bimodal. For some reason, the duration of the taboo is rarely in the neighborhood of one year. Usually, it is either very long (lasting a year and a half or more) or very short (lasting just a few weeks or months). With just a few exceptions, there is a big difference, in respect to duration of the taboo, between societies rated *long* and societies rated *short*.

The long post partum sex taboo has several obvious consequences for the mother who must observe it. Her children are spaced. During the time she cares for a new baby, she is sexually continent. Also, this period of continence recurs with each birth. Her adult life is divided into alternating phases of roughly equal duration: first a period of sexual activity, then a period of continence, then another period of sexual activity, then another period of continence, and so on, until she ceases to bear children. We might infer that, according to the phase she is in, she is first relatively husband-centered, then relatively child-centered, then again husband-centered, and so on. I impute to the long post partum sex taboo this effect: it makes the mother more sexually interested in her children and more sexually arousing to them. In Chapter 2 this assumption is examined in detail.

As to *why* many primitive peoples insist on this long sex taboo, we can only guess. One reason may be that, since it acts to space births, it is beneficial for the health of mothers and young children. John Whiting has pointed out that the long post partum sex taboo is largely concentrated in: (1) the disease-ridden tropics (in South America, Africa, New Guinea, and Oceania); (2) hunting-nomad groups, who must be continually on the move (North America, and perhaps Australia). (J. W. M. Whiting, personal communication.) Maybe one reason for its occurrence is its value for individual and group survival.

Polygyny

Only a small number (about 30 per cent) of the primitive societies in my samples are strictly monogamous. Most of them allow polygyny. It is my impression that, in most primitive societies, polygyny is more than "allowed." It is preferred—at least by men. For men, it is the ideal and privileged state, a mark of success and prestige. However, even in the polygynous societies not all men are blessed with two or more wives; some men have only one. Therefore, the *variable* here is the *percentage* of polygynous marriages within a society. There have been two attempts to measure this variable, one by G. P. Murdock (1957) and the other by J. W. M. Whiting and Roy G. D'Andrade. I shall use the more recent ratings, by Whiting and D'Andrade. The ratings are rough estimates of the percentage of *married women* who share their husbands with co-wives. The ratings divide societies into three groups: high polygyny (at least 40 per cent of all married women in the society are polygynous);

low polygyny (between 1 per cent and 39 per cent of married women are polygynous); no polygyny (or strict monogamy).

There is a major difference between this variable and the duration of the post partum sex taboo. Presumably, in a society observing the long post partum sex taboo, the taboo applies equally to *all mothers*. This is not true for polygyny. In the polygynous society, some mothers are polygynous and some are not. The variable—percentage of polygyny—is the percentage or proportion of mothers (or, more accurately, married women) to whom this condition (polygynous marriage) applies.

The obvious consequence of polygyny is that the wife does not "own" her husband; she shares him with one or more co-wives. What does this mean? For one thing, it must mean that the polygynous husband tends to have less of an emotional investment in any single wife. He does not have "all his eggs in one basket." The meaning for the co-wife is less clear. I suspect that polygyny has a general "lowering" effect on the emotional importance of the husband-wife bond, and that this applies to the wife as well as to the husband; she also "invests less" in her husband, and "invests more" in other relationships. Shortly, we shall examine some evidence which indicates that this may be so.

Mother-Child Household

The usual arrangement for a polygynous family is for each wife to occupy a separate house. The husband either "rotates"—that is, sleeps first in the house of one wife, then in the house of another—or occupies still another house of his own. Occasionally, the polygynous family may occupy a "polygynous household"—husband and co-wives all sleep in the same house. This usually occurs when co-wives are sisters (Murdock and Whiting, 1951). Generally, if a family is monogamous, husband and wife sleep in the same house; in my samples, there are only rare exceptions to this rule. In other words, the following generalization is possible: if marriage is polygynous, husband and wife usually maintain separate houses; if marriage is monogamous, husband and wife nearly always occupy the same house. For most societies in my samples, the percentage of mother-child households (households containing mother, children, and occasionally other relatives, but no regular father) is approximately equal to the percentage of polygynous marriages.

The ratings of frequency of mother-child households were also made by Whiting and D'Andrade. The ratings make a two-way division: "high" (over 40 per cent of all households in the society are estimated to be mother-child) and "low" (less than 40 per cent are estimated to be mother-child).

The Diluted Marriage Complex: Cause and Effect

As I said before, the three variables are positively correlated with each other. The three conditions—*long* post partum sex taboo, *high* percentage of polygynous marriage, and *high* percentage of mother-child households—tend to occur together in the same societies. Why should this be? Why are these customs so tightly patterned? The best guess, I think, is that frequent polygyny acts to "cause" the other two.

The mother-child household seems like a way of handling

friction between co-wives. Monogamous spouses nearly always live together in the same house.[2] Polygynous spouses usually live in different houses, *unless the co-wives are sisters* (Murdock and Whiting, 1951; Whiting and D'Andrade). In other words, it looks as if the mother-child household is only "necessary" for polygynous families, in which the co-wives are not sisters (nonsororal polygyny). Of course, this absolute statement must be qualified: there are a few exceptions.

It is harder to make a case for frequent polygyny as a "cause" for the long post partum sex taboo. Perhaps this rule of prolonged sexual continence for the mother is less trying for her husband if he has another wife to turn to. If this is so, it might be easier and more likely for a society to adopt the long post partum sex taboo, if a high proportion of its men had several wives.

I will not speculate further about the reasons for the close association between these customs. I do want to say something here about their *consequences*, vis-à-vis the emotional relations within the family. Tentatively, I propose the following: these conditions—long post partum sex taboo, polygyny, and mother-child household—represent "diluted" marriage. When these customs are in force, husband and wife are (on the average) less "close," less mutually involved, less emotionally dependent on each other—in other words, "less married."

There is some indirect cross-cultural evidence indicating that these customs make mothers "closer" to their children. That is, as the mothers become "less husband-centered" they

2. I know of the following exceptional cases, in which monogamous spouses customarily sleep in separate houses: Ashanti, Dahomey, Hupa, Malaita, Pomo, Mundurucu, Rajput, and Yurok.

Table 1.
Mother-Infant Sleeping Arrangements Compared with Frequency of Polygyny, Frequency of Mother-Child Households, and Duration of the Post Partum Sex Taboo

Frequency of Polygyny	Mother and Nursing Child Customarily Sleep in the Same Bed			Mother and Nursing Child Customarily Sleep in Different Beds		
High	Arapesh	M	P	Ganda	M	P
	Araucania	m	P	Jivaro	m	P
	Bhil	m		Kapauka	M	
	Gusii	M	p			
	Hausa	M	P			
	Kurtachi	M	P			
	Kwoma	m	P			
	Lovedu	M	P			
	Mende	M	P			
	Nambicauru	m	p			
	Riff	m				
	Siriono	m	p			
	Tallensi	M	P			
	Tanala	M	p			
	Tiv	M	P			
	Wogeo		P			
Low	Alor	m	p	Aleut	m	
	Ashanti	M	p	Comanche	m	
	Camayura	m		Gilyak	m	
	Copper Eskimo	m	p	Koryak	m	p
	Igorot	m	p	Ojibwa	m	P
	Lepcha	m	p	Pomo	M	
	Malekula	m		Pilaga	m	P
	Manus	m	p	Thai	m	
	Montana	m		Trobriands	m	P
	Navaho	m	p			
	Papago	m	p			
	Samoa	m	P			
	Siwai	m				
	Silwa	m	p			
	Tarahumara		p			
	Tlingit		p			
	Toda					
	Yagua	m	p			

Table 1 (cont.)

Frequency of Polygyny	Mother and Nursing Child Customarily Sleep in the Same Bed		Mother and Nursing Child Customarily Sleep in Different Beds		
Absent	Andamans	m		Ainu	m	p
	Aymara	m	p	Cuna	m	
	Chenchu	m	p	Iroquois	m	
	Dobu	m		Kaska	m	
	Ifaluk	m	P	Lapp	m	p
	Ifugao	m		Omaha	m	
	Rajput	M	P	Yuchi	m	
	Semang	m				
	Tepoztlan	m	P			
	Tzeltal	m				
	Witoto	m	P			

Societies are divided into three groups, according to frequency of polygyny: "high" (40 per cent or more wives are polygynous), "low" (less than 40 per cent), and "absent" (strict monogamy).

The entry "M" beside the name of a society indicates a rating of "high" (over 40 per cent) on frequency of mother-child households. The entry "m" indicates a "low" rating on frequency of mother-child households.

The entry "P" beside the name of a society indicates a "long" post partum sex taboo. The entry "p" indicates a "short" post partum sex taboo.

This same form is followed in Tables 2 and 3.

All ratings on these three variables are listed in Appendix VIII.

become "more child-centered." This evidence is given in Tables 1, 2, and 3.

Table 1 indicates that these mothers tend to be *physically* closer to their children; they and their young sleep together in the same bed (or, if there are no beds, sleep side-by-side.[3] That is, as the percentages of polygyny and of mother-child households increase, the likelihood increases that mother and nursing child will sleep in the same bed. The trend is not very impressive, since this is the most common sleeping arrangement for all types of primitive societies (whether "high" or "low" on the diluted marriage variables). Also, the trend does not hold for the post partum sex taboo.

Table 2 indicates that these mothers tend to be more at-

3. Mother-child sleeping arrangements were also rated by Whiting and D'Andrade.

Table 2.
Initial Indulgence of Dependency Compared with Frequency of Polygyny, Frequency of Mother-Child Households, and Duration of the Post Partum Sex Taboo

Frequency of Polygyny	Societies Rated at or above the Median on Intial Indulgence of Dependency			Societies Rated below the Median on Initial Indulgence of Dependency		
High	Arapesh	M	P	Thonga	M	P
	Azande	M	P			
	Dahomey	M	P			
	Kurtachi	M	P			
	Kwoma	m	P			
	Murngin	m	p			
	Siriono	m	p			
	Tanala	M	p			
	Venda	M	P			
	Wogeo		P			
Low	Bena		P	Alor	m	p
	Comanche	m		Ashanti	M	p
	Copper Eskimo	m	p	Baiga	m	p
	Maori	m	p	Bali	m	p
	Navaho	m	p	Kutenai	m	
	Paiute	m		Lepcha	m	p
	Papago	m	p	Manus	m	p
	Trobriands	m	P	Malekula	m	
	Yagua	m	p	Samoa	m	P
				Tikopia	m	
Absent	Andamans	m		Ainu	m	p
	Chenchu	m	p	Hopi	m	p
	Lapp	m	p	Dobu	m	
	Pukapuka	m		Ifugao	m	
				Kwakiutl	m	P
				Marquesas	m	p
				Witoto	m	P
				Lakher	m	p

tentive and succorant. The rating used—"initial indulgence of dependency"—assesses how much a young child's dependent demands are indulged and rewarded (Whiting and Child, 1953: 91–93). Societies "high" on all three diluted marriage variables—frequency of polygyny, frequency of

Table 3.
Average Age of Weaning Compared with Frequency of Polygyny, Frequency of Mother-Child Households, and Duration of the Post Partum Sex Taboo

Frequency of Polygyny	Societies Rated at or above the Median* on Average Age of Weaning			Societies Rated below the Median on Average Age of Weaning		
High	Arapesh	M	P	Siriono	m	p
	Azande	M	P	Tanala	M	p
	Dahomey	M	P			
	Jivaro	m	P			
	Kurtachi	M	P			
	Kwoma	m	P			
	Thonga	M	P			
	Venda	M	P			
	Wogeo		P			
Low	Bali	m	p	Alor	m	p
	Copper Eskimo	m	p	Baiga	m	p
	Lepcha	m	p	Bena		P
	Manus	m	p	Chiricahua	m	P
				Comanche	m	
				Kutenai	m	
				Lamba	m	p
				Malekula	m	
				Maori	m	
				Navaho	m	p
				Papago	m	p
				Trobriands	m	P
				Yagua	m	p
Absent	Ainu	m	p	Hopi	m	p
	Chenchu	m	p	Kwakiutl	m	P
	Omaha	m		Lakher	m	p
				Lapp	m	p
				Marquesas	m	p
				Pukapuka	m	

* For the Whiting and Child sample, the median age of weaning was two-and-a-half years.

mother-child households, and duration of the post partum sex taboo—tend strongly to be "high" on "initial indulgence of dependency."

Table 3 indicates that in societies "high" on the diluted marriage variables nursing is prolonged.[4]

In other words, there is some reason for believing that these customs, which appear to have some "separating" effect on the husband-wife relationship, bring mother and child even closer together. Quite possibly this arrangement has its advantages. But it also seems to have its problems. Peoples with the diluted marriage complex appear to be unusually phobic and taboo-ridden, particularly about matters involving sex.

Customs of the Second Group

The other customs, which are associated with the diluted marriage variables, are largely concerned with taboo and avoidance. Many of these customs are grotesque; they seem senseless and unnecessary. They appear to us to be extreme burdens and hardships.

To illustrate these customs, I shall trace part of the life-cycle in an ideal-type society. This society has most, but not all, of the customs in this group:

1. When a boy in this society nears the age of puberty, he ceases to sleep in the parental home. He moves to a bachelor-house.

2. Near this time, he is initiated. He passes through a series of rite-of-passage trials. He is frightened, beaten, secluded from women, and circumcised.

3. When he marries, he avoids his mother-in-law. They both observe these avoidance rules: can't touch each other;

4. Average age of weaning was rated by Whiting and Child (1953).

can't look eye-to-eye; can't use each other's personal name; can't be alone together; can't speak to each other. He also avoids other of his wife's relatives.

4. When a girl in this society begins to menstruate, she is also treated to a rite-of-passage ceremonial. She has now acquired malignant power, due to her menstrual bleeding. The power must be neutralized. After the first purifying ceremonies, she must observe recurring taboos as long as she continues to menstruate. She spends her periods in a special menstrual hut, out of the sight of men. She cannot cook for her husband (during her periods). During her life she may be blamed for some misfortune—failure of crops or hunting, sickness, death, displeasure of the gods—because somehow, despite all precautions, she has contaminated with her menstrual blood.

5. When she marries, she avoids her father-in-law and her husband's uncles.

Other things characterize this society: extreme fear of sorcery, totemism, and further superstitions about the dangers inherent in sex.

Order of Presentation

We have now reveiwed the phenomenon. It is a network of positive correlations between the diluted marriage variables and the customs in the second group. The book will follow these steps:

In Chapter 2, I propose the hypothesis. One part of the hypothesis is an assumption about the long post partum sex taboo: that it intensifies the son-to-mother sex attraction.

Starting with Chapter 4, the hypothesis is tested and documented.

Chapter 10 is a summary of evidence that bears on the hypothesis. It also summarizes all correlations between the duration of the post partum sex taboo and the "second group variables"—menstrual taboos, kin-avoidances, etc.

In Chapter 9, polygyny and mother-child households are again briefly discussed.

2

THE OEDIPUS COMPLEX
HYPOTHESIS

I SHALL FIRST DEFINE WHAT I
mean by "Oedipus complex." Throughout this book, the term
has a very limited meaning—limited mainly by what can be
tested and measured here, and what can't be. *By Oedipus
complex, I mean the sex attraction of a boy for his mother.*
I do *not* mean rivalry felt toward the father. I shall always
refer to the Oedipus complex of boys; I shall have nothing to
say about girls.

To get a better understanding of this definition, and on the
hypothesis it leads to, we had best review what psychoanalysts
have meant by the term "Oedipus complex." Here is a very
brief and simplified account of the Oedipus complex and its
effects, according to Freud and Fenichel:

1. Young boys customarily become sexually attracted to
   their mothers.

2. As a result, they feel hostile and rivalrous toward their fathers.
3. This has lasting effects on their personalities. Here are some of the results of the Oedipus complex:

   a. Unconscious fantasies, which continue to influence a man's motives and view of the world. Largely through the action of unconscious fantasies, the Oedipus complex also influences:
   b. Attitudes toward sex, particularly sexual fears, inhibitions and avoidances.
   c. Moral standards and guilt.
   d. Mental illness. (Freud, 1933:122) (Freud, 1936:44) (Fenichel, 1945:88–93, 170, 196–209, 231)

In these studies, I shall test only statements "1," "a," and "b" above. Nothing will be said directly about mental illness, moral standards, or guilt. Also, I do not have substantial evidence on father-son rivalry. I *do* have considerable evidence that bears these questions:

Do boys become sexually attracted to their mothers?
Does this have lasting effects on their attitudes toward sex?
Are these effects mediated by unconscious fantasies?

In other words, in this book the following general hypothesis (or, if you like, hypotheses) will be tested: *Young boys— at least under optimal conditions—become sexually attracted to their mothers. This generates lasting sexual fears and avoidances. These fears are (at least in one instance) mediated by unconscious fantasies.* "Optimal conditions" refers to factors that make the mother more seductive—primarily, the long post partum sex taboo. "In one instance" refers to castration anxiety, as reflected in menstrual taboos.

The hypothesis will be tested in later chapters. But first, we need to discuss the assumptions that underly the hypothesis. This background discussion will be organized around the following questions:

1. Are young children capable of having sexual desires?
2. If so, what forms do these sexual desires take? How are they manifested in behavior?
3. What is the Oedipal sex attraction?
4. Does the Oedipal sex attraction have persisting effects? What are these effects?

In answering each of these questions, some pre-existing evidence will be reviewed. The first question can be answered pretty conclusively; the second question can also be impressively documented. These first two questions are primarily questions of fact; they are answered with factual data. The last two questions are primarily questions of definition; in answering them, I shall be discussing assumptions rather than presenting facts. However, answers to the last two questions will also be *introduced* by means of factual data.

The treatment will not be a complete review of pre-existing evidence on the Oedipus complex. Instead, it will be a sampling of evidence. One great source of data will be more-or-less overlooked: clinical evidence, furnished by psychoanalysts. In sampling the evidence that bears on these questions, I have tried to choose data that "stands by itself" (as an answer to a particular question), requiring little or no interpretation.

We shall now address ourselves to the questions.

1. *Are young children capable of having sexual desires?*
The only problem here is defining what one means by "sexual." I will omit this problem of definition. Instead, I shall review some behavior which, by almost any definition, would be considered "sexual."

In the first place, male infants in the first year of life ordinarily have erections (Halverson, 1938). Kinsey, Pomeroy, and Martin go so far as to conclude that: "Erection may occur immediately after birth and, as many observant mothers (and few scientists) know, it is practically a daily matter for all small boys, from earliest infancy and up in age" (Kinsey, Pomeroy, and Martin 1948: 164).

As boys grow older, apparently they keep on having erections, although there is little evidence on how frequently erections occur. Also, there is no way of knowing whether this statement is accurate for all boys, most boys, or only some boys.

In what other ways do children express their sexual desires? We can group their obvious sexual expressions into three spheres: (1) sex play—genital contact or exhibitionism; (2) other kinds of body contact, resulting in apparent sexual pleasure; (3) "acting out" or play, which—although it is not sex play—seems to give clear signs of sexual preoccupation.

For sex play, let us turn again to the "Kinsey report":

The most specific activities among younger boys involve genital exhibition and genital contacts with other children. Something more than half (57 per cent) of the older boys and adults recall some sort of pre-adolescent sex play. This figure is much higher than some other students have found . . . ; but it is probably still too low, for 70 per cent of the pre-adolescent boys who have contributed to the present study have admitted such experience, and there is no doubt that even they forget many of their earlier activities. It is not improbable that nearly all boys have some pre-adolescent genital play with other boys or girls. Only about one-fifth as many of the girls have such play (Kinsey, Pomeroy, and Martin, 1948: 165–167).

Later, they add: "Most of this pre-adolescent sex play occurs between the ages of eight and thirteen" (Kinsey, Pomeroy, and Martin 1948: 167). There are reports of sex play (involving genital contact) by much younger children (Henry, 1944). However, I know of no large, controlled quantitative study, like the Kinsey study, that specifically treats it.

The best source on the "second sphere"–apparent sexual pleasure from other sorts of body contact—is a study of the Navaho, reported by Clyde Kluckhohn. The report describes sexual pleasure during nursing. In this study, over forty Navaho children were observed by eighteen field workers. Observation began at birth and continued, at repeated short intervals, for several years (Kluckhohn, 1947: 38). Until toilet-trained, Navaho boys wear pants with the bottoms out, making it easy to observe erections. Here are a few extracts from the workers' field notes:

Tony (a boy of twenty-six months) kept fighting for her breast, and half stood up on his feet, bending across her knees to nurse and at the same time manipulating his genitals with one hand and wiggling in a decidedly passionate manner. Presently he fell asleep and she held him on her lap. He woke at intervals and nursed more quietly, lying on her lap while she stroked his hair. Just before we left, he was lying on his back in her lap, when he began wiggling and fighting for her breast again, and had a prolonged erection. His mother, noticing it, played with him and stroked his penis while he nursed. If she left off, he continued by himself. He seemed very pleased and even left off nursing once to smile at all about him.

Finally he relaxed and crawled away, his sister playing with him for a while, and then his brother tussled with him.

At 9:12 Jake (a boy of two-and-a-half) nursed for four minutes. As he nursed, his mother patted him on the head, fondled his hair, and also patted his lower leg. He nursed greedily and noisily, giving vent to pants of ecstacy. He nursed first on the left breast. While doing this, he fondled the right breast and pulled out the nipple. Then he nursed briefly on the right breast. Now—five minutes later —he is going after the left breast again. His mother at first makes a gesture of protest, then lets him have it. But he sticks at it less than a minute. Two minutes later he is back at it again.

Having played with each breast again for a few minutes, Jake now dawdles in his mother's lap—is tickled by her and laughs rather hysterically. At 9:45 his mother is lying down. Jake tries to get breast, but she won't have it at first and sits up. He says: "My mother is stingy." He cries and whines. After a couple of minutes, she gives him first the left breast. Then he takes the right. She grooms his head briefly as he nurses.

Between 10:00 and 10:40 Jake was eating constantly: orange, tomato, bread, meat. He sat near his mother and touched her several times. Once she kissed him passionately on the mouth (Kluckhohn, 1947: 69–70).

In summarizing the field notes, Kluckhohn says:

By the time most children are nine months old it is also plain that they find libidinous pleasure in nursing and in handling the mother's breast (Kluckhohn, 1947: 58).

The erotic manifestations accompanying nursing are particularly plain with children past a year-and-a-half. There is also no doubt whatsoever that this is seen more often with boys than with girls (Kluckhohn, 1947: 69).

Boys find weaning a more upsetting experience than do girls. . . . Perhaps the best guess as to an explanation is the greater erotic significance of nursing for Navaho boys (or a higher energy level—

more active in general? Perhaps both?) As has been pointed out, mothers stroke the genitals of boy nurslings, and the active passionate manipulation of the mother's breast during the later years of nursing is almost exclusively characteristic of boys (Kluckhohn, 1947: 77).

Something should be said about nursing in primitive societies. Needless to say, it is always by breast (never by bottle). Also, by our standards, it is of extremely long duration. Whiting and Child, in rating the average age at weaning, found only one primitive society in which duration of weaning is ordinarily less than one year—the Marquesans. Usually, a child is nursed for at least two years; often he is nursed much longer (Whiting and Child, 1953: 342–343).

The third sphere—"acting out" of sexual preoccupation— you have probably seen with your own eyes, in your own observations of children. Sometimes the sexual preoccupation is more obvious than at other times. Here, necessarily, we must leave the quantitative studies altogether and turn to simple descriptive accounts. For an example, I have chosen an account of sexual preoccupation that is so obvious that interpretation is unnecessary. The actor is a Pilaga boy, engaged in doll-play. The reporters are the anthropologists Jules and Zunia Henry.

Yorodaikolik. Trial XII. 11–3–37. Points to sister doll and says "This one has no genital." Makes a very big one. Says: "Suña, Tapáñi says she has a big vulva" (1). He shows it to the examiner. Yorodaikolik remarks that self doll has no penis. Says: "Look, I know how to make a penis." Puts penis on self doll. Squashes it (2). Scratches it (3) and says: "The penis' opening." Says it looks like a vulva. Does the same to brother doll (4). Puts a new vulva on mother doll. Puts breasts on brother doll, and says that he's putting breasts on Denikí. Puts small blob of clay into vagina of sister doll, saying "The vagina's clitoris." Puts tiny breasts on sister doll and closes its eyes with clay (5). Says, "The covering of its eyes. O *way!* Blind!" He makes the abdomen, a clay blob on the abdomen. Says: "O *way!* Blind!" Asks for father doll. Picks up scissors. Lays them down. Picks up sister doll and says "O *way!*" Self doll and brother doll are side by side.

Puts sister doll next to self doll, then brother doll, then mother doll. Pushes scissors closer to mother doll. Puts clay on head of sister doll and calls it "its hair." Puts extra nipple on mother doll's breast. Removes it and puts it on brother doll's head, calling it a hat. Handles scissors again. Asks for bubble pipe. Says he's thirsty. Drinks. Asks for hockey ball (a very heavy wooden ball about an inch and a half in diameter) and immediately puts it on mother doll's head (6). Picks up sister doll and puts hockey ball beside mother. Places sister doll beside mother doll. Places brother doll beside mother doll. Then places brother doll beside sister doll, self doll next to brother doll, then scissors. Treats the scissors like a doll. Pushes metal object into mother doll's foot (7). Picks up hockey ball. Yatákana looks in, and Yorodaikolík puts down hockey ball. He puts sister doll on genital of mother doll *1*, then across neck of mother doll. Puts brother doll on top of sister doll *2*, self on top of all *3*, and says "A heap." In answer to examiner's question, "Why is there a heap?" Yorodaikolík says "They are having intercourse." Yorodaikolík again puts sister doll across the breasts of the mother doll. Places self on sister doll *4*, and brother doll on top of all *5*. Changes brother doll to position on top of sister doll *6*. Then takes away self and brother dolls. Puts head of self doll into cup of water and says "I'm bathing." Puts legs of self doll into cup. Repeats. Puts self doll and brother doll (8) completely into cup. Takes out brother doll and says: "Denekí drowned (9). I, on the other hand, did not drown." Picks up scissors, looks angrily at Naichó at door, holds scissors up and puts them down again. Picks up hockey ball and rolls it on mother doll's face (10). Makes shoes for mother doll. Stands sister doll on head. Takes shoes off mother doll's feet and puts them on sister doll's head, saying: "The hat's brim." Puts sister doll aside on toy box within reach. Pulls up sleeves of self doll, drinks the water in which he had bathed the two dolls, and says: "I'll stop now." (Henry and Henry, 1944)

The Pilaga children may be unusually preoccupied with sex. The Henry paper is peppered with such examples. However, the accounts of psychoanalytically oriented children's workers are full of play that is interpreted as sexual acting-out (Isaacs, 1933, Klein, 1948). How many of these interpretations you believe depends on your theoretical preferences. You may believe all of them, or most of them, or some of them. But it is very hard to believe none of them.

2. *What forms does children's sexuality take? How is it manifested in behavior?* In a minimal way, this question has already been answered. I shall now expand the answer by trying to characterize childhood sexuality. Freud characterized young children as "polymorphous perverse." He meant that, compared to normal adults, their sex drive is more diffuse, and less centered in the genitals and in genital pleasure (Fenichel, 1945: 61). This may be so. What is very clear is that *children respond sexually to a great range of stimuli*. Compared with normal adults, many more things are "sexy" to children.

To document this point, we turn once again to Kinsey, Pomeroy, and Martin. They give a long list of stimulus situations that led to erection. The age of the boys at the time they had these experiences is not given; I assume that most of the boys were fairly "old" (eight to fifteen). Also, the authors do not give frequencies; we do not know which situations more often produced erection. The list is based on their own interviews, and on a previous study by Ramsey (1943). It is presented here in full.

Nonsexual Sources of Erotic Response among Pre-Adolescent and Younger Adolescent Boys

Chiefly physical: sitting in class; friction with clothing; taking a shower; punishment; accidents; electric shock; fast elevator rides; carnival rides; Ferris wheel; fast sled riding; fast bicycle riding; fast car driving; skiing; airplane rides; a sudden change in environment; sitting in church; motion of car or bus; a skidding car; sitting in warm sand; urinating; boxing and wrestling; high dives; riding horseback; swimming.

Chiefly emotional: being scared; fear of a house intruder; near accidents; being late to school; reciting before a class; asking to go front in class; tests at school; seeing a policeman; cops chasing him; getting home late; receiving grade card; big fires; setting a field afire; hearing revolver shot; anger; watching exciting games; playing in exciting games; marching soldiers; war motion pictures; other movies; band music; hearing "extra paper" called; harsh words; fear of punishment; being yelled at; being alone at night; fear of a big boy; playing musical solo; losing balance on heights; looking over edge of building; falling from garage, etc.; long flight of stairs; adventure stories; national anthem; watching a stunting airplane; finding money; seeing name in print; detective stories; running away from home; entering an empty house; nocturnal dreams of fighting, accidents, wild animals, falling from high places, giants, being chased, or frightened (Kinsey, Pomeroy, and Martin 1948: 164–165).

I tried to group these erection-provoking situations into categories, and came up with this: violence (or threat of it) to self—10 cases; violence, self not involved—13; locomotion —18; other fear-situations—15; tactile stimulation to penis from inanimate objects—5.

One striking feature of this list is the parallel between

some of the items in it and psychoanalysts' interpretations of fantasy sex-symbols. Another striking feature is the great range and variety of situations that, although one would expect them to be sexually "neutral," may provoke a sexual response. A large number of these situations have to do with aggression, violence, and fear of violence. For some vivid examples of the association between sex and aggression, let us turn again to the Pilaga children, as described by the Henrys.

> . . . Pilaga children pass hours each day in violent sexual games of a rather simple character. One of these is what we have called the genitalia-snatching game. In this game the children go hurtling after one another trying to touch each other's genital. Usually the boys chase the girls. Often they throw them down, and try to touch the girl's genital, while she shrieks with excitement. Sometimes the fall hurts, and she cries. When the boys have caught one girl, the other little girls dash up and beat off the boys. Then the boys chase the other little girls, and the situation is repeated. The play may go on for hours, and it is accompanied by the excited screams of the children. This blending of violence and sexuality extends to many details of play . . .

> *Attacks on genitalia*—Darotoyí, in a state of high exultation, attacks the genitals of his entire family (in doll play). In Trial I, he attacks the genital of the baby doll and the penises of the father and brother dolls. He behaves similarly in Trial V, except that he attacks the genital of the older sister and the mother also. Yorodaikolík's remark in Trial IV that the sister doll is deflowered, and his attack on her vagina in Trial VI, are other aspects of the same drive toward attack on the genitals.

> Attack on the genitals is the converse of *fear* of attack on the genitals. In everyday life attacks on the genitals—real, feinting, and verbal—are common enough. Below are a few examples.

> 1. Nagête, playing with Yorodaikolík, pushes him over and handles his penis, saying: "I'll cut it off."

2. Diwá'l screams and screams at Yorodaikolík: "Come here! Come here!" When he does go home, his mother, Nenarachí, and Piyärasáina scold him poisonously. Nenarachí says: "You will be killed." Piyärasáina says: "Your penis will be cut off."

3. Araná and Nagête put a dead nestling in Denikí's face. Denikí seems half frightened, half amused. He leans against Nagête's arm. Then she touches his penis and says: "It is bleeding." His penis, however, is not bleeding. Tapáñi says: "It's bleeding." Araná opens the bird's mouth and puts Denikí's penis in it, saying: "It is devoured, it is devoured." Denikí starts to whimper, but does not touch the bird. Either Araná or Nagête at last takes the bird away. Denikí goes out.

4. Yorodaikolík is sitting near the fire. His mother says: "Your testicles." Yorodaikolík moves away. His mother picks up a firebrand and puts it between his legs, moving toward his genitalia. He immediately bursts into tears and leans on his mother's breast. She strokes his head and he soon stops.

5. Nenarachí says to Simiti. "You'd better guard your vagina, because, if you don't, a man will come along, take you away, and rape you. Then you'll be a poor little thing when your vagina bleeds."

6. Sidingki makes a jab at Simiti's vulva with a ten-inch hunting knife. She retreats. Sidingki says to JH: "She's going to show you her genitals."

7. JH offers his watch to Dañakána so that she may listen to the tick. She withholds in embarrassment. JH withdraws the watch. Nagête, Nenarachí, and Piyärasáina insult her in a steady stream, until she weeps and goes home. The insult most often repeated is: "She is fed up with her big wormy vagina."

. . . Thus in everyday life *there is a constant veering between sexuality and violence, and often the two are inextricably blended.* An examination of the experimental material from this point of view seems pertinent. Before going ahead, however, we should like to point out that it has always seemed to us that for the children sexual intercourse itself has a certain hostile component. This may readily be inferred from the foregoing data. There are, however, many other indications of the way in which the sexual act and hostility are blended in the minds of the children. A common threat is: "I'll have intercourse with you," and it passes from girl to girl as well as from boy to boy and boy to girl. The boy speaks of succesful entry as: "I hit it" (as with a projectile), and failure to enter as "I missed it." The little girls (and, indeed, the adults too) believe that menstruation is caused by violent entrance of the vagina; and it can be seen that they scratch the little boys when they attempt intercourse. The great extent to which violence is associated with the sexual act leads to such angry remarks as that of the little foreign girl (i.e., from another village) : "They wanted to mount us!"

In view of this situation, we have often been tempted to list every act representative of intercourse in the experiments as hostile. We have refrained, however, . . . (selected from Henry and Henry, 1944).

Perhaps, for these charming people, the association between sex and aggression is unusually strong. Or, perhaps they are only unusual for their relative lack of inhibitions. For the more inhibited European and American children, it is hard to know to what extent sex and aggression are cognitively and emotionally linked. The Kinsey data, as well as many clinical case histories, indicate that in our society this linking probably is not unusual.

Let us return to the more general question of the diffuse and variegated nature, for children, of possible sexual stimuli. Why should this be?

Kinsey, Pomeroy, and Martin offer the following explanation: the sexual response is at first generalized, and becomes more specific with learning. I quote:

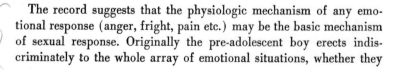

The record suggests that the physiologic mechanism of any emotional response (anger, fright, pain etc.) may be the basic mechanism of sexual response. Originally the pre-adolescent boy erects indiscriminately to the whole array of emotional situations, whether they be sexual or non-sexual in nature. By his late teens the male has been so conditioned that he rarely responds to anything except a direct physical stimulation of genitalia, or to psychic situations that are specifically sexual. In the still older male even physical stimulation is rarely effective unless accompanied by such a psychologic atmosphere. The picture is that of the psychosexual emerging from a much more generalized and basic physiologic capacity which becomes sexual, as an adult knows it, through experience and conditioning (Kinsey, Pomeroy, and Martin 1948: 165).

There may be a good deal of truth to the above explanation. Still, it can be supplemented by another explanation, suggested by psychoanalytic theory: children are "diffuse" in their sexual reactions because many things "remind" them of sex. Many apparently neutral stimuli may function as *sex symbols*. This sex symbolism exists on a level of cognitive functioning that is primitive, illogical, and more-or-less unconscious and nonverbal, and has frequently been described as "fantasy" or "primary process" (Fenichel, 1945: 47–48; Freud, 1958: 588–609; Rapaport, 1951: 693–694). In short, another possible reason for the diffuse nature of children's sexual reactions is that, in children's more-or-less unconscious fantasies, many objects may symbolize sexual stimuli or activity.

It may not be that unconscious fantasy explains the variety of childhood sexual stimuli. Whatever is the case, I must add unconscious fantasy as one more sphere of sexual activity in children. Demonstrating that such a phenomenon exists is something else again. Quantitative studies do not help us here. For evidence on unconscious sexual fantasies, we must turn to psychoanalytic case studies. Obviously, space does not permit even a fair sampling of such case-record evidence. I will give only one example, drawn from a case-study by Melanie Klein. It consists of a dream followed by a story, related by a four-year-old boy. Sex is represented by such images as: "The big motor went on top of the electric car"; "The electric car had a connecting rod too"; "The motors stayed there in the night too"; "The garden was very beautiful, it was up on the roof. I always took a ladder to get up to it." Genital injury to the father is represented by: "They took his gun away from him; he could only walk like this." (Here he doubles himself up.) He continued kindly, "Then the soldiers gave him a decoration and a bayonet because they had taken his gun from him."

. . . He begins with the description of a dream. "There was a big motor that looked just like an electric car. It had seats too and there was a little motor that ran along with the big one. Their roofs could be opened up and then shut down when it rained. Then the motors went on and ran into an electric car and knocked it away. Then the big motor went on top of the electric car and drew the little one after it. And then they all got close together, the electric car and the two motors. The electric car had a connecting-rod too. You know what I mean? The big motor had a beautiful big silver iron thing and the little one had something like two little hooks. The little one was between the electric car and the motor. Then they drove up a high mountain and came down quickly again. The motors stayed there in the night too. When electric cars came they knocked them away and if any one did like that" (with an arm) "they went backwards at once." (I explain that the big motor is his papa, the electric car his mama and the little motor himself, and that he has put himself between papa and mamma because he would so much like to put papa away altogether and to remain alone with his mamma and do with her what only papa is allowed to do.) After a little hesitation he agrees but continues quickly, "The big and little motors then went away, they were in their house, they looked out of the window, it was a very big window. Then two big motors came. One was grandfather, the other was just papa. Grandmamma was not there, she was" (he hesitates a little and looks very solemn) ". . . she was dead." (He looks at me, but as I remain quite unmoved, he goes on.)—"And then they all drove down the mountain together. One chauffeur opened the doors with his foot; the other opened with his feet the thing that one turns round" (handle). "The one chauffeur became sick, that was grandpapa." (Again he looks at me interrogatively but seeing me undisturbed continues.) "The other chauffeur said to him, 'You dirty beast, do you want your ears boxed, I will knock you down at once.' (I enquire who the other chauffeur was.) He: "Me. And then our soldiers throw them all down; they were all soldiers—and smash the motor and beat him and smear his face with coal and stuff coal in his mouth too"; (reassuringly) "he thought it was a sweetie, you know, and that is why he took it and it was coal. Then everyone was a soldier and I was the officer. I had a beautiful uniform and" (he holds himself erect) "I held myself like this, and then they all followed me. They took his gun away from him; he could only walk like this." (Here he doubled up.) He continued kindly, "Then the soldiers gave him a decoration and a bayonet because they had taken his gun from him. I was the officer and mama was the nurse" (in his games the nurse is always the officer's wife) "and Karl and Lene and Anna" (his brother and sisters) "were my children and we had a lovely house too—it looked like the king's house from the outside it was not quite finished; there were no doors and the roof wasn't on but it was very beautiful. We made for ourselves what was wanting." (He now accepts my interpretation of the meaning of the unfinished house, etc., without any particular difficulty.) "The garden was very beautiful, it was up on the roof. I always took a ladder to get up to it. All the same I always managed to get up to it quite well, but I had to help Karl, Lene and Anna. The dining-room was very beautiful too and trees and flowers grew in it. It does not matter, it's quite easy, you put down some earth and then the things grow. Then grandpapa came into the garden quite quietly like this" (he imitates the peculiar gait again), "he had a shovel in his hand and wanted to bury something.

Then the soldiers shoot at him and" (again he looks very solemn), "he dies." After he has gone on talking for a long time about two blind kings of whom he now himself says that the one is his papa and the other his mamma's papa, he relates, "The king had shoes as long as to America, you could get inside them and there was plenty of room. The long-clothes babies were put to bed in them at night" (Klein, 1948: 48–50).

How many of these images you accept as sex symbols depends on your theoretical preferences. If you accept this sort of interpretation, I am sure you could add to my list. I termed sex symbolism as *more-or-less* unconscious because it is a matter of degree the extent to which the symbolic meanings are both clearly and specifically recognized. This little boy, with Miss Klein's prompting, seems to have a good deal of conscious awareness; however, it is doubtful that even he could explain many of the symbols that he used. Psychoanalytic literature is full of such examples which, if a certain interpretation is accepted, appear to be sex symbols, used with little or no conscious awareness. The above example is a particularly good one.

Something else should be said about the sphere of unconscious fantasy as a "place" or medium for sexual preoccupation. Up to now, I have treated only sex symbols: symbolic connections, symbolic meanings. It is also a part of psychoanalytic theory that children (and adults too) have complete "unconscious fantasy-thoughts." Here is an example: "Feces equals penis; if I defecate, I lose my penis; I am afraid to defecate; I will be constipated." These unconscious fantasy-thoughts can be fantastic. They even run counter to conscious knowledge of reality, usually in children. Being complete "thoughts," they lead to "conclusions" which influence behavior: "I will be constipated." Also, they may have a drive or motive quality: "I am afraid to defecate; therefore I will be constipated." Again, you will not accept the reality of the unconscious fantasy-thoughts if you do not accept psycho-analytic interpretations. One reason psychoanalysts believe in them is that, at times, when it seems that a patient's uncon-scious fantasy-thought has been reached, interpreted, and changed, the patient's behavior changes, indicating that the fantasy-thought had previously been influencing the patient's behavior (Klein, 1948: 13–67; Freud, 1956: 149–289).

The sexual fantasy-thought which is presumed to be "classic" or most typical in children is the castration fantasy or castration anxiety—fear of genital injury (Freud, 1933: 122–123; Freud, 1936: 49; Fenichel, 1945: 77–78). One chapter of this book, the chapter on menstrual taboos, will be devoted, in part, to testing the hypothesis that there is such a thing as castration anxiety.

This concludes the reply to the first two questions. Before we go on, we had better review them.

1. *Are young children capable of having sexual desires?* Yes.

2. *How are the sexual desires manifested in behavior?* Through: (1) play involving genital contact or exhibition-ism (Kinsey); (2) obvious sexual pleasure at other kinds of body contact (Kluckhohn); (3) "acting-out" play that shows sexual preoccupation, although there is no body contact (Henry); (4) unconscious fantasy (Klein). Children were characterized as unusual for the wide range of apparently neutral stimuli that excite them sexually (Kinsey), and for their "mixing" of sex and aggression (Kinsey, Henry).

The first two questions are primarily questions of fact; they have been answered with factual data. Except for one instance—unconscious sexual fantasies—the facts stand by themselves as answers to the questions; they need little or no interpretation. The next question is different. It is primarily a question of definition. I will introduce the answer to it with a few facts, and conclude with some definitions.

3. *What is the Oedipal sex attraction?* There is evidence indicating that mothers may sexually stimulate their children, and that the mother's own behavior is one determinant of the degree and intensity of the child's sexual preoccupation.

We have already examined one such piece of evidence: the Kluckhohn study. It indicates that something about nursing sexually excited the Navaho children. What was it? There are two main possibilities. One is that the body contact by itself excited them. The other possibility is that the nursing was also sexually exciting to the mother, on a rather mild level, and because she was sexually aroused she further stimulated the child by kissing, caressing and teasing, and by merely communicating her own sexual interest by means of numerous cues. In fact, we do know that women are capable of being sexually aroused by nursing (Ford and Beach, 1951: 46). Both possibilities are probably true to some extent.

The next piece of evidence comes from the Henrys' account of the Pilaga. In considering the reasons why the Pilaga children should be so sexually active, they state:

The desire of a little boy to have intercourse with his mother appears in Darotoyí II, and in Yorodaikolík V, VIII and IX. Yorodaikolík was once observed to masturbate on the buttocks of his mother who was lying down. She did nothing to stop him. Darotoyí was never observed to do this. In the development of this kind of behavior in little boys, a number of factors must be taken into consideration. First is the pregnancy and lactation taboo on intercourse, and the long period of abstinence it imposes on the women as well as on the man. During this period, two women were observed to use the feet of their infant sons to masturbate, i.e., they held the feet of the babies, eight and fifteen months respectively at the time of the observation, pressed against their genitals. Another important factor is that mothers manipulate the genitals of their infant sons. It is likely also that the straddled position of the child on its mother's hip in carrying would have some effect in focusing the child's sexual interests (Henry and Henry, 1944).

In other words, they conclude that the reason Pilaga boys sometimes show sexual interest in their mothers is because the mothers sexually stimulate them. Apparently, by implication, this is also a reason for the Pilaga children's great sexual activity. The same two possible reasons why the mother is sexually stimulating are given: (1) mere body contact—the carrying position, genital manipulation; (2) the mother's own sexual interest in the child. The Henrys conclude that one reason why the mother uses the child for sexual gratification is because she herself is sexually frustrated during the time she observes the pregnanacy taboo and the post partum sex taboo (the Pilaga observe the long post partum sex taboo. The Navaho do not).

The last piece of evidence I shall give on this point is drawn from our own society. It comes from a study by René Spitz and Katherine Wolf. The study describes genital self-stimulation by infants. Three samples were used. The first sample is sixty-one infants in an orphan home institution, without mothers. Each nurse had, on the average, ten infants to care for. The second sample is 170 infants in a penal institution for women; they were (to some extent, at least) cared for by their mothers. The third sample is seventeen infants in private homes, all characterized by a "good" mother-child relationship. Children in the second sample were observed during controlled time-intervals. For the first and third samples, the observation method is not described.

Here is how the three samples compared, as regards genital self-stimulation (or masturbation):

In the first sample—the "orphan home" children—infants were observed throughout the first eighteen months of their lives (presumably at scattered time intervals). Only one child (out of a sample of sixty-one) was observed in genital self-stimulation.

In the second sample—the penal home children (with mothers present)—infants were observed for (on the average) the first fifteen months of life. Twenty-one (out of a possible 170) were observed to masturbate.

In the third sample—the children in private homes (with "good" mothers)—observation lasted for one year after birth. All but one (out of seventeen) were seen masturbating.

Age at observation is given because it appears to be an important variable. For the second sample, Spitz and Wolf show that genital self-stimulation seldom occurred before the infant was ten months old. In other words, the age difference makes the contrast between these three sample even more striking.

What does this data tell us? If just the first and third samples are considered, it means: infants with mothers masturbate; infants without mothers don't (or, at least, do so much less frequently). What does the difference between the second and third samples tell us? Spitz and Wolf explain the difference by saying that a good number of the penal-institution mothers were "cold" and "rejecting," while the private-home mothers were more "warm." They give a number of reasons why some of the penal home mothers were rejecting. There is one obvious situational reason: the babies, to some extent, are the reason their mothers are in jail.[1]

Spitz and Wolf specifically address the question: how does a mother sexually stimulate a child; is it mere body contact, or is it the way the mother feels? As far as *genital* body contact is concerned—diaper changing, washing the genital region, treating rashes—they do not think the institutionalized children were "deprived"; they received just as much stimulation of this sort as did the private-home children. They conclude that the crucial variable is not body contact but maternal warmth—the way the mother feels toward the child (Spitz and Wolf, 1949: 85–120). The implication is that generalized maternal nurture or mother-love, in and of itself is, to some extent, sexually stimulating to the infant.

I have established my original point, although it probably needed no establishing: it is possible for a mother to stimulate her child sexually. From here I will move on to a deduction; it may also seem obvious and unnecessary, but it is important. This is the deduction:

Depending on her behavior, feelings or needs, a mother may be more or less sexually stimulating to her child. If she is very stimulating, her child will tend to perceive her as a "sex object" i.e., as a source of many sexual stimuli, and as an important satisfier (or at least an arouser) of sexual urges. If she is not very stimulating, her child will tend less to per-

1. It is interesting, though, in the light of my hypothesis about the effect of the long post partum sex taboo, that the penal-home mothers were sexually continent; the private-home mothers were not.

ceive her as a "sex object"; fewer sexual stimuli, and perhaps fewer and less intense sexual urges will be associated with the sight, sound, feel, name, and concept of "mother."

You may note that we have now singled out two major "sex variables" or "sex dimensions" in children. One is the general level of preoccupation with sex. The other is the degree to which the mother is perceived as a sex object—the importance of the mother in the child's "sex life." If we had the measuring instruments, we should be able to give any child a score on both variables or dimensions. Probably the two dimensions are positively correlated. If a mother is particularly "seductive," her child would probably be "high" on both dimensions—on general preoccupation with sex, and on importance (to him) of the mother as a sex object. But they are two separate dimensions; they are not the same thing.

The Oedipal sex attraction refers to the *second dimension*. Later, I shall be trying to measure its intensity, in a crude and indirect way. In doing so, I will not regard the measurement as applying to the average intensity of children's sexual preoccupation. I will be trying to measure the average "intensity" with which—or the degree to which—boys see their mothers as sex objects. "See the mother as a sex object" means several things. It means hoping for, daydreaming of, expecting and seeking sexual excitement from the mother, by means of various kinds of body contact. It also means the degree to which the mother has sexual attributes in the boy's unconscious fantasy life. How much do both sex symbols and mother symbols tend to be "sexy mother symbols." How important is the "sexy mother" in the boy's unconscious fantasy-thoughts. As an example of what I mean, I would guess that in the story told by Melanie Klein's little boy (see pp. 30–

32), "electric car," "lovely house," and "beautiful garden" are not mere mother symbols or sex symbols; they are "sexy mother symbols," or symbols of a mother-who-may-give-sexual-stimulation.

While we are on the subject, something should be said about the "antecedents" of the Oedipal sex attraction (or, as I shall call it, the Oedipus complex): what determines whether it is "high" or "low," intense or mild? By definition, an important antecedent is the mother herself, or something about the mother. This brings back the question: what is it about the mother that stimulates; is it degree and nature of body contact between mother and child, or is it the way the mother feels toward the child? I assume it is both factors, intermingled. However, in my attempts to measure antecedents, I have focused on a condition that should influence how the mother feels. If I had done it the other way, I might have asked (in my ratings) such questions as: Do mother and infant sleep in the same bed? For how long? What sort of clothing do they wear when they sleep together? Does the mother routinely carry her infant about? How does she carry him? Does she nurse him by breast? For how long? Instead, I have used a variable which, I reasoned, should make the mother, because of her feelings, more sexually stimulating to the child. This variable is the long post partum sex taboo. When it is in force, a mother is not allowed to have sexual intercourse. I reasoned that this condition should make it more likely that the mother would redirect more of her sexual interest toward her child. The mechanism I assume operates is displacement.[2] From nursing and fondling the child, she

2. When the organism is deprived of an object of drive-reduction, it tends to seek reduction of this drive through responses directed toward other (substitute) objects (Dollard and Miller, 1950: 172–173).

would seek sexual gratification, probably of a rather mild level, somewhat analogous to the gratification of sexual foreplay. She would also, probably, seek gratification from observing the *child's* sexual excitement. She would be more apt to masturbate him, "tempt" him, and "tease" him. In short, she would be more "seductive." As a result, the child would be more apt to, and to a greater extent would see her as a "sex object."[3]

To summarize the cause and effect assumptions that lie behind the cross-cultural tests: (1) the long post partum sex taboo intensifies the mother's sexual interest in her child; (2) this intensifies the child's sexual interest in her; (3) this in turn intensifies, or makes more likely, the *effects* of the Oedipus complex. I will have more to say about these effects in a moment. We can apply cross-cultural measures at two points in this series of cause and effect assumptions: the beginning and the end. We can measure the duration of the post partum sex taboo and (with other assumptions) effects of the Oedipus complex. The two other "variables"—intensity of the mother's sexual interest in the child, and intensity of the child's sexual interest in the mother—remain as unmeasured "intervening

3. I assume that the entire "diluted marriage complex" has this effect; polygyny and the mother-child household, to the extent that they represent marriage that is less important and less satisfying (to the mother), have an effect that is to some degree parallel to that of the post partum sex taboo. In Chapter 1, we saw that these two customs do seem to "intensify" maternal nurture and mother-child body contact (dependency indulgence, side by side sleeping arrangements, and prolonged nursing). This, in itself, should have some intensifying effect on the Oedipal sex attraction. However, I assume that the long post partum sex taboo, which implies specifically sexual frustration of the mother, has a more direct influence on the Oedipus complex. I have concentrated on the post partum sex taboo as an "antecedent," and have generally ignored the other two. They are treated briefly in Chapter 9.

variables." The whole series of cause and effect assumptions will be tested, by correlating the duration of the post partum sex taboo with other ratings of the assumed effects on the Oedipus complex.

There is one aspect of these assumptions that is logically awkward: I must ignore girls. In societies observing the long post partum sex taboo, girls as well as boys have mothers who are, periodically, sexually continent. If this makes mothers act more "seductively," and if this affects boys, then it probably has some effect on girls too. The "consequent variables" I shall use—menstrual taboos, kin-avoidances, etc.—usually represent custom-complexes that involve women just as much as they involve men. I assume that these customs are caused (to some extent) by the effects of the Oedipus complex as they are "carried" by men. Actually, the women's feelings about these customs may be important too; but I take no account of them. Perhaps the long post partum sex taboo makes female children more preoccupied with sex. Perhaps it increases female homosexual trends. Whatever the effect of the long post partum sex taboo on female children, it will not be considered in the hypotheses. Though this is logically awkward, a "double-barreled hypothesis" would have been even more awkward. This course makes the hypotheses logically simpler and more economical.

I will now summarize what has been said in answer to the question: *What is the Oedipal sex attraction?* The Oedipal sex attraction was defined as the sex attraction felt by a boy toward his mother. It may be more or less intense. The intensity dimension is the degree to which the boy seeks and hopes for sexual stimulation via body contact with his mother, and the degree to which, in his fantasy-life, both sex symbols and mother symbols tend to be "sexy mother symbols." What determines intensity? The determinant that was singled out was the mother's own actions. Evidence was given indicating that a mother can sexually stimulate her child, and by doing so can make him more sexually preoccupied. What about the mother's actions is stimulating? Is it just the amount of body contact she affords, or is it indications she gives as to her own feelings? It is probably both. However, the antecedent measure will tap (by inference) the mother's feelings—her own sexual interest in her child. The cause-and-effect assumptions behind the cross-cultural hypotheses will be: (1) the long post partum sex taboo intensifies the mother's sexual interest in her child; (2) which intensifies his sexual interest in her; (3) thus intensifying, or making more likely, effects (in adult men) of the Oedipus complex.

4. Does the Oedipal sex attraction have persisting effects (in adults)? What are these effects? As mentioned in the beginning of this chapter, many effects are imputed to the Oedipus complex. However, we shall be concerned with only two: sexual fears, and unconscious fantasies concerning sex. In "answering" this question, I shall introduce only one piece of evidence—from experiments on hypnotically induced dreams. This evidence will serve as a sort of introduction; all it indicates (for our purposes) is that adults are capable of having unconscious fantasies about sex, or, at least, that there is such a phenomenon as unconscious sex symbolism (in adults).

These experiments are reported by Karl Schroetter. The procedure is as follows: the subject is put into hynotic trance, told what to dream about, and then instructed to dream. After having the dream, the subject relates it.

EXPERIMENT 5. *Subject:* Miss B.

Suggestion: You will dream of sexual intercourse with your friend B, first in a normal, then in an abnormal fashion. You are to *forget* the suggestion and then to dream of it symbolically. *No further explanation was given.*

Dream (in hypnosis): Sunday afternoon. I am expecting my friend B. We want to celebrate his name-day. He brings a bottle of wine wrapped in a coat. Upon his request I take a glass from the cupboard and hold it up to him; he pours out some wine. I am frightened by that, cry out and drop the glass. It breaks and the wine spills over the floor. I am very angry with B. for ruining the rug. He consoles me: "I'll make up for that. Give me another glass for the wine." I bring another one. He wants to pour out the rest of the wine carefully into the glass. But after pouring a few drops, he snatches away the bottle.

[remarks omitted]

EXPERIMENT 6. *Subject:* Miss B.

Suggestion: You will dream that you have intercourse with a man, French fashion. (The experimenter knew that this kind of intercourse was known to her by that name.)

Dream (in hypnosis): I feel as if a mass is descending upon me from the upper edge of my eye, preventing me from seeing, and settles on my shoulders like heavy wings. I wrap myself up in it entirely as if it were a hooded cape and go to a masked ball to look for B. I enter. A multitude of people running around, noise, stench, candles burning. Then I see—in fact I saw nothing—B in a corner with a wench. "Oh, you are here, I knew you'd come." Then he wants to shake hands with me, but pulls back his hand and searches his pockets for his gloves. He doesn't find them. Then he takes out a cigarette and puts it in his mouth. I want to snatch it away from him and burn myself badly. He says: "What are you doing?"

[remarks omitted]

EXPERIMENT 7. *Subject:* Miss E., pharmacist, age 24.

Suggestion: You will dream that you have homosexual intercourse with your girl friend L. You will forget the suggestion and then dream. (No suggestion to symbolize.)

Dream (the following night) : I sit in a small dirty cafe holding a tremendous French newspaper. There is hardly anyone there, except a few peddlers. A woman with a strong Yiddish accent asks me twice: "Don't you need anything?" I don't answer, burying myself in the paper. She comes a third time. I angrily put down the newspaper and recognize in her my acquaintance L. She holds a threadbare suitcase with a sticker on it that reads: "For ladies only!" She is dressed like an old woman, in dirty rags, with a kerchief on her head. "Don't you want to come with me, I am on my way home." I leave the cafe with her and we go through an unfamiliar street, but soon find ourselves in Mariahilf, where she lives. On the way she hangs onto me; I find this unpleasant but suffer it in order not to offend. Before her house she pulls an enormous bunch of keys out of a bag, selects a key and gives it to me: "I trust only you with it; it is the key to this case. You might like to use it. Just watch that my husband doesn't get hold of it; I couldn't stand that. He is so indiscreet, always wanting to prowl around among my things. I can't stand that." "I don't get a word of what you are saying." "Just don't give me away, my husband must not find out." She goes into the house, leaving me with the key.

Remarks: Miss L., the friend, is Jewish, while the dreamer is of Aryan origin (Schroetter, 1951: 241–244).

These, and similar experiments by others (Rapaport, 1951), tell us that adults are capable of representing sexual activities and objects by images that are not manifestly sexual. In other words, adults are capable of unconscious sex symbolism, of a type similar to that imputed to Melanie Klein's little boy. I say "unconscious" because I am fairly sure that these ladies did not consciously recognize the symbolic connections they had made.

To elaborate the hypothesis, as regards the effects of the

Oedipus complex, some other things must be assumed that are not so clearly documented. Evidence does exist on these points, but it is clinical evidence—it does not stand by itself; it requires interpretation to be accepted as evidence. Here are these assumptions:

1. The sex symbolism of adulthood is a carry-over of the sex symbolism of childhood. That is, to a large extent, adults recognize (more or less unconsciously) the same sex symbols as they did when they were children. The adult retains some of the same unconscious fantasies he had as a child.[4]

2. This "infantile fantasy life" in adults consists of both symbolic meanings and complete fantasy-thoughts, which may have a motive quality (for example, the castration fantasy).

3. The Oedipal sex attraction has an effect on adults' unconscious fantasies because, as for children, it determines the likelihood that mother symbols and sex symbols will both tend to be "sexy mother symbols." If the Oedipal sex attraction was relatively intense, this will be likely; if it was relatively mild, this won't be so likely. Also, if the Oedipal sex attraction was relatively intense, it will more likely influence, color, or be a "theme" in the adult's complete unconscious fantasy-thoughts.

Via unconscious fantasy, the Oedipus complex determines the degree to which the concept, "mother," and the concept, "sex partner," are confounded. An adult who experienced an intense Oedipal sex attraction will continue to view his mother as a potential

4. Psychoanalysts believe that fantasies become, and remain, unconscious through the agency of repression. If repression is extensive, more childhood unconscious fantasy will persist. Presumably, repression is specific to topics or motives; if *sexual* repression is particularly extensive, more unconscious sexual fantasy will persist. In turn, one determinant of the extensiveness of repression is the severity of sanctions: if sex training is severe, sexual repression will be relatively extensive, and persisting unconscious sexual fantasies will be numerous. In effect, this points to another "antecedent" of effects of the Oedipus complex: severity of sex training. Generally, in this book, this antecedent will be ignored (Fenichel, 1945: 57, 91, 95).

source of sexual stimulation. He will also view his actual or potential sex partner as having maternal attributes. She will remind him of his mother. Having sexual intercourse with her will remind him of (or suggest to him) having sexual intercourse with his mother.

4. The last assumption is that this confounding of "mother" and "sex partner" is apt to be frightening. At least, it is apt to make sexual thoughts and activities frightening. This is so because sexual designs on the mother inevitably collide with negative sanctions of various sorts (Balint, 1954: 70–80).

The above are four interlocked assumptions. That is, the later assumptions rest, to some extent, on the previous ones. On the basis of these assumptions I have singled out the following lasting effects of the Oedipus complex: (1) unconscious fantasies that are influenced by the Oedipal sex attraction; and (2) anxiety about sex, due to the confounding of "mother" and "sex partner."

I will now review the "consequent variables" that will be used, and state, in a general way, how they represent effects of the Oedipus complex.

One consequent variable—menstrual taboos—represents a motive stemming from unconscious fantasy-thoughts: castration anxiety. It is assumed that the extensiveness of menstrual taboos is determined, to some degree, by the intensity and frequency (among men) of castration anxiety. It is further assumed that intensity and frequency of castration anxiety is influenced by the intensity of the Oedipus complex.

Another set of consequent variables—those considered in the chapter entitled "Sexual Problems"—represent anxiety about sex. Generally, I assume that they are influenced by the level of anxiety about sex, which in turn is affected by intensity of the Oedipus complex.

Kin-avoidance represents a sort of mixture. I assume that it reflects a phobic attitude toward incestuous sexual relations, which stems from Oedipal fantasies and desires.[5]

Two of these interpretations stem from the writings of Geza Roheim. As far as I know, he was the first to suggest (in a vague and indirect way) that fear of menstruating women is caused by castration anxiety, that kin avoidances are caused by a phobic attitude toward incest, and that both of these are caused by the Oedipus complex (Roheim, 1945: 174; Roheim, 1947: 10).

I will now summarize the answer to the last question: *Does the Oedipus complex have persisting effects (in adults)? What are these effects?* There is evidence that adults employ unconscious sex symbols, in a manner similar to children. The following assumptions were made: (1) adults have unconscious fantasies that carry over from their childhood; (2) these fantasies include both symbolic meanings and fantasy-thoughts; (3) the Oedipus complex has the same effect on an adult's fantasy-life as it does on children's fantasy-life: it determines the degree to which the concepts "mother" and "sex object" are confounded; (4) confounding of "mother" and "sex object" leads to anxiety about sex.

In this study, there will be one major attempt to make a deduction from the effects of an unconscious fantasy-thought (castration anxiety). There will be numerous attempts to measure the effects of sex anxiety.

This concludes the discussion of assumptions underlying

5. There are further consequent variables that fall beyond the boundaries of my rather narrow Oedipus complex hypothesis: initiations, totemism, and perhaps sorcery. To explain these, an extra formulation must be added—father-son rivalry. Possibly, this factor also partly accounts for menstrual taboos.

the general hypothesis of this study. The general hypothesis is: *young boys, at least under optimal conditions (post partum sex taboo), become sexually attracted to their mothers. This generates lasting sexual fears and avoidances. These fears are (at least in one instance—menstrual taboos) mediated by unconscious fantasies.*

I will now preview the results on which this book will report. On balance, the cross-cultural evidence gives massive, impressive support to the hypothesis. When the cross-cultural evidence is added to pre-existing evidence from other sources, the Oedipus complex hypothesis (as narrowly defined here) is substantially documented. The probability is high that it is, approximately, valid.

3

THE CROSS-CULTURAL
METHOD

BEFORE PRESENTING THE
cross-cultural evidence, I should say something about how the
evidence was gathered. This chapter will describe the cross-
cultural research method, as I have practiced it.

The Case

The raw material, or raw data, of cross-cultural research
comes from written accounts by anthropologists (ethnographies). The ethnographies we use describe *primitive* societies: societies without modern science and technology. These
societies are usually (but not always) quite small, containing only a few hundred or a few thousand people. They are
usually rather isolated and culturally distinct: only nomi-
nally are they part of larger nations. They are characterized

49

by a great many superstitions, supernatural explanations for events, magical practices, and "make-believe" entities (ghosts, witches, etc.).

Today, many of these primitive societies are greatly changed, due to contact with Western culture. Some of the ethnographies, particularly those dealing with the North American Indians, describe how it was "in the old days," before deculturation. Other ethnographies are current accounts of primitive societies that were not (at the time of the ethnographer's visit) radically changed by Western contact. Usually current accounts of radically deculturated societies are excluded from my samples.

In most research methods of social science, a "case" is a single person. The sample that is studied is a collection of persons, each person constituting a separate "case." Cross-cultural research is different in this respect: *the case is an entire primitive society* (or a community that is taken to represent an entire society) (Whiting, 1954). The cross-cultural sample is made up of many primitive societies, each society representing a separate case.[1]

Later, I shall have more to say about the cross-cultural sample.

The Variable

The cross-cultural researcher measures variables. Here are some of the variables that will be used: *duration* of the

1. You may have heard the term "cross-cultural" before, used to describe comparisons between two or three societies. When I use the term, I always mean large-sample studies, usually, those with more than thirty societies in the sample in which quantified data is treated.

post partum sex taboo; *severity* of sex training; *extensiveness* of menstrual taboos; *presence* of initiations for boys. For each variable measured, there is assigned to societies scores or ratings along some sort of "high/low" continuum. A society may be rated "long" or "short" for duration of the post partum sex taboo; "severe" or "mild" for severity of sex training; "present" or "absent" for presence of initiations. For extensiveness of menstrual taboos, a society may be scored 5, 4, 3, 2, or 1 on an extensiveness scale; societies scored "5" have the most extensive menstrual taboos; societies scored "1" have the least extensive.

Each variable subsumes one or several *customs* (Whiting, 1954). The variable "duration of the post partum sex taboo" is based on just one custom (or narrowly defined custom-category)—the post partum sex taboo. Other variables are based on several customs. In general, I try to follow this strategy when rating societies in regard to some variable: (1) I code several customs "present" or "absent"; (2) I then arrange these customs into a scale; (3) I score societies on the variable according to where they fall on the scale. Below, I shall describe the scales. First, let us consider coding.

Coding

You may wonder why we speak of "measurement," if all we do is read ethnographies and decide whether certain variables are "high" or "low." The cross-cultural researcher actually does measure (if in a rather crude way), since his decisions about the societies' scores are made in a standardized manner. He has no yardstick, but he has a substitute for a yardstick—coding rules.

In the appendices are coding rules for all the variables I have tried to measure. They are detailed instructions to the coder. The cross-cultural coder (the person who applies the coding rules), when deciding whether a custom is "present" or "absent" in a particular society, is supposed to base his decision on a precise, literal application of the coding rules. The rules are supposed to be detailed enough so that the judgment comes automatically; the coder should not have to guess, intuit, or employ his own personal criteria to make a judgment.

The coding rules resemble a yardstick in that they provide a standardized basis for judgment. When applied to case after case, they do not change in any respect (as bases for personal intuitions might). They also resemble a yardstick in that they allow a repeatable, de-personalized judgment. If two coders working separately apply them to the same case, they should come up with the same judgment.

In repeatability (or reliability) my coding rules are inferior to a yardstick. About 20 per cent of the time, coders use them and come up with different answers. This is partly because the ethnographic descriptions are sometimes vague; in order to apply the rules, the coder sometimes must guess what the ethnographer means. Partly, it is because the rules are not precise enough; for some cases they do not automatically make the decision for the coder (even when the ethnographer has not been vague).

My coding rules are applied, separately, by *three* cross-cultural coders. (The only exception to this is the coding of folklore.) The final code, for each case, is decided by majority rule. Using several coders allows us to estimate the repeatability, or reliability, of the coding rules. For example, 94 per cent of the time the coders agreed as to whether *menstrual huts* were "present" or "absent" in a society; 82 per cent of the time they agreed as to whether *the belief that menstrual blood is dangerous to men* was "present" or "absent." The rules for coding *menstrual huts* come much nearer to the yardstick, in repeatability, than do the rules for coding *danger to men*.

Scales

For some variables, the society's score was assigned directly by the coders. For example, when I measured *the father's obedience demands*, the coders' job was to score societies on this variable—either "severe" or "mild." For other variables—extensiveness of menstrual taboos and severity of kin-avoidances—the coders did not assign the final score. Here, their job was to code "present" or "absent" a number of *code-categories*; each of the code-categories represented a specific custom or group of customs. For example, the coders of menstrual taboos coded the following code-categories "present," "absent," or "no information": menstrual huts; cooking taboo; sex taboo; belief in danger to men; many other menstrual taboos. After societies had been coded for these code-categories, I arranged the code-categories into a cumulative or Guttman-type scale. Then each society was given an over-all score on extensiveness of menstrual taboos; its score was equal to the "highest" scale point (or code-category) for which it had been scored "present." The same method was used for scoring societies on severity of kin-avoidances.

A final type of scale used is a composite index. I will use two composite indices: a composite index of sex anxiety, and a composite predicter of castration anxiety. Each is composed of scores on still other variables, which are combined to produce composite scores. For example, the *sex anxiety index* is made up of six variables: severity of sex training, premarital intercourse prohibited, duration of the pregnancy sex taboo, presence of sexual explanations for illness, presence of sexual avoidance therapy, and sexual intercourse usually punished in folklore. All of these variables but the last are the work of previous researchers. A society's score on *sex anxiety* is derived from its scores on these other variables.

To conclude, I measure variables in three ways: (1) high/low ratings, made directly by the coders; (2) Guttman scales, made up of coder-judgments on code-categories; (3) composite indices, composed of still other variables.

Other cross-cultural researchers frequently use still another method. Their coders rate a variable along some continuous dimension; duration (in months) of the post partum sex taboo, percentage of polygynous marriages, or severity of some aspect of child-rearing (judged intuitively on a seven-point scale). After the coder's judgments are assembled, societies may be sorted into "highs" and "lows"—divided at the median score or at some arbitrary cutting-point. I shall rely heavily on ratings of this sort, made by other researchers.

These are the cross-cultural variables (to be used here) that were measured by others:[2]

Ayres (1954): duration of the pregnancy sex taboo (used in the sex anxiety index).

2. The following people conceived, supervised, and made available these ratings. They did not necessarily do the coding.

Bacon, Barry, and Child (1954): diffusion of nurturance; general pressure for obedience; severity of punishment for disobedience.

Fischer and Whiting (1957): totemism with food taboos.

Ford and Beach (1951): premarital intercourse prohibited (used in the sex anxiety index).

Murdock (1957): rules of descent and residence; sex-division of labor.

Whiting and Child (1953): severity of sex training; severity of aggression training; severity of punishment for masturbation; importance of physical punishment as a technique of discipline; average age of weaning; initial indulgence of dependency; sexual explanations for illness, sexual avoidance therapy (both used in the sex anxiety index); dependency explanations for illness; dependency avoidance therapy; fear of humans (sorcery-fear); over-all fear of others.

Whiting and D'Andrade: percentage of polygyny; percentage of mother-child households; propinquity of sleeping arrangements; change of residence for adolescent boys.

Whiting and Kluckhohn: duration of the post partum sex taboo.

Whiting, Kluckhohn, and Anthony: initiation ceremonies for adolescent boys.

There are the variables I measured: extensiveness of menstrual taboos; severity of kin-avoidances (avoidance of mother-in-law, daughter-in-law, or sister);[3] frequency of castration-suggestive incidents in folklore; frequency of father-son conflict in folklore; sexual intercourse usually punished

3. Kin-avoidance ratings were done in collaboration with Roy G. D'Andrade.

in folklore; strictness of the father's obedience demands; importance of the father as a disciplinarian; whether or not breasts are considered special sexual stimuli; intensity of sex anxiety; composite predicter of castration anxiety. In addition, I made informal judgments on these topics: presence or absence of menstrual pads; presence or absence of joking relationships; and certain facts about the patterning of kin-avoidances.

Cross-Cultural Measurement: Step-by-Step

To summarize the chapter so far:

The raw material comes from ethnographies. Each primitive society is treated as a separate case.

A variable is measured on a high/low dimension. Measurement is accomplished by means of coding rules. The societies are scored on the variable, using one of several kinds of scaling devices.

These scales will be more fully described when we begin to use them.

To review further, and to introduce the topics to follow, we will now go through a cross-cultural study chronologically—the ratings of menstrual taboos.

1. First, I decided on my hypothesis: menstrual taboos are caused (partly) by castration anxiety. Then I made a prediction: menstrual taboos would be positively correlated with other specified variables.

2. I decided on the sample: it would include all societies that have been previously rated for either the post partum sex taboo or for severity of sex training.

3. I read all ethnographic descriptions (which were available to me) of these societies, searching for accounts of menstrual taboos, and noting page references.

4. After reading the accounts, I drew up the rules for coding certain menstrual customs (code-categories) "present" or "absent."[4] Two of us (John K. Harley and myself) tried them out on about a dozen cases. Our findings did not agree. The rules were changed, and we agreed fairly well. The coding rules were then "set" in their final form.

5. Two coders were given the ethnographies, the page references to accounts of menstrual taboos, and the coding rules for judging certain menstrual customs "present" or "absent." I served as the third coder (this was the only time I did). Each coder applied the rules to each case in the sample, and made his judgments. He worked separately, never communicating with the other coders. When the coding was finished, average agreement was computed (it was fairly high); the societies were assigned final scores (on the code-categories) by majority rule.

6. The code-categories were arranged into a Guttman scale. Societies were assigned scale-scores on extensiveness of menstrual taboos.

7. I tested for the correlations I had predicted. Menstrual taboos were correlated with the other variables; a test of significance was applied.

4. By this time, I had made my own informal ratings. I knew approximately what the Guttman scale-pattern was. I also had an approximate idea of how menstrual taboos would correlate with the other variables.

The Ethnographic Data

While we are considering measurement, something should be said about the quality of the ethnographic reports on which these measures are based.

In the first place, this data is frequently incomplete. I would estimate that for every variable I tried to measure at least one third of all the ethnographies I scanned contained no information. In other ethnographies the variable was mentioned, but was described vaguely, from the viewpoint of the coder who had to apply the coding rules. These cases either proved uncodable or led to frequent disagreements between the data of the coders. Then, of course, other ethnographies gave descriptions that were clear, complete, and eminently codable.

The best way to get a feeling for the quality of the ethnographic reports is to actually read some, so some examples will be given at this point. They are accounts that were used to code mother-in-law avoidance. The coders had to judge "present" or "absent" the following avoidance rules (code-categories): can't talk about sex; can't talk directly; can't look eye-to-eye; can't eat together. They were also to code if the ethnographer indicated that "no avoidance rules" applied to a man and his mother-in-law. There were a few more code-categories, which we needn't consider now. The complete coding rules are given in Appendix IV.

Thirteen examples follow. I have tried to choose them so that they are roughly representative of the range of the accounts, and of the proportion of "good" to "bad" accounts. I will start with accounts that were "good" from the viewpoint of the coders—that is, they made coding relatively easy. I will gradually work down the scale, and conclude with accounts that were uncodable.

1. . . . A strict reciprocal avoidance is observed between *veivungoni* (this includes the man to mother-in-law relationship). Sexual intercourse is tabu between them. They avoid meeting, speaking to one another, and never look at one another. When they are together they keep the head and eyes lowered and avoid saying more than is necessary. The words come slowly and heavily in a trembling voice. Jokes and references to sex are prohibited. . . . Those standing in the vungo relationship do not address one another with personal names but use the polite second person plural. . . . *Veivungoni* may enter the same house, eat together, drink in the same kava circle and eat one another's left over food. Although sleeping in the same house is not allowed, it is quite common for a widowed mother-in-law to live in the house of the son-in-law (L. Thompson, 1940).

2. This is the most important of all taboo relationships. . . . But his relations with all his female *waris*, and with the actual mother of his wife in particular, are hedged about with the strictest taboos that are known in this society. . . .
A man must not see the face of his female *waris*, nor her hair. For this reason she carries about with her constantly a kind of pointed hood made of pandanus leaves, which, when her *waris* is present or expected, or where there is a chance of meeting him by accident, she keeps on her head, and pulls, if necessary, over her face. Most particularly she must never be seen by him while eating, and if she has to eat in his presence, she goes as far away from him as possible, pulls her hood over her face, and eats behind it. On encountering in the bush a party of which any relation a woman calls *waris* is likely to be one, she will leave the path and hide behind the tree 'till they have gone. . . . Further restrictions on the relations between a man and his mother-in-law and other female *waris* are as follows: They must not defecate within sight of one another (in the ordinary way no shame is attached to being seen in the act of defecating). They must not touch one another. They must not sleep

in the same house. They must not chew areca nut in the presence of each other. They must not speak to one another directly, but must converse through the wife. They must not say each other's personal name, nor even a substitute name. This taboo ceases to operate when the wife's mother is very old . . . (Blackwood, 1935: 72–73, 74).

3. It is obligatory for the husband to avoid his mother-in-law, his father-in-law, his mother-in-law's mother, and his father-in-law's mother. With these individuals there is no choice or alternative.
[avoidance behavior described]
The attitude and behaviour of the parties to an avoidance relationship are identical in every respect with the elements of polite-form relationship with the exception that the principals are prevented from ever meeting face to face. All negotiations between them must be carried on through a third person, usually the wife of the married man; for, of a married couple, only the man avoids any of his wife's relatives. There is a general term, reciprocally used, which can be translated "that one whom I avoid." It is employed in speaking of any person with whom an avoidance relationship has been established.

The avoidance relationship necessitates some manner of warning from others to those in an avoidance relationship who are inadvertently about to come into each other's view. Bystanders are most obliging in this respect, and the usual warning, "Do not walk there," is constantly heard (Opler, 1941: 216–218).

4. No avoidance is practiced between men and their mothers-in-law. In fact, no avoidance relationships exist (Bennett and Zingg, 1935: 223).

5. Generally speaking, there are no formalized obligatory patterns of kinship behavior. Brother-sister avoidance, parent-in-law taboos, joking relationships, etc., are lacking. However, patterns of relative reserve and freedom are clearly noticeable between certain relatives.

Although there are no taboos between parents-in-law and children-in-law, the relationships between these relatives are the most reserved of all . . . it is strange that no mother-in-law taboo has arisen to help in keeping peace between the families, but this has not happened (Holmburg, 1950: 56, 57).

6. During the first few years of wedlock a man never communicated directly with his parents-in-law, his wife serving as an intermediary for either party. In the course of time—especially after the arrival of children—the rule is relaxed, that is, at first only between father-in-law and son-in-law, who henceforth converse with fair freedom from restraint. Finally, the wife's mother also addresses her daughter's husband, though a certain reserve is maintained inasmuch as they avoid meeting or addressing each other when by themselves. In case of a chance encounter the son-in-law gives the woman a wide birth (Nimenaju, 1946: 125).

7. A Lepcha is expected to respect his parents and grand-parents, his parents-in-law, and his sons- and daughters-in-law. Of these "respect-ful" situations by far the most important is that between a Lepcha and his parents-in-law. A person is more respectful to his spouse's parents than to his own; he uses more honorific words to them and is careful never to use directly obscene language in front of them. A person must never witness his parents-in-law copulating nor must he be seen doing so by them. Should either of these situations arise the elders will be ashamed and angry.

The tensest of all situations, and one which lasts during the whole life-time of both parties is the relationship between a man and his wife's mother, and a woman and her husband's father. These relationships are always rather strained and uncomfortable. If for instance a man's mother-in-law says something immodest, the man himself will feel uncomfortable, and may get up and go away. . . . Once he has brought his wife home a man still has to avoid the crudest sexual phrases in front of his parents-in-law, but it is considered a rather amusing and risky game to sail as near the wind as possible.

. . . Adult brothers and sisters should not, and on the whole do not, touch one another except in cases of actual necessity, such as helping a person work or if they are ill. This prohibition does not extend to dressing the hair, which can be performed by anybody for anybody else, with the exception of a son- or daughter-in-law and parent-in-law of the opposite sex (Gorer, 1938: 147).

8. A man must show formal deference to his parents-in-law or their representatives, especially in the early years of marriage, and always in ceremonial situations. When he encounters them, or visits them, he sits down to greet them in the posture of respect—crossed legs, bowed and hatless head—adopted before a chief, a high ritual functionary, or an ancestor shrine. He is a "stranger" in their house and they in his house. He is "shy" of them, and must be on his best behavior in their presence.

. . . There is no prohibition against talking to or in the presence of an affine about sexual matters (Fortes, 1949: 119, 123).

9. Between mother-in-law and son-in-law there is reserve and a measure of avoidance—he may never go into the inner part of her hut where her bed is, and the food she cooks for him will be brought by someone else—but the restrictions on his behavior are slight compared to those imposed on his wife (Wilson, 1950: 128).

10. Mothers-in-law are treated with respect and deference, but not avoided (Burrows, 1948).

11. . . . Husband and wife are segregated from the wife's relatives until family ties are established, and it is only after the birth of children that these customs which keep the wife's family at a distance are allowed to lapse. . . .

Hostility and opposition are created by bride-wealth and by a whole range of taboos like mother-in-law avoidance, and patterns of behavior like the pattern of submissiveness which the husband has to enact, for these establish new relations which are characterized by opposition and necessitate estranged and distant inter-communications (Evans-Pritchard, 1934: 174).

12. When a marriage takes place children-in-law and parents-in-law at first avoid each other. After a time, however, the only trace of this avoidance is that they do not use one another's names (Hogbin, 1931: 418).

13. A man must avoid his mother-in-law, father-in-law, brother-in-law and his wife's mother's brother (Berndt and Berndt, 1942: 150).

You may have noticed the following things about these accounts: they are always brief; they are sometimes vague (in respect to the code categories); they seldom contain any statement that a specific avoidance custom is absent.

The extent of the vagueness problem depends, partly, on the reasonableness of the demands put on the data. Perhaps, if my coding rules had been different, the coders would have had less trouble agreeing.

The rarity of reported absences is a problem I handle in a rather complicated way, by means of scaling. However, the most important rule I follow in this regard is as follows: if nothing can be coded either present or absent, the society is not scored; it is excluded from the sample.

Finally, how was this data gathered? Did the ethnographer talk to one or two informants, observe a small village, check his findings in several villages, or randomly sample the entire society? Did he use a standardized questionnaire, or standardized behavior-observations, or gather his data in an informal, uncontrolled way?

In fact, we do have a general idea of how these people gathered their data. By the standards of most social psychologists and sociologists who gather quantified data in our own society, the ethnographers' methods were primitive. At the very best, they questioned several informants (and checked to see if the informants agreed with each other), informally observed how men actually acted toward their mothers-in-law (to see if behavior matched informants' accounts), and visited several villages in the society (to see if there were differences between them).[5] Often, they did not—or could not—take all these steps.

Given the magnitude of their task, they did the best they could. If you are working by yourself, and have about two years to make a general study of an entire society, you have little time for elaborately controlled data-gathering. To a large extent, the ethnographers' methods of data-gathering were informal, unstandardized, and uncontrolled. What can be done with data like this?

One thing we can do is use only that part of the data which looks like it is least subject to reporting-error. This I have attempted. Generally speaking, there are two levels of ethnographic data: descriptions of actual behavior, and reports of specific rules (or norms or prohibitions) that govern behavior. When an ethnographer operates on the first level, he usually characterizes behavior with some descriptive term, and then gives examples. He may say something like this: "Children are expected to be obedient. Their parents are strict about this. When a child does disobey, he is usually spanked." He may then illustrate this with a few anecdotes. Sometimes, a descriptive term is given without illustrations: "Obedience demands are strict"; "Brother and sister are shy toward each other"; "A man has a warm relationship with his maternal uncle." And then, occasionally, behavior is described and not summarized or evaluated by means of descriptive terms.

When an ethnographer operates on the second level, he merely notes what the rules are: "A man can't eat with his

5. The ethnographer's problem of sampling within a society has been discussed by Whiting, (1954: 526).

mother-in-law"; "A brother is not supposed to touch his sister"; "When a woman menstruates, she must go to a special menstrual hut."

Whenever possible, I have tried to base my ratings on this second level—on mere statements of the rules that govern behavior—in the belief that it is probably less subject to reporting-error. This is not too limiting, since most ethnographies are largely concerned with the *formal* content of culture—rules and beliefs—and devote less space to descriptions of how people actually behave. One gets the impression that ethnographers often do sense the difficulties of truly and reliably reporting behavior, in all its subtlety and variety, and as a practical compromise concentrate on reporting the formal rules. Coding the rules does present problems. Occasionally, it is hard to decide whether an ethnographer is reporting a rule or describing behavior. For instance, he may say: "When a woman menstruates, she goes to a menstrual hut." Is this a formal rule, or merely something women like to do? (We code it as a formal rule, although, strictly speaking, it is a behavior-description.) Sometimes an ethnographer describes behavior that violates the formal rule. For example, he may state that brother and sister are not supposed to discuss sex, but that in fact a boy frequently brags to his sister about his sexual exploits. What do you code here: the rule or the actual behavior? (We code the rule.) The main difficulty with coding formal rules is that it forces us to make an extra assumption about the data: that the rule usually does represent actual behavior—that usually the rule is obeyed. Sometimes, I am sure, this assumption is incorrect.

Ratings of post partum sex taboo, menstrual taboos and kin-avoidances are based on descriptions of formal rules.

Most of the other ratings are based, to a greater or lesser degree, on behavior-descriptions. The child-rearing ratings by Whiting and Child, Bacon, Barry and Child, and myself, rely very heavily on descriptions of behavior. They also involve evaluations—more or less intuitive, informal judgments—of "severity," "indulgence," "strictness," and the like, made by ethnographer and/or coder.

Because of the above inconsistencies, I am confident that slips occur in data-processing. Some of the individual scores are inaccurate. All the variables are tainted, to some degree, by measurement error. However, some variables are probably more fallible than others. I suspect that, generally, the ratings based on formal cultural rules are most accurate, and ratings based primarily on behavior-descriptions, particularly the child-rearing ratings, are the least accurate.[6]

The Samples

There are two kinds of samples: (1) the collection of cases measured for some variable, and (2) the collection of cases that underly a correlation. In a moment we will consider the second kind; now we shall discuss the first.

6. I do not think that measurement error is so great as to pose an impossible handicap. It has been fairly easy to find strong correlations between cross-cultural variables. I don't believe this could have happened if most of the cross-cultural ratings were grossly inaccurate.

Although I cannot prove it, I think that measurement error occurs randomly—in respect to the correlations we shall deal with. If this is so, measurement error must nearly always weaken the correlation. If error was truly great, we would rarely get strong correlations. Since fairly pronounced cross-cultural correlations occur frequently, I must conclude that measurement error does not reach major proportions. Probably, though, most of the correlations are weakened somewhat by randomly-occurring measurement error.

Each variable we use represents a separate sample. For the variable "duration of the post partum sex taboo," the sample is all societies rated for the duration of the post partum sex taboo. The same applies for the other variables.

These samples overlap. All the societies we use are in several of them. However, no single society is present in all the samples.

Sample-choice for the variables I measured was predetermined by previous cross-cultural samples. For kin-avoidances, menstrual taboos, and "breasts a sexual stimulus," I tried to include only those societies that had been previously rated by Whiting and Kluckhohn on duration of the post partum sex taboo.[7] For the ratings of folklore, and of the father's role, the samples were limited to all societies that had been previously rated for menstrual taboos. For each of these variables, sample-size fell short of its optimal limits, since many societies were uncodable.

For the two composite indices, the samples were also predetermined by previous samples.

I believe (although I am not sure) that the samples for most of the other variables rated by other researchers were selected by the "gold is where you find it" principle; since rateable cross-cultural cases are always at a premium, these researchers gathered all the cases they could.

Now let us consider the "second kind" of sample: the collection of cases rated for *both* of two variables we wish to correlate. In the first place, in any cross-cultural study this

7. A few more cases were added: for the menstrual taboo sample, all societies scored for severity of sex training by Whiting and Child; for the kin-avoidance sample, all societies given propinquity ratings by Whiting and D'Andrade; for both of these samples, several more cases that accrued as a result of ethnographer-interviews.

is *not* a random sample. The sample has not been chosen by a completely random method, such as referring to a table of random numbers. Neither is it a representative or stratified sample. All societies in the world do not have an equal chance to be represented in it. By the "gold is where you find it" principle, a society cannot get into the sample unless it is reported (and unless the report is known and accessible). Some areas of the world—Africa, Melanesia, and western North American (the "American Indians")—are relatively well-reported; hence, they are "over-represented" in the samples. Other areas—Asia, South America—are poorly reported, and hence "under-represented."

Also, some cases in the sample are probably not independent of each other. Some societies probably do, in indirect ways, influence each other, in respect to the two variables being correlated; they are in contact with each other in the same geographic area, or they represent the same linguistic stock (indicating a historical connection).

The great danger in sampling is that sample-choice will "rig" the results of a correlation, that it will artificially inflate the apparent association between two variables. I have taken two precautions against this. First, I have deliberately excluded from the samples all "civilized" societies—societies characterized by modern science and technology, and by relatively little superstition (sometimes, though, it is hard to draw the line between "civilized" and "primitive" societies). To my knowledge, civilized societies are uniformly "low" on all the variables we will be correlating (*sex anxiety* and *severity of sex training* are possible exceptions). If they had been included, most of the correlations would have been a good deal stronger. I excluded them to guard against "rigged" results. I thought there might be something special about civilization, or modern science, which "depresses" scores on all the variables I wanted to correlate. In other words, I thought civilized societies might conform to my predictions for special reasons, which had little to do with the cause-effect relationships I hypothesize.

Nonindependence of cases may also inflate correlations. The way I deal with this problem is described in Appendix I. Briefly, the method involves "re-running" the correlations on new samples. In these new samples, each of Murdock's Culture Areas is represented by no more than one primitive society (Murdock, 1957). These "new correlations" are always in the same direction as were the "original correlations," and nearly always of approximately equal strength (i.e., equal in strength to the original correlations). On the basis of these results, I am confident that possible non-independence of cases does *not* seriously distort the results. It may distort one or two of the correlations, but it has little if any over-all inflating effect on the entire correlation-network, taken as a whole.

Precautions against Cheating

As in other sorts of research methods, it is easy to cheat while doing cross-cultural research—that is, distort the data in such a way as to strengthen the correlations you predict or "want to find." Several things can be done about this. In those areas where it is in his power to distort the data, the researcher can try to be honest. He can also, to some extent, remove the data-processing from his own control. He can arrange it so that he has no control over (1) the selection of cases, (2) assignment of scores, and (3) the assignment of page-references (the pages in the ethnographies that are coded). I took all these precautions except the last. The samples were defined by previous ratings. The coding was done by other persons. The coders could not cheat, since they were ignorant of the hypotheses to be tested and of the other variables to be correlated. I arranged code-categories into scales, but the nature of the scales was dictated, in large part, by the ethnographic data itself. I *did* control the assignment of page-references. My data-gathering would have been even more stringently controlled if someone else, who was ignorant of the hypothesis and predictions, had scanned the ethnographies and decided on the pages to be coded.

An additional precaution against cheating is replication of the study. It would be rather easy to fully replicate any cross-cultural study. The ethnographies—the raw data—remain in the libraries, after the study is over. The researcher should certainly have a full copy of his coding rules and ratings. I hope that someone will take my studies seriously enough to replicate them. But I doubt that this will happen since—to date—no one has replicated a cross-cultural study.

Drawing Conclusions from the Data

First, I had better define what I mean by a "correlation." When I "correlate" two variables, I compare them to see if they "behave" in a parallel, or opposite, manner. This can always be represented by a table, as follows:

	Number of Societies "High" on Variable X	Number of Societies "Low" on Variable X
Number of Societies "Low" on Variable Y	1	7
Number of Societies "High" on Variable Y	8	2

Variables X and Y in this table behave in a parallel manner. Most societies high on variable X are also high on variable Y, and vice versa. When one variable "goes up" the other variable "goes up"; when one "goes down" the other "goes down." In this particular example, there are three exceptions to this rule. This sort of parallel behavior, trend, or association between two variables I shall term a *positive correlation*. If the trend were in the opposite direction—that is, if the trend was for societies high on variable X to be low on variable Y—I would call it a *negative correlation*. (I will rarely deal with negative correlations.) When the table shows no trend, for example, if each cell in the table above contained four or five cases, I will say that the two variables appear to be *uncorrelated*.

The strength of the correlation can be formally estimated by means of various sorts of statistics. The statistic I usually use is Chi Square; at times, I use correlation coefficients.[8] For most correlations, I will not report a statistic; however, you will usually be able to estimate, by inspection, the strength of the trend—you can look at the Table. My primary interest is not the strength of a positive correlation, but the likelihood that it could have occurred by chance. I estimate this likelihood by means of *tests of significance*.

The test of significance "considers" two things: (1) the strength of the correlation, and (2) the number of cases in the sample (Edwards, 1954: 369–370). If the correlation is strong and the sample is large, the significance test will indicate that the association between the two variables is prob-

8. Since I seldom employ correlation coefficients, I shall be using the term "correlation" rather loosely. It is synonymous with "trend," "association," or "parallel behavior of two variables."

ably not due to "accident" or chance. As correlation-strength or sample-size diminishes, the probability increases that the correlation (whether positive or negative) is merely due to chance.

The test of significance represents likelihood of chance occurrence with a "P value." A P of 0.05 means "there are five chances in 100 that a correlation of this strength, based on a sample of this size, could have occurred by chance or accident." When reporting a correlation, I will usually give the direction of the correlation (positive or negative) and the P value; I will seldom report the Chi Square or correlation coefficient value.[9]

Although these P values are not completely illegitimate, they are not completely legitimate either. They should be "taken with a grain of salt." They are based on samples that are neither random nor stratified, and which probably include some nonindependent cases. (Also, of course, they are probably "penalized" to some extent by randomly-occurring measurement error.)

When the P value reaches the conventional level for rejecting the null hypothesis (0.05 or less), I will conclude that the correlation probably isn't due to chance[10] (Edwards, 1954:

9. Even though I often predict the direction of a relationship, I shall always report P values based on a two-tailed test of significance (Edwards, 1954: 257).

10. When the P value doesn't reach this level—when it is greater than 0.05—I should, perhaps, accept the null hypothesis. That is, I should conclude that the positive correlation is merely due to chance. In practice, I don't do this. A number of correlations (particularly in the chapter on menstrual taboos) are in the predicted direction, but fall short of statistical significance (P is greater than 0.05); in such cases I usually draw no conclusions at all. Or, I may summarize a number of such correlations, and allow you to draw your own conclusions.

255–258). I will say (or imply) that there probably is a relationship—some sort of causal connection—between the two variables. The smaller the P value, the more confident the statement; if P is 0.001, non-chance is more probable than when P is 0.05. To all such statements of probability you should make a small mental subtraction—an allowance for the partial illegitimacy of the P value.

I will generalize from the sample-correlation to the "population"—in this case, I suppose, all primitive societies. If two variables are significantly correlated, I will conclude that if all primitive societies were scored the two variables would still be correlated. From significant correlations, I will draw this further conclusion: within all primitive societies, the two variables are probably causally connected.

What kind of causal relationship is it? I assume that it is never a one-to-one cause-effect relationship. Rather, the two variables are joined in rather complex causal systems. One variable "causes" or influences another in conjunction with still other (unmeasured) variables. The cause-effect relationship may very well be indirect; it may also be circular or reciprocal. In a certain percentage of cases, the cause-effect relationship between the pair of variables being correlated is probably "over-ridden" or "canceled out" by other causal factors; these are the "exceptional cases."

What is the direction of causation? What causes what? The correlation doesn't say. I can state that variable X causes variable Y. The data may be consistent with this statement (if variables X and Y are positively correlated); or, the data may be inconsistent with the statement (if variables X and Y are uncorrelated). But the correlation itself does not say which variable is "antecedent," or causal, to the other.

All I can do is assemble correlations that may be more or less consistent with my causation-statements. I can never directly demonstrate the direction of causation.

This assembly of evidence is more convincing (in respect to a causation-statement) if the correlations are predicted before the facts are known. So, whenever possible, I have tried to predict. Here is the sequence:

1. First, I stated my general hypothesis (outlined in Chapter 2). Briefly, it is this: maternal seduction (of children) leads to anxieties concerning sex (when they become adults), by means of persisting unconscious fantasies.

2. Then, making further assumptions, I impute "meanings" to variables. For example, I assumed that the long post partum sex taboo makes maternal seduction more likely and "intense," thereby also making sexual or Oedipal anxieties more likely. In other words, the meaning I impute to the long post partum sex taboo is that it is an antecedent, cause, or intensifier. I also assume that certain child-rearing variables are antecedents. Other variables—menstrual taboos, kin-avoidances—I assume are "effects" or "consequences" of the Oedipus complex.

3. On the basis of the general hypothesis, and on the basis of the "meanings" I have imputed to these variables, I then make predictions. For example, I predict that duration of the post partum sex taboo and extensiveness of menstrual taboos will be positively correlated, because (I assume) the post partum sex taboo *causes* (or intensifies) menstrual taboos. That is, it is one of several causes or "antecedents."

4. *After* the prediction is made, the ratings are done and the prediction is tested. If the correlation is in the expected

direction (positive) and statistically significant, I feel the prediction has been borne out; the evidence is consistent with (1) the general hypothesis and (2) the special assumptions I made, when I imputed "meanings" to the variables.

At times the correlation is in the expected direction, but it falls short of statistical significance. At such times I suspend judgment. Perhaps, if the sample was larger or the ratings more accurate, it would have been significant. Or, perhaps the prediction was at fault: either the general hypothesis, or the special assumptions about the "meanings" of the variables, were, somewhere, incorrect.

5. I keep track of all predictions. After the testing, I will summarize them all. Then you can see how many predicted the direction of the correlation and how many didn't, and how impressive are the P values.

My predictions are tested in Chapters 5 and 6. In other chapters, I present further correlations that are usually consistent with the general hypothesis, but these correlations were *not* formally predicted. The one exception is the correlation between duration of the post partum sex taboo and presence of initiations for boys, predicted by Whiting, Kluckhohn, and Anthony. (Their prediction was based on a different version of the Oedipus complex hypothesis.)

Summary

To summarize the last part of the chapter:

The ethnographies are sometimes incomplete and sometimes vague, in respect to the variable being measured. Customs are seldom reported to be absent. The ethnographer's data-collection methods are rather informal. Some measurement error must exist. I would guess that error is minimized when we do not try to code actual behavior, but instead code the cultural rules that govern behavior.

My samples were predetermined by previous samples. The samples are neither random nor stratified. Civilized societies are excluded from them. Probably, they include some nonindependent cases; the problem of nonindependence is treated in Appendix I.

It is easy to cheat. I take several precautions to "keep myself honest."

I term parallel behavior, or association, between two variables a "correlation." In the text, a correlation will usually be represented by a table; its probability of chance-occurrence is represented by a P value. Citing P values is slightly illegitimate, due to sample-deficiencies.

I will conclude that a significant correlation ($P = 0.05$ or less) probably represents a causal connection between two variables, which applies to all primitive societies. I assume the causal connection is always partial, and never one-to-one.

The correlation does not tell the direction of causation. It may or may not be consistent with a cause-effect statement that specifies direction of causation.

Whenever possible, the general hypothesis is tested by means of the prediction method. All tests of predictions are reported and then summarized. Additional correlations, which were not formally predicted, are also reported.

Having disposed of methodology, let us move on to the findings.

4

SEXUAL PROBLEMS

Ｉn this chapter we shall examine some correlations that were not formally predicted, but which do seem consistent with the general hypothesis. They suggest that people in societies with the long post partum sex taboo tend to be (1) unusually worried about the sexuality of children, and (2) unusually anxious about the general topic of sex.

Sex Restrictions on Children

Sex Training. There is some tendency for the long post partum sex taboo societies to be "high" on severity of sex training (as measured by Whiting and Child). See Table 4.

Change of Residence. In most societies with the long post partum sex taboo, boys, when they reach the age of puberty, no longer sleep at home. They move to a bachelor-hut, or to some other sleeping quarters in the neighborhood. Occasionally, as among the Nyakusa and the Trobriand Islanders, they move to a different community. Whiting and D'Andrade have made ratings on whether or not a change of residence for adolescent boys is customary (i.e., whether it is or is not the custom for most boys). Table 5 shows the strong correlation between long post partum sex taboo and change of residence.

Frequency of mother-child households seems to exert a powerful effect on occurrence of change of residence. All societies rated "high" for mother-child households have change of residence for adolescent boys (Appendix VIII). When these societies are taken out of the sample, there is still a positive correlation between long post partum sex taboo and change of residence, but it is now much less impressive.

Table 4.
Severity of Sex Training Compared with Duration of the Post Partum Sex Taboo

Duration of the Post Partum Sex Taboo	Number of Societies Rated at or above the Median on Severity of Sex Training	Number of Societies Rated below the Median on Severity of Sex Training
Long	13	6
Short	10	12
	(Not Significant)*	

* When two dichotomized variables are correlated, the chi-square test of significance (for two-by-two tables) will be used (Edwards, 1954: 367–372).

What is the "meaning" of change of residence? I propose that this custom reflects, among other things, fear of sexual attachment and/or sexual relations between mothers and their adolescent sons. This interpretation is supported by the fact that, within my sample, the custom is universal for all

Table 5.
Duration of the Post Partum Sex Taboo Compared with Occurrence of a Change of Residence for Adolescent Boys

Duration of the Post Partum Sex Taboo	Change of Residence for Adolescent Boys Is Customary	Change of Residence for Adolescent Boys Is Not Customary
Long	Arapesh	Araucania
	Azande	Ifaluk
	Dahomey	Jivaro
	Fiji	Kwoma
	Ganda	Pilaga
	Hausa	Tepoztlan
	Hupa	Witoto
	Kipsigi	
	Kiwai	
	Kurtachi	
	Lovedu	
	Malaita	
	Mende	
	Nuer	
	Nyakusa	
	Ooldea	
	Pondo	
	Rajput	
	Tallensi	
	Samoa	
	Thonga	
	Tiv	
	Trobriands	
	Venda	
	Wogeo	
Short	Ashanti	Ainu
	Gusii	Alor
	Hopi	Aymara
	Koryak	Baiga
	Lakher	Bali
	Lamba	Cagaba
	Murngin	Copper Eskimo
	Nambicauru	Kazak
	Silwa	Lapp
	Tanala	Lepcha
	Timbira	Manus
		Maori
		Marquesas
		Nama Hottentot
		Navaho
		Papago
		Siriono
		Tarahumara
		Truk
		Yagua

$$P = 0.002$$

societies with a "high" percentage of mother-child house-holds.

To summarize, both *change of residence for adolescent boys* and *severe sex training* appear to reflect concern over the sexuality of children. Both are positively correlated with the long post partum sex taboo. This suggests that the long post partum sex taboo intensifies the Oedipus complex.

Later, we shall look at another set of customs that frequently appear to reflect concern over the sexuality of (adolescent) children—initiation ceremonies. Initiations also tend to accompany the long post partum sex taboo.

Sex Anxiety

I made a composite index of sex anxiety by intercorrelating a number of variables that tapped sexual avoidances, fears and restrictions, and then choosing those variables that "clustered"—that is, those variables that were positively associated with all the other variables in this group.[1] These are the variables in the sex anxiety index: *severity of sex training* (Whiting and Child, 1953); *premarital intercourse prohibited* (Ford and Beach, 1951; Ford, 1945); *duration of the pregnancy sex taboo* (Ayres, 1954); *sexual intercourse usually punished in folklore* (Appendix VII); *presence of sexual explanations for illness* (Whiting and Child, 1953);

1. One of these variables was discarded because it was generally uncorrelated with the others—*extra-marital liaisons prohibited,* rated by Clellan S. Ford (Ford and Beach, 1951; Ford, personal communication). One of the variables I included in the composite index—*sexual intercourse usually punished in folklore*—was positively correlated with only three of the five other variables. The other five variables were all positively correlated with each other.

presence of sexual avoidance therapy (Whiting and Child, 1953). The assignment of a label to this composite index— *sex anxiety*—is, of course, arbitrary. Perhaps the label should be more vague; "sexual problems index" might be more apt.

The derivation of, and rationale for, this composite index is given in Appendix II.

Societies are scored on *sex anxiety* in this manner: their "low" scores (on the component variables) are subtracted from their "high" scores. For example, the Ashanti received three "high" scores (*severe* sex training, *long* pregnancy sex taboo, sexual intercourse before marriage *prohibited*), and one "low" score (sexual explanations for illness *absent*). Their one low score was subtracted from their three high scores; the result was a score of +2 on sex anxiety.

In Table 6, duration of the post partum sex taboo is cor- related with intensity of *sex anxiety*. It is a statistically sig- nificant positive correlation. This, I feel, is a substantial piece of evidence favoring the general hypothesis: the long post partum sex taboo does (usually) seem to accompany sexual fears.

Breasts

We shall look at one more bit of evidence. It is interesting, in the light of Kluckhohn's description of nursing among the Navaho, that in some primitive societies breast-feeling plays little part in the sex-play of adults. Apparently, in a few primitive societies, the woman's breasts are not even con- sidered sexual stimuli. These tend to be the long post partum sex taboo societies. The positive correlation between duration

Table 6.
Duration of the Post Partum Sex Taboo Compared with Intensity of Sex Anxiety

Intensity of Sex Anxiety	"Long" Post Partum Sex Taboo	"Short" Post Partum Sex Taboo
4	Dahomey Kiwai Kwoma	Manus
3	Arapesh Kwakiutl	
2	Chiricahua Lesu	Alor Ashanti Navaho
1	Chagga Witoto	Sanpoil
0	Azande Kurtachi	Lamba Papago
−1		Hopi Murngin Tanala
−2	Thonga Jivaro	Yagua
−3	Bena	Baiga
−4	Masai Trobriands	Ainu Chenchu Bali Copper Eskimo Lakher Lepcha Marquesas Siriono

$$*P = 0.03$$

* In all cases where a dichotomized variable is correlated with a 5- or 9-point scale, the test of significance is based on a test for linear trend (Armitage, 1955).

Table 7.
Duration of the Post Partum Sex Taboo Compared with Whether or Not Breasts are Considered Sexual Stimuli

Duration of the Post Partum Sex Taboo	Breasts Are Considered Sexual Stimuli	Breasts Are Not Considered Sexual Stimuli
Long	Lesu Trobriands	Kurtachi Kwakiutl Kwoma Ulithi
Short	Alor Baiga Chukchee Gusii Lakher Lepcha Manus Marquesas Mohave Rwala Bedouin Tarahumara Truk	Navaho Siriono

*P = 0.04

* Fisher-Yates Test of Significance (Finney, 1948).

of the post partum sex taboo and *breasts not sexual stimuli* is given in Table 7. The correlation is strong and significant, although based on few cases.

The coding rules and results for the variable, *breasts not sexual stimuli*, are given in Appendix V.

What does the data in Table 7 mean? If non-breast-feeling represents an avoidance—that is, if it is motivated by fear— then it may be motivated (or partly caused) by fears generated during "sexy nursing." In other words, it may represent an Oedipal fear. However, if it is an avoidance it is different from some other avoidances we shall examine. There are no reports that breast-feeling is "against the law," negatively sanctioned, or discouraged by superstitions. It is reported as just a simple "omission"; it simply "isn't done."

Summary

The long post partum sex taboo is positively correlated with two variables that probably reflect, to some degree, concern over the sexuality of children: *severity of sex training,* and *change of residence for adolescent boys.* It is also positively correlated with a composite index of *sex anxiety,* and with the variable, *breasts not sexual stimuli.* All correlations but the first are statistically significant. None of these correlations were formally predicted. However, all of them are consistent with the notion that the Oedipus complex intensifies anxieties about sex, and that the long post partum sex taboo intensifies the Oedipus complex.

5

MENSTRUAL TABOOS

IN SEVERAL WAYS, THE MENstrual taboo study was particularly fruitful. For one thing, the menstrual taboo scale is, relative to other cross-cultural scales, very "good." Also, many predictions were made in advance of the data. The strategy of this study was as follows:

1. Following Roheim's suggestion, I interpreted menstrual taboos as reflecting castration anxiety (Roheim, 1945: 174). I hypothesized that the extensiveness or elaboration of menstrual taboos is caused (partly) by frequency and intensity of castration anxiety, current in the population that observes the taboos.

2. I reviewed psychoanalytic sources for the hypothesized origins of castration anxiety. From this review, there emerged a number of child-rearing practices (behaviors and attitudes of the parents) which, according to the psychoanalytic theorists, aggravate castration fears.

3. I matched these practices against cross-cultural ratings of child rearing. I chose from the cross-cultural literature (mainly from Whiting and Child and from Bacon, Barry, and Child) some child rearing variables that seemed to draw on these aggravating conditions. Usually, the cross-cultural variable represented the "castration anxiety aggravator" only partially and indirectly.

4. I measured extensiveness of menstrual taboos with a Guttman scale.

5. I predicted positive correlations between extensiveness of menstrual taboos and these child-rearing variables. The assumption was that the child-rearing ratings represented *antecedent variables,* extensiveness of menstrual taboos was a *consequent variable,* and in all cases intensity of castration anxiety was an (unmeasured) *intervening variable.*

6. I tested my predictions.

Other comparisons were also made, which we will review later.

The Variable

The term "menstrual taboos" refers to special avoidance customs that menstruating women must observe. These customs are rationalized by superstitions: either the menstrual blood, or the woman herself, is believed to be dangerous. Such customs and beliefs are common in many parts of the world. J. G. Frazer gives this list of (mostly ancient) European menstrual taboos:

Amongst the civilized nations of Europe the superstitions which cluster round this mysterious aspect of woman's nature are not less extravagant than those which prevail among savages. In the oldest existing cyclopaedia—the *Natural History* of Pliny—the list of dangers apprehended from menstruation is longer than any furnished by mere barbarians. According to Pliny, the touch of a menstruous woman turned wine to vinegar, blighted crops, killed seedlings, blasted gardens, brought down the fruit from trees, dimmed mirrors, blunted razors, rusted iron and brass (especially at the waning of the moon), killed bees, or at least drove them from their hives, caused mares to miscarry, and so forth. Similarly, in various parts of Europe, it is still believed that if a woman in her courses enters a brewery, the beer will turn sour; if she touches beer, wine, vinegar, or milk, it will go bad; if she makes jam, it will not keep; if she mounts a mare, it will miscarry; if she touches buds, they will wither; if she climbs a cherry tree, it will die. In Brunswick people think that if a menstrous woman assists at the killing of a pig, the pork will putrefy. In the Greek island of Calymnos a woman at such times may not go to the well to draw water, nor cross a running stream, nor enter the sea. Her presence in a boat is said to raise storms (Frazer, 1951: 702).

Here is another example—menstrual taboos among the Balinese:

But once a month, during menstrual time, a wife's life is not a happy one; to her physical handicap is added the powerful taboo of pollution (sebel) which then falls upon her; she is forbidden to go into the temple, into the kitchen or the granary, or to the well. She may not prepare food nor, of course, make offerings or participate in feasts, and the wife of a high priest may not even speak to her exalted husband. No man would dream of sleeping in the same room with a woman in this condition; the average man moves into the house of a friend, but the wife of a nobleman has to look for a place to sleep, far from her husband. In the palace of a prince there is often a secluded compartment where his wives retire while menstruating. When the period is over, a woman has to be purified again with sprinkling of holy water before she can resume normal life.

Perhaps because the Balinese believe that a man can be bewitched, losing all his will to the woman who can anoint his head with menstrual blood, they have such mortal horror of being near a woman during the time of menstruation (Covarrubias, 1937: 156).

Here is one more example—the Kwakiutl of Vancouver Island:

Whenever thereafter a woman menstruated she remained in isolation until the flow of blood ceased. Menstrual blood was thought to be dangerous and was carefully collected in cedar bark and buried. Should a menstruating woman contaminate any of the fishing or hunting gear, fish and game would elude capture. Should she cook for her husband, some of the blood might get into the food and harm him. Should she make love to him, the blood would make him sick. The menstrual fluid was thought to be especially dangerous to sick people. While a woman remained in seclusion, her mother, sister, or some other female member of the household would supply the food and water that she needed. After the flow ceased, she washed herself carefully every day for four days and was then permitted once more to mingle freely in the community. The malignant power which menstrual blood was believed to have for human beings extended to monsters; therefore when women were traveling, they kept some menstrual blood in a bit of shredded bark to be used to poison a monster should one appear (Ford, 1941: 35).

As these examples suggest, there is a luxuriant variety of menstrual taboos. Each society adds its own special variations. However, some menstrual customs (or narrow custom-categories) are widely distributed; they occur frequently, in many parts of the world. I picked out three of these: the menstruating woman is secluded in a special menstrual hut; the menstruating woman is not allowed to cook for men; the menstruating woman is not allowed to have sexual intercourse.

The coding of menstrual taboos is described in Appendix III. Each of these three menstrual customs represented a separate code-category, to be coded "present," "absent," or "no information" for each society in the sample. The other two code-categories were looser and more inclusive: belief that menstrual blood is dangerous to men, coded "present," "absent," or "no information"; and other menstrual taboos (not included in the other code-categories), coded "many," "few or none," or "no information."

These code-categories patterned cumulatively. This is the pattern:

If a society was judged "present" for *menstrual huts,* it was never judged "absent" for any of the other code-categories.

If a society was judged "present" for the *menstrual cooking taboo,* it was never judged "absent" for *many other menstrual taboos,* the menstrual *sex taboo,* or belief in *danger to men* from the menstrual blood (however, it might be judged "absent" for *menstrual huts*).

If a society was judged "present" for *many other menstrual taboos* ("many" for other menstrual taboos), it was never judged "absent" for *sex taboo* or *danger to men* (however, it might be judged "absent" for *menstrual huts* or *cooking taboo*). Here occurred the only "error" in the cumulative pattern: the Lakher, coded "present" for *many other menstrual taboos* and "absent" for *sex taboo.*

Refer to Appendix III for a more detailed account of the coding. I will merely point out now that this cumulative effect is only to a very minor extent an artifact of the coding procedures. These menstrual taboos actually "behave" this way: they follow a cumulative pattern that is *identical* for all but one of the codable cases.

Societies were scored on *extensiveness of menstrual taboos* with the following Guttman scale, made possible by the cumulative pattern:

5. Menstrual huts.
4. Menstrual cooking taboo.
3. Many other menstrual taboos.
2. Both menstrual sex taboo and belief that menstrual blood is dangerous to men coded "present."

The following were the conventions for assigning to societies scale-scores on *extensiveness of menstrual taboos:*

A society's score was equal to the highest scale-point (code-category) for which it had been coded "present."

If a society was scored "present" for none of these scale-points, its score was equal to the scale-point immediately below the lowest point for which it had been scored "absent." For example, if the society was coded "absent" for either *sex taboo* or *danger to men* (or for both), it was assigned the lowest possible scale-score—1. If a society was coded "absent" for point 3 and "no information" for point 2, its score on *extensiveness of menstrual taboos* was 2.

For a few societies, these two conventions were not enough. For example, Ooldea is coded "present" for point 2 and "absent" for point 5. Should its score on *extensiveness of menstrual taboos* be 2, 3, or 4? Such cases were scored by this added convention: when points 2 and 3 were unreported, they were checked "present"; when points 4 and 5 were unreported, they were checked "absent." By this means, Ooldea is scored 3 on *extensiveness of menstrual taboos*. The practical effect of this convention is to group those societies whose "real score" is uncertain near the "middle" of the menstrual taboo scale (Appendix III).

This scale empirically demonstrates a continuum of extensiveness, and gives an empirical basis for placing societies on the continuum. The "high" societies have what the "low" societies have, plus something extra. For example, a society scored 5 has the menstrual taboos of a society scored 2 (sex taboo and belief in danger to men of menstrual blood), plus these added customs: menstrual huts, menstrual cooking taboo, and "many" other menstrual taboos. Also, the scale roughly represents the full range of menstrual taboos. "High" societies have "many" other menstrual taboos; "low" societies have "few or none" other menstrual taboos.

Menstrual Taboos and Castration Anxiety

I interpret menstrual taboos as reflecting castration anxiety. In this section I shall explain this interpretation.

In the first place, what is castration anxiety? A more accurate, if less colorful, name for it is *fear of genital injury*. It is described as a fantastic fear, which follows from a great variety of unconscious fantasy-thoughts that have to do with injury to the genitals:

> The nature of the danger that is believed to be threatening the penis likewise varies. It might be believed that the penis is endangered by a masculine enemy, that is, by a penetrating, pointed tool, or by a feminine enemy, that is, by an encompassing instrument, depending upon whether the father or the mother appeared as the more threatening person, or depending upon what special fantasies the boy has had about sexual intercourse. Persons with oral fixations

may fear that the penis will be bitten off, which results in confused ideas made up of both oral and genital elements.

Sometimes specific experiences shape rather grotesque forms of castration fear (Fenichel, 1945: 78).

Freud and his followers believed that castration anixety is the classic or most typical fear that results from the Oedipus complex. They felt that, as the characteristic Oedipal fear, castration anxiety is the prime motive for repressing the sexual wishes toward the mother and rivalrous feelings toward the father (Freud, 1933: 123; Mullahy, 1952; 21–28; Munroe, 1955: 203–208; Roheim, 1950: 63–74).

When persisting in adults, castration anxiety is described as a more or less unconscious fear that may underlie other fears, such as sexual fears and inhibitions, fear of blood, sharp objects or mutilation, or may motivate more elaborate neurotic symptomatology (Fenichel, 1945: 170, 197, 199, 209, 231, 274, 326, 344; Freud, 1933: 122–123). Since it is unconscious, its presence must be inferred. The psychoanalytic case literature is replete with instances of inferred castration anxiety.

Castration anxiety characterizes *males*, although analogous fantasies may be entertained by females (Balint, 1954: 78–82; Fenichel, 1945: 77–83). Needless to say, my discussion is specific to castration anxiety as felt by males.

To summarize: following psychoanalytic theorists, I assume there is such a widespread and common phenomenon as castration anxiety, felt by males. It is a fantastic fear of genital injury, resulting from a variety of unconscious fantasy-thoughts that have to do with genital injury. It "starts" in early childhood, as a result of the son-to-mother sex attraction (and as a result of other factors, to be reviewed presently). It is more or less unconscious. It may persist into adulthood (my assumptions about the persistence into adulthood of Oedipal fears were outlined in the latter part of Chapter 2). When it does, it may motivate a variety of fearful, phobic, avoiding, or neurotic reactions.

How does castration anxiety "cause" menstrual taboos? In the first place, I assume that the sight or thought of a person who bleeds from the genitals (a menstruating woman) is frightening to a person who has intense castration anxiety. It is a reminder of genital injury. Beyond this, I would not care to speculate too much about how the fear of this "reminder" is translated into institutionalized avoidance. I do assume that the various superstitions about the malignant power of menstruating women are projections or results of this fear-of-the-reminder-of-the-fantasied-expectation-of-genital-injury. Also, the avoidances are a way of "handling" or "doing something about" the fear. Quite possibly, the menstruating woman arouses phobic reactions in some men, analogous to phobias toward snakes, spiders, etc.

I do think that the institutionalized avoidance rules are a different order of phenomena than individual fear-reactions. If the avoidance rules represent phobia, then they are "institutionalized phobia." They do not coincide exactly with each person's phobic tendencies. Probably, in societies with extensive menstrual taboos, some men have little "need" for them. However, I do assume that there is some congruence between extensiveness of menstrual taboos and both intensity and frequency (in the population) of castration anxiety.

The taboos may be more or less extensive. When they are very extensive (menstrual huts, cooking taboo, many other

menstrual taboos) this represents extreme avoidance-measures. I assume that the extremity of avoidance-measures is
contingent, to some degree, on intensity of fear (on the magnitude of personal needs for avoidance-measures).

Also, when the taboos are extensive they must be very
burdensome and inconvenient not only to women but also to
men. I assume that these burdensome taboos will not be "put
up with" indefinitely if they are not needed; if, with passing
generations, castration anxiety "goes down" in a population,
the menstrual taboos will also "go down" (i.e., become less
extensive).

This issue—the congruence between personal anxieties and
institutionalized avoidance rules—is treated in more detail in
the next chapter.

Needless to say, I do not assume that there is one-to-one
causal relationship between frequency and intensity of castration anxiety and extensiveness of menstrual taboos. I assume
that extensiveness of menstrual taboos responds to many
causal factors; castration anxiety is just one of them. I spent
considerable time in a search for some of the other causal
factors. This search is described toward the end of the chapter.

We shall now examine two pieces of preliminary evidence
that are congenial to the notion that menstrual taboos reflect
castration anxiety.

Menstrual Taboos and Sex Anxiety

In Table 8, extensiveness of menstrual taboos is correlated
with intensity of sex anxiety. It is a fairly pronounced positive correlation, highly significant. If extensiveness of menstrual taboos is an indicator of frequency and intensity of

Table 8.
Extensiveness of Menstrual Taboos Compared with Intensity of Sex Anxiety

Intensity of Sex Anxiety	EXTENSIVENESS OF MENSTRUAL TABOOS				
	5	4	3	2	1
4	Dahomey	Kiwai Kwoma			Manus
3	Arapesh Kwakiutl				
2	Ashanti		Lesu	Chiricahua Navaho	Alor
1	Sanpoil			Witoto	
0	Papago	Lamba Kurtachi	Azande		
—1		Wogeo		Murngin	Tanala Hopi
—2	Paiute		Thonga	Jivaro	Pukapuka
—3		Baiga	Bena		
—4		Bali	Lakher Copper Esk.	Ainu Lepcha Siriono	Masai Chenchu Marquesas Trobriands

$$\rho = 0.40$$
$$P = 0.01$$

castration anxiety, we would expect this positive correlation. Castration anxiety is itself a sex-connected fear, and according to the psychoanalytic theorists underlies other sex-connected fears.

Danger to Men

Frazer, in his general treatment of taboo, states that taboos are instituted to protect the tabooed person, and also to protect others from him (or her) (Frazer, 1951: 260). If this is so, menstrual taboos are unusual in that they appear to reflect hardly any solicitude for the safety of the menstruating woman herself. Only two cases in the sample, the Arau-

canians and the Warrau of South America, seem at all preoccupied with protecting her. Rather incidental recognition
of danger to the menstruating woman is reported for nine
other societies.

A number of societies have the belief that the menstruating
woman can endanger the whole community by bringing supernatural punishment or by blighting the food supply. She may
also be dangerous to special categories of persons, such as
sick people. However, there were no reports of menstruating
women being dangerous to other women (with the exception
of individual females who fell into one of these special categories). For only one society, the Ojibwa, was it reported that
the menstruating woman is dangerous to young children.

By far the dominant belief (reported for forty societies)
appears to be that menstruating women are dangerous to men.
The reason usually given for such customs as the use of
menstrual huts, the menstrual cooking taboo, or the menstrual
sex taboo is that these avoidance-measures protect men. The
avoidance measures are rationalized as guarding against
danger, which is usually conceived as some sort of contamination as a result of touching either the woman, her blood, or
things she has touched, which (for men) leads to sickness,
injury or loss of magical power. The seven societies in which
this belief appears to be absent have, as the scale implies, few
if any menstrual taboos.

The emphasis on danger to men could be interpreted as an
"admission" that extensive menstrual taboos reflect fears that
are specific to men. What is very clear is that usually it is
specifically men who are in danger of contamination, not
children, or other females, or the menstruating woman herself. In other words, the avoidance-measures apply *between*

the menstruating woman and men. It is only men who need the "protection." This does seem consistent with the notion that menstrual taboos reflect castration anxiety, a fear specific to men.

Castration Anxiety: Aggravating Conditions

As I stated in the introduction to this chapter, I reviewed the psychoanalytic literature for the conditions of childhood that are supposed to aggravate castration anxiety (i.e., make severe castration anxiety more likely). I found mention of three general classes of "aggravating conditions": "seduction" of the (male) child by his mother; punishment (or implied punishment—threats) of his sexual activity; and the perceived danger of rivalrous behavior toward the father. We shall now take up these aggravating conditions one by one, describe how they were "matched" against cross-cultural variables, and describe the predictions and tests.

Maternal Seduction. A number of writers mention *the mother's own sexual interest in her child* as an "antecedent" or "intensifier" of Oedipal problems in general, and castration anxiety in particular. This, in turn, is said to be greater *when the mother herself is sexually frustrated* (Fenichel, 1945: 91, 93; Horney, 1937: 83; Thompson, 1951: 39). These statements, I feel, give a rather clear mandate to the long post partum sex taboo as an intensifying condition for castration anxiety (Chapter 2). So my first prediction was that extensiveness of menstrual taboos would correlate positively with the duration of the post partum sex taboo. The assumptions underlying the prediction were: (1) the long post partum sex taboo, by sexually frustrating mothers, causes them to be more seductive to their young children; (2) this acts to raise the general level of castration anxiety among these young children; (3) to some extent the castration anxiety, among men in the population, is a determinant of the extensiveness of menstrual taboos.

Table 9 shows the correlation between extensiveness of menstrual taboos and duration of the post partum sex taboo; it is in the expected direction (positive) and is statistically significant.

Also mentioned are "situational determinants"—opportunity to see the mother nude, observation of parental intercourse, and extent of body contact with the mother. These conditions, by influencing the intensity of the son-to-mother sex attraction, may also exert an influence on castration anxiety (Mullahy, 1952: 22–23). As I stated in Chapter 2, we will not use measures of such "situational determinants." I do think, however, that they are generally much "higher" in the sample-societies than they are among ourselves. This is due to two near-universal conditions in these primitive societies—the one-room house, and breast-feeding for at least two years—and to a third condition that seems to be quite common: mother and young child sleeping side by side, or in the same bed (Whiting and D'Andrade; Whiting and Child, 1953: 70–71).

I made one more try in this area—to find another intensifier of the son-to-mother sex attraction. Although I did not find mention of it in the psychoanalytic literature, I reasoned that the importance of the mother, as opposed to other persons, as a "sex object" should have an effect on the Oedipal sex attraction. Often, in primitive societies, the mother shares her caretaking with other women or older children. I reasoned

Table 9.
Extensiveness of Menstrual Taboos Compared with Duration of the Post Partum Sex Taboo

Extensiveness of Menstrual Taboos	DURATION OF THE POST PARTUM SEX TABOO	
	Long	Short
5	Arapesh	Ashanti
	Cheyenne	Maria Gond
	Dahomey	Papago
	Dakota	Sanpoil
	Hupa	Warrau
	Ifaluk	
	Kwakiutl	
	Malaita	
	Ojibwa	
	Tiv	
	Ulithi	
4	Ganda	Baiga
	Gesu	Bali
	Kiwai	Lamba
	Kurtachi	Nama Hottentot
	Kwoma	
	Manam	
	Wogeo	
3	Araucania	Aymara
	Azande	Chukchee
	Bena	Copper Eskimo
	Lesu	Lakher
	Nyakusa	Maori
	Ooldea	Rwala Bedouin
	Thonga	Eastern Timbira
		Tungus
2	Arapaho	Ainu
	Chiricahua	Gros Ventre
	Jivaro	Kazak
	Tallensi	Lepcha
	Witoto	Murngin
		Navaho
		Siriono
		Tarahumara
		Tarasco
1	Bassa	Alor
	Bulu	Chenchu
	Masai	Gusii
	Samoa	Hopi
	Trobriands	Manus
		Marquesas
		Mohave
		Ontong Java
		Tanala
		Zapotec

$P = 0.02$

that when there are a number of significant "mother-figures" to absorb the child's sexual interest, he would have less sexual interest in his "real" mother—he would "focus" less on her.

Bacon, Barry, and Child rated a variable they term "diffusion of nurturance." It is an assessment of the degree to which the mother shares her caretaking duties with others; it applies to the nursing period—the first two or three years of a child's life, before he is weaned (Bacon, Barry, and Child, 1954). I predicted a *negative* correlation between diffusion of nurturance and extensiveness of menstrual taboos. My reasoning was: (1) "high" diffusion of nurturance leads to relatively little "focusing" on the mother (by the young child) as a sex object; (2) this "lowers" the intensity of the son-to-mother sex attraction; (3) this has a "lowering" effect on castration anxiety, leading to (4) relatively mild and non-extensive menstrual taboos.

In Table 10, diffusion of nurturance is correlated with extensiveness of menstrual taboos. The trend is in the expected direction (negative), but it is weak and nonsignificant.

Punishment of the Child's Sexual Activity. Punishment for (or threats about) masturbation is a frequently mentioned antecedent of castration anxiety (Fenichel, 1945: 75; Mullahy, 1952: 21; Munroe, 1955: 206; Roheim, 1950: 64). So the menstrual taboo scale was correlated with Whiting and Child's ratings of *severity of punishment for masturbation.* I predicted a positive correlation. Table 11 gives this comparison. The correlation was in the expected direction and was statistically significant.

Fenichel also states that the general attitude of parents to sex, which may be either permissive or restrictive, has an important bearing on the likelihood of castration anxiety (Fenichel, 1945: 95). So the Whiting and Child variable

Table 10.
Extensiveness of Menstrual Taboos Compared with Diffusion of Nurturance

Extensiveness of Menstrual Taboos	Societies Judged at or above the Median on Diffusion of Nurturance	Societies Judged below the Median on Diffusion of Nurturance
5	Arapesh Ashanti Ifaluk Dakota Kwakiutl Papago	Cheyenne Dahomey Hupa Malaita Ojibwa Paiute Ulithi
4	Bali Ganda Kurtachi	Kwoma Lamba Wogeo
3	Bena Lesu Maori Nyakusa Araucania Thonga	Aymara Azande Chukchee Timbira
2	Arapaho Chiricahua Lepcha Murngin Navaho Tallensi	Ainu Jivaro Siriono
1	Alor Hopi Marquesas Masai Pukapuka Samoa Trobriands	Chenchu Manus Ontong Java Tanala

$$P = 0.28$$

Table 11.
Extensiveness of Menstrual Taboos Compared with Severity of Punishment for Masturbation

Extensiveness of Menstrual Taboos	Societies Judged at or above the Median on Severity of Punishment for Masturbation	Societies Judged below the Median on Severity of Punishment for Masturbation
5	Arapesh	Dakota
	Ashanti	
	Dahomey	
	Paiute	
	Sanpoil	
	Tiv	
4	Kurtachi	Baiga
	Kwoma	Bali
	Wogeo	
3		Maori
2	Chiricahua	Kazak
		Lepcha
		Navaho
		Siriono
1	Manus	Alor
	Tanala	Hopi
		Marquesas
		Pukapuka
		Samoa
		Trobriands

$P = 0.01$

severity of sex training, used as an over-all estimate of the strictness of sex-sanctions on children, was correlated with extensiveness of menstrual taboos. A positive correlation was again predicted. This correlation is given in Table 12. It is in the predicted direction and (barely) statistically significant.[1]

1. There is some contamination between the two Whiting and Child measures. Severity of punishment for masturbation was one of the subscales that contributed to the final rating of over-all severity of sex training (Whiting and Child, 1953: 77).

Table 12.
Extensiveness of Menstrual Taboos Compared with Over-All Severity of Sex Training

Extensiveness of Menstrual Taboos	Societies Judged at or above the Median on Severity of Sex Training	Societies Judged below the Median on Severity of Sex Training
5	Arapesh	
	Ashanti	
	Dahomey	
	Dakota	
	Kwakiutl	
	Paiute	
	Papago	
	Sanpoil	
	Tiv	
4	Kurtachi	Baiga
	Kwoma	Bali
	Wogeo	Lamba
3	Azande	Bena
	Flathead	Lakher
	Rwala Bedouin	Lesu
		Maori
		Thonga
2	Chiricahua	Ainu
	Navaho	Lepcha
		Murngin
		Siriono
		Witoto
1	Alor	Chenchu
	Hopi	Marquesas
	Manus	Masai
	Ontong Java	Pukapuka
	Samoa	Trobriands
	Tanala	

$$P = 0.05$$

Danger of Rivalrous Behavior toward the Father. This is the first of several times, throughout this book, that I shall depart from my self-imposed limitation and deal with Oedipal (father-son) rivalry. Psychoanalysts state that frequently the father may be feared as a potential "castrater." The reasoning (simplified here) is: (1) the son-to-mother sex attraction generates sex-based rivalrous feelings toward the father; (2) this leads to destructive fantasies of various sorts, in which sex and aggression may be "mixed" and confabulated; (3) among these are fantasies of retribution from the father—sexual or sex-connected injuries (Freud, 1933: 122; Freud, 1936: 44; Roheim, 1950: 221–227; Fenichel, 1945: 78; Sachs, 1934: 63–64).

In this section I shall review a number of factors which, I reasoned, might intensify and/or make more likely these retribution-fantasies and, as a result, intensify castration anxiety.

My first prediction in this area was a positive correlation between *severity of aggression training* (rated by Whiting and Child) and extensiveness of menstrual taboos. My reasoning was that the general strictness of sanctions against aggression (by the child) would be one determinant of the likelihood of retribution-fantasies (resulting from aggressive wishes). Table 13 shows this correlation. It is positive but nonsignificant.

My second prediction was a positive correlation between *importance of physical punishment as a technique of discipline* (rated by Whiting and Child) and extensiveness of menstrual taboos. I reasoned that genital injury (a form of violence) would be a more likely retaliatory fear when physical punishment was preferred (by the parents), rather than when nonviolent means of discipline were preferred—such as withdrawal of love, ridicule, withdrawal of privileges, or threats of various sorts. This correlation is shown in Table 14. It is positive, but slightly short of statistical significance.

Table 13.
Extensiveness of Menstrual Taboos Compared with Severity of the Socialization of Aggression

Extensiveness of Menstrual Taboos	Societies Judged at or above the Median on Severity of Aggression Training	Societies Judged below the Median on Severity of Aggression Training
5	Arapesh Ashanti Dakota Kwakiutl Paiute Papago Sanpoil	Dahomey Tiv
4	Kiwai	Baiga Bali Kwoma Lamba Kurtachi Wogeo
3	Azande Maori Rwala Bedouin	Bena Copper Eskimo Lakher Lesu Thonga
2	Ainu Chiricahua Jivaro Lepcha	Murngin Navaho Siriono
1	Alor Hopi Samoa	Chenchu Manus Marquesas Masai Ontong Java Pukapuka Tanala Trobriands

$$P = 0.18$$

Table 14.
Extensiveness of Menstrual Taboos Compared with Importance
of Physical Punishment as a Technique of Discipline

Extensiveness of Menstrual Taboos	Societies Judged at or above the Median on Importance of Physical Punishment	Societies Judged below the Median on Importance of Physical Punishment
5	Ashanti	Arapesh
	Dahomey	Dakota
	Kwakiutl	Tiv
	Paiute	
	Sanpoil	
4	Baiga	Bali
	Kiwai	Kurtachi
	Kwoma	Wogeo
3	Azande	Bena
	Lesu	Copper Eskimo
	Maori	Lakher
	Rwala Bedouin	Thonga
2	Ainu	Chiricahua
	Jivaro	Murngin
	Lepcha	Siriono
1	Alor	Chenchu
	Hopi	Manus
		Marquesas
		Masai
		Ontong Java
		Pukapuka
		Samoa
		Tanala
		Trobriands

$$P = 0.07$$

I made several predictions in the area of obedience-demands. I felt that the obedience issue was closely tied with attitudes toward, and latitude for, rivalry on the part of the child: strict obedience-demands means relatively little tolerance of rivalrous actions; severe punishment for disobedience means, among other things, severe "retribution" for rivalrous actions.

Table 15.
Extensiveness of Menstrual Taboos Compared with General Pressure for Obedience

Extensiveness of Menstrual Taboos	Societies Judged at or above the Median on General Pressure for Obedience	Societies Judged below the Median on General Pressure for Obedience
5	Cheyenne	Ashanti
	Dahomey	Arapesh
	Kwakiutl	Hupa
	Ojibwa	Ifaluk
	Tiv	Malaita
		Paiute
		Papago
		Dakota
		Ulithi
4	Bali	Wogeo
	Ganda	
	Kurtachi	
	Kwoma	
	Lamba	
3	Araucania	Aymara
	Chukchee	Azande
	Maori	Bena
	Nyakusa	Lesu
	Thonga	Timbira
2	Arapaho	Ainu
	Chiricahua	Lepcha
	Jivaro	Murngin
	Siriono	Navaho
		Tallensi
1	Alor	Hopi
	Chenchu	Ontong Java
	Manus	Pukapuka
	Marquesas	Samoa
	Masai	Tanala
	Trobriands	

$P = 0.65$ (not in expected direction)

The first two variables in this area were rated by Bacon, Barry, and Child. They assess obedience-socialization from all socializing agents (not just the father or the mother); the ratings pertain, roughly, to obedience-socialization during the "latency period" (five to twelve) (Bacon, Barry, and Child, 1954).

I predicted a positive correlation between *general pressure for obedience* and extensiveness of menstrual taboos. My reasoning was that when pressure for obedience is "high," rebelliousness is taboo, and retaliation-fantasies (for rebellious or rivalrous wishes) are more likely. Table 15 shows the zero correlation between *general pressure for obedience* and extensiveness of menstrual taboos. This is the only time, in these studies, when a prediction as to the direction of trend was not vindicated by the data.

I also predicted a positive correlation between *severity of punishment for disobedience* and extensiveness of menstrual taboos. My reasoning was much the same: if a child is severely punished for rebellious actions, he will be more likely to fantasy a future retribution for his rivalrous motives. Table 16 shows this correlation. It is in the expected direction but nonsignificant.

At this point I made my own child-rearing ratings. The first was *the severity of the father's own obedience demands* (*not* the obedience demands of all socializing agents in general); the second was *whether or not the father is expected to be the main disciplinarian* (of the male child). These ratings were made for the birth-to-six-years age period. They are described in Appendix VI.

I predicted that both variables would be correlated positively with extensiveness of menstrual taboos. For *severity of the father's obedience demands*, the reasoning was essentially the same as for *general pressure for obedience*. This correlation is given in Table 17. It is in the expected direction, but nonsignificant.

Table 16.
Extensiveness of Menstrual Taboos Compared with Severity of Punishment for Disobedience

Extensiveness of Menstrual Taboos	Societies Judged at or above the Median on Severity of Punishment for Disobedience	Societies Judged below the Median on Severity of Punishment for Disobedience
5	Ashanti	Arapesh
	Dahomey	Cheyenne
	Ifaluk	Dakota
	Kwakiutl	Hupa
	Ojibwa	Malaita
	Ulithi	Paiute
		Papago
		Tiv
4	Bali	Wogeo
	Ganda	
	Kurtachi	
	Kwoma	
	Lamba	
3	Aymara	Araucania
	Bena	Azande
	Chukchee	Lesu
	Maori	Timbira
	Nyakusa	
	Thonga	
2	Ainu	Arapaho
	Chiricahua	Lepcha
	Jivaro	Murngin
	Siriono	Navaho
		Tallensi
1	Alor	Chenchu
	Manus	Hopi
		Marquesas
		Masai
		Ontong Java
		Pukapuka
		Samoa
		Tanala
		Trobriands

$$P = 0.18$$

Table 17.
Extensiveness of Menstrual Taboos Compared with Strictness of the Father's Obedience Demands

Extensiveness of Menstrual Taboos	Father's Obedience Demands Judged "Strict"	Father's Obedience Demands Judged "Mild"
5	Ashanti	Malaita
	Dahomey	Papago
	Kwakiutl	Ulithi
4	Kiwai	Bali
	Kwoma	Manam
	Lamba	Wogeo
3	Bena	Araucania
	Lesu	Maori
	Thonga	Ooldea
		Timbira
2		Lepcha
		Navaho
		Siriono
		Tallensi
1	Gusii	Alor
	Hopi	Chenchu
	Tanala	Manus
		Ontong Java
		Samoa
		Trobriands
		Zapotec

$P = 0.20$

I reasoned that, when the father is the main disciplinarian, the child will more likely expect "retribution" from him for a wide range of antisocial acts (or fantasied acts); an act (or wish) that collides with social sanctions will be apt to bring expectation of paternal punishment. For this reason, castration anxiety (if it is often a retribution-from-father-fear) should be "higher" when the father is the main disciplinarian. This variable is correlated with extensiveness of men-

Table 18.

Extensiveness of Menstrual Taboos Compared with Whether or Not the Father Is the Main Disciplinarian

Extensiveness of Menstrual Taboos	Societies in Which the Father is Judged to Be the Main Disciplinarian	Societies in Which the Father is Judged Not to Be the Main Disciplinarian
5	Ashanti Malaita Papago Ulithi	Cheyenne Dahomey
4	Kiwai	Bali Wogeo
3	Thonga	Lesu Timbira
2	Tallensi	Lepcha Murngin Navaho Siriono Tarasco
1	Gusii	Alor Hopi Manus Pukapuka Samoa Tanala Trobriands Zapotec

$$P = 0.02$$

strual taboos in Table 18. The correlation is positive and significant.

This concludes the series of tests based on the third hypothesized aggravator of castration anxiety—danger of rivalrous behavior toward the father. It is the first evidence, presented here, on Oedipal rivalry. I must conclude that it is mildly favorable evidence; it is not as strongly favorable as the previous evidence that bore on the son-to-mother sex attraction. Possibly this is because the Oedipal rivalry tests are based on less satisfactory indices and less well-founded deductions (as to the "meaning" of variables).

A Composite Predicter of Castration Anxiety

I then combined all these variables which, presumably, draw on different aspects of the "antecedents" of castration anxiety, into a *composite predicter of intensity of castration anxiety*. To assign scores on this composite index, I followed the same conventions as for the *composite index of sex anxiety*. A society was scored on this variable if it was rated for at least *four* of these ten "antecedent variables." All ten of the component variables were weighted equally. A society's score was arrived at by subtracting its "low" scores ("low" ratings on the antecedent variables) from its "high" scores ("high" ratings on the antecedent variables).[2] For example, if a society got three "high" scores (*long* post partum sex taboo, *severe* sex training and *high* importance of physical punishment as a technique of discipline) and two "low" scores (*low* severity of aggression training, father *not* the main disciplinarian), its score on the *composite predicted* is +1. If it got two "high" scores and four "low" scores, its score on the *composite predicter* would be −2. And so forth.

Finally, to equalize chances to attain any score on the *composite predicter*, the minimum score was set at −4, and the maximum score was set at +4. For example, if a society

2. Exception: a rating of "low" on *diffusion of nurturance* was counted here as a "high" or "plus" rating, since it was predicted that "low" diffusion of nurturance would have an intensifying effect on castration anxiety.

was "high" on one of the antecedent variables, and "low" on six of them, it would receive the lowest possible score on the *composite predicter:* —4.

In other words, this is an attempt to summarize, in a crude way, the various possible sources (in childhood experience) of castration anxiety. Combining these various sources gives an over-all estimate (or "prediction") of frequency and intensity of castration anxiety current in a society, assuming that the psychoanalytic formulations, and my special assumptions about the "meaning" of these "antecedent variables," are approximately valid. *If* menstrual taboos reflect castration anxiety, we would expect a positive correlation between scores on this *composite predicter of castration anxiety* and extensiveness of menstrual taboos. Table 19 shows this correlation.[3] It is a strong one. More important, the *P* value is extraordinarily low.

Castration-Suggestive Incidents in Folklore

Up to this point, the scheme of this study had been as follows: (1) *antecedent variables,* reflecting conditions of childhood, were correlated with a *consequent variable*—extensiveness of menstrual taboos; (2) in all cases, castration anxiety was assumed to be the (unmeasured) *intervening variable.* I then wanted to further test my hypothesis by relating menstrual taboos to another proposed *consequence* of castration anxiety: incidents suggestive of castration in myths and folktales.

3. Formal prediction (that is, prediction that is solely based on theory) is not involved here, since I already knew that all but one of the component antecedent variables were positively correlated with menstrual taboos.

What sort of story-episodes might be suggestive of castration (i.e., genital injury)? The most obvious would be actual cases of genital injury. Psychoanalytic writers mention other sorts of events that may, in fantasy, be equated with castration. One of these is severing—incidents in which part of a person's body is cut off. A less obvious castration-suggestive incident is physical injury of any kind (Fenichel, 1945: 78, 197, 200, 209, 262; Freud, 1958: 357, 366–367, 387).

The next question is: would the folktales of people with great castration anxiety be unusually "high" in castration-suggestive incidents, or would it be unusually "low"? Does great castration anxiety lead to preoccupation with genital injury, which reflects itself in many "castration motifs" in folklore? Or, does it lead to unusual avoidance of subjects that suggest castration, thus having the opposite effect on folklore? Or does it somehow do both, thereby wiping out any simple, direct relationship?

Since I did not feel I could predict the direction of relationship, folklore seemed like a "poor bet." I was also skeptical for another reason. Previously, when working with avoidance, I assumed that their burdensomeness and inconvenience "regulated," to some extent, the congruence between the avoidance rules and personality tendencies. Folktales, not being "inconvenient," did not seem to have this advantage. I suspected that factors such as "cultural lag" might blur or completely wipe out any crudely measured relationship between folklore characteristics and current personality tendencies. Still, I felt it necessary to match menstrual taboos against some other consequent-index of castration anxiety, so I went ahead. As it turned out, I was needlessly pessimistic.

Folktales (and myths) were coded for three "variables,"

Table 19.
Composite Predicter of Intensity of Castration Anxiety Correlated with Extensiveness of Menstrual Taboos

Composite Predicter Score	EXTENSIVENESS OF MENSTRUAL TABOOS				
	5	4	3	2	1
4	Ashanti Dahomey Kwakiutl Ojibwa	Kiwai Kwoma		Chiricahua Jivaro	
3	Paiute Sanpoil		Azande		
2	Ulithi	Ganda Kurtachi	Chukchee Nyakusa Rwala		
1	Cheyenne Tiv	Lamba	Thonga	Ainu	
0	Arapesh Hupa Ifaluk Malaita		Aymara	Arapaho	Alor Manus
—1			Araucania Maori		
—2	Dakota Papago	Wogeo	Bena	Tallensi	Hopi Tanala
—3		Baiga	Lesu		Masai
—4		Bali	Lakher Timbira	Lepcha Murngin Navaho Siriono	Chenchu Marquesas Ontong Java Pukapuka Samoa Trobriands

$$\rho = 0.55$$
$$P = 0.000001$$

the three classes of castration-suggestive incidents mentioned above: frequency of genital injury, frequency of severing, and frequency of all types of physical injury. The rather complicated coding and rating procedures are given in Appendix VII. Here is a brief summary:

For most sample societies, all available folk literature was coded. In the interests of reliable measurement, an extremely formalized coding system was used. This system "misses" many physical injury incidents (perhaps about 30 per cent) that are vaguely described or, for other reasons, do not satisfy the coding rules.

The unit for coding (a single "incident") is each phrase that contains a subject, object and active verb. The frequency-score for a society (on each of the three variables) is the average number of incidents per 1,000 words of folklore text. For example, the Murngin had 22,250 words of literary text; there was one scored incident of genital injury, no cases of severing, and twenty-one cases of physical injury of all sorts. The Murngin's scores on the three variables were as follows: *genital injury*—0.04; *severing*—0.00; *all physical injury*—0.94.

Since I did not feel that I could predict direction of relationship, my prediction was only that there would be some sort of pronounced trend or correlation between these folklore-variables and extensiveness of menstrual taboos.

The results were surprising in a number of ways. In the first place, genital injury and severing rarely occurred; this was generally true for almost all the sample-societies. Genital injury was completely absent for 62 per cent of the sample; the only case with fairly frequent genital injury was the Trobriand Islanders. Severing incidents were seldom completely absent; however, the average was only six severing incidents per society. Low frequencies make scores on these two variables extremely unstable. That is, if, for a society with 50,000 words of literary text, one more story was found that contained one additional "incident" (of either genital injury or severing), this would frequently change the society's score from "low" to "high." This problem is particularly acute for the variable *frequency of genital injury* (coder-agreement was also lowest for this variable: 50 per cent). On the grounds of score-instability, I discarded *frequency of genital injury* as a measure too invalid to use. For whatever it is worth, there is no apparent relationship between extensiveness of menstrual taboos and frequency of genital injury in folklore.

The third variable, *all types of physical injury,* yielded much higher frequencies; it averaged fifty-two incidents per society. It also yielded the best coder-agreement—78 per cent.

In Table 20 extensiveness of menstrual taboos is correlated with *frequency of severing* and *frequency of all types of physical injury*. The correlation is neither positive nor negative: it is *curvilinear*. For *severing* the trend is nonsignificant; for

Table 20.
Extensiveness of Menstrual Taboos Compared with Frequency of Castration-Suggestive Incidents in Folklore

Extensiveness of Menstrual Taboos	Severing: Average Frequency Score for Societies at Each Point on the Menstrual Taboo Scale	All Types of Physical Injury: Average Frequency Score for Societies at Each Point on the Menstrual Taboo Scale
5	0.17	1.79
4	0.21	2.28
3	0.33	3.20
2	0.22	1.73
1	0.19	1.52
	*P = 0.30	*P = 0.001

* Test of significance for the correlation ratio (ϵ), using the F test.

all physical injury it is highly significant. Both the extreme "low" and extreme "high" societies on menstrual taboos tend to have relatively little physical injury in their folktales. Societies near the "middle" of the menstrual taboo scale tend to have much more frequent physical injury in their folktales.

These are rather peculiar findings. They suggest that, within a certain range, castration anxiety does increase overt preoccupation with castration (castration-motifs in literature), but that after castration anxiety exceeds a certain "tolerance level" it has the opposite effect; then, it leads to "avoidance-tendencies" which override "preoccupation-tendencies."

Summary of Evidence on Menstrual Taboos

In Table 21 I summarize all the evidence on the castration anxiety interpretation of menstrual taboos. Seven of the four-

Table 21.

Summary of Evidence on the Castration Anxiety Interpretation of Menstrual Taboos

Measures Correlated with Menstrual Taboos	Trend in Expected Direction	Probability of Chance Occurrence
Intensity of Sex Anxiety		0.01
Duration of Post Partum Sex Taboo	Yes	0.02
Diffusion of Nurturance	Yes	0.28
Severity of Punishment for Masturbation	Yes	0.01
Over-all Severity of Sex Training	Yes	0.05
Severity of Aggression Training	Yes	0.18
Importance of Physical Punishment	Yes	0.07
Pressure for Obedience	No	0.65
Severity of Punishment for Disobedience	Yes	0.18
Strictness of Father's Obedience Demands	Yes	0.20
Whether or Not Father is Main Disciplinarian	Yes	0.02
Composite Predicter of Castration Anxiety		0.000001
Frequency of Severing in Folktales		0.30
Frequency of All Types of Physical Injury in Folktales		0.001

teen correlations are statistically significant. Nine of the ten predictions about direction of trend were vindicated by the data.

A few of these variables are contaminated by each other; the correlational evidence does not directly indicate direction of causation; castration anxiety has been "measured" only indirectly. Still, making allowance for that, I find all of this evidence extremely compelling. I think it gives strong support to the following conclusions:

1. The psychoanalytic concept "castration anxiety" does approximately describe a real phenomenon.

2. At least in many of these primitive societies, castration anxiety is common among adults, and a strong enough motive to exert some influence on their behavior (on their social customs).

3. Extensiveness of menstrual taboos is, to an important extent, contingent on frequency and intensity of castration anxiety.

4. There is also some approximate validity to psychoanalytic formulations about the origins of castration anxiety.

Finally, support has been given to the general hypothesis: young boys—at least under optimal conditions—become sexually attracted to their mothers; this generates lasting sexual fears and avoidances; *these fears are mediated by unconscious fantasies.*

The Search for Other Causes

The rest of this chapter shall report on my attempts to find other factors that exert an influence on menstrual taboos. On the whole, this search was fruitless. I say "fruitless" because, although these tests were usually negative, they were based on indirect indices; therefore, they usually gave only weak and tentative evidence for ruling out these other possible causal factors.

My menstrual taboo study was preceded by a previous cross-cultural survey of menstrual customs by Clallan S. Ford, to whom I am in considerable debt. As a tentative suggestion, Ford proposed that fear of menstrual blood might somehow be connected with a sort of general eliminative-disgust reaction; in other words, abhorrence of menstrual blood may be a function of disgust for feces (Ford, 1945: 14). At the time, he had no way to test this notion. However, since Whiting and Child have rated *severity of toilet training*, I think it can now be indirectly tested (Whiting and Child, 1953). The assumption underlying the test is that severity of toilet training reflects the "intensity" of disgust for feces. If this is so, and if fear of menstrual blood is associated with disgust for feces, we could predict a positive correlation between extensiveness of menstrual taboos and severity of toilet training. As a matter of fact, the correlation is zero.

Ford advanced another hypothesis that was not so tentative: to some extent, menstrual taboos are made unnecessary by effective means for catching the menstrual flow (such as menstrual pads); therefore, when these means are present menstrual taboos are few. His data supported this hypothesis (Ford, 1945: 17–19). My data do not. However, there are relatively few ethnographic reports on this question. For my sample, I was able to judge menstrual pads "present" or "absent" for twenty-three societies. For these twenty-three cases, there is no obvious association between extensiveness of menstrual taboos and presence of menstrual pads; but most of the sample is still unaccounted for.[4]

I expected that menstrual taboos might be influenced by the amount of inconvenience they cause, since, when extensive, they must withdraw women from the labor force and disrupt family life. So I compared extensiveness of menstrual taboos with three other variables: importance of women's contribution to the subsistence economy; frequency of polygyny; and frequency of nuclear households (households composed of a father, a mother, and children, with no other relatives or co-wives).

Importance of women's contribution to the subsistence economy was estimated with a formula suggested by Dwight B. Heath (1958). The estimate is based on Murdock's ratings of *sex-division of labor,* given in his "World Ethnographic Sample" (Murdock, 1957). I thought that the degree to which women are needed to "bring home the bacon" might have a "depressing" effect on extensiveness of menstrual taboos: the more important women's work, the less elaborate the taboos. The test did not show this. There was a zero correlation between extensiveness of menstrual taboos and *importance of women's contribution to the subsistence economy.*

I reasoned that two conditions should make menstrual taboos especially disruptive to the household (and inconvenient to men): monogamous marriage, and nuclear households.

4. My informal judgments were as follows: menstrual pads present: Ifaluk, Bena, Maori, Tungus, Chiricahua, Navaho, Alor, Hopi, Pukapuka, Samoa, Tanala. Menstrual pads absent: Kwakiutl, Sanpoil, Kwoma, Araucania, Aymara, Lesu, Lepcha, Siriono, Tarasco, Gusii, Trobriands, Zapotec.

On this basis, I predicted that extensiveness of menstrual taboos would correlate positively with percentage of polygyny, and that it would correlate negatively with frequency of nuclear households.

There is a moderate positive correlation between extensiveness of menstrual taboos and percentage of polygyny; however, this correlation is subject to another interpretation (see Chapter 9).

Most of the societies characterized by nuclear family households (Murdock, 1957) cluster at the very bottom of the menstrual taboo scale; but these societies are also "low" or "absent" on percentage of polygyny.

In other words, there is some rather weak and ambiguous evidence that amount of disruption to family-life may act on menstrual taboos as a "depressing" influence.

Finally, I thought that menstrual taboos might, to some extent, be a function of the status of women; perhaps they occur when women occupy an especially lowly, exploited position. There is no direct cross-cultural index of women's status. The best indirect index appeared to be rules of descent and residence. I expected that women's prestige and privilege would usually be relatively high in societies with matrilineal descent and/or matrilocal residence; it would be lowest in patrilineal and/or patrilocal societies. On this basis, I predicted that extensiveness of menstrual taboos would correlate positively with presence of patrilineal descent and presence of patrilocal residence, and that it would correlate negatively with presence of matrilineal descent and presence of matrilocal residence (ratings of rules of descent and residence also come from Murdock's "World Ethnographic Sample"). These predictions also failed; extensiveness of menstrual taboos was uncorrelated with rules of descent and residence.

This concludes the tests for other possible causal factors.

We now move on to the study of kin-avoidance, in which the Oedipus complex hypothesis is tested again.

6

KIN-AVOIDANCE

in collaboration with Roy G. D'Andrade

HIS CHAPTER REPORTS MY second attempt to test the Oedipus complex hypothesis, via prediction (the first attempt being the menstrual taboo study). Whereas menstrual taboos afforded many possible "antecedents," only one antecedent is correlated with kin-avoidances —the post partum sex taboo. My assumptions about the post partum sex taboo remain the same. The only new assumption added here is the "meaning" of kin-avoidance, which we assume to be a phobic reaction to the idea of incest.

This particular study was a joint effort between myself and Roy D'Andrade. We have divided this chapter into the following parts:

1. Kin-avoidance: defined and described.
2. The hypothesis and prediction.
3. The scale of severity of kin-avoidances.

4. Test of the prediction.
5. Other facts about avoidance: the pattern of focal avoidance relationships and their extensions; persons who are not avoided; the avoidance syndrome.
6. Other possible correlates of kin-avoidances.

Kin-Avoidance Defined

Avoidance, in the sense of a curtailment or limit set on intimacy between persons, is a matter of degree. Husband and wife perhaps come nearest to the "zero point" on the "avoidance scale." All of us, in most of our daily social contacts, observe certain avoidance customs. We wear clothes, abstain from sexual behavior, etc. These "mild," "usual" avoidance customs we take for granted. In this study, we shall be concerned with more extreme, grotesque avoidances—extreme enough to catch the ethnographer's eye and be reported in ethnographies. Here are a few examples:

Mother-in-law avoidance, among the Araucanians of South America:

A man was forbidden to take things directly from his mother-in-law, to gaze upon her, and to eat or converse with her. If they were indoors, a partition was usually erected between them; if they met outdoors by chance, a woman was permitted only to ask after her daughter's welfare. These customs no longer prevail (Titiev, 1951: 44).

Sister avoidance, among the Cheyenne:

The Cheyenne young man was not permitted to speak to his adult sister. While the little children of a family played together until they approached manhood and womanhood, still, young men might not speak to their sisters after the latter had grown up—when they were about fifteen years old. Until very recently this law has been rigidly observed. If a man went to the lodge of his brother-in-law to speak to him, or to get some article, and found him absent, he did not address the wife—his own sister—on the matter, but spoke to a child about it. Thus, he might ask a little child—even a new-born babe—in the mother's hearing, for the article which he required; or might give it a message for his brother-in-law. If he came to borrow something, very likely the wife presently took the article and put it down somewhere in his sight, and after a time the man took it and went away. The message left with the child in the wife's hearing was always delivered. The practice continued until old age (Grinnell, 1923: Vol. I, 155).

What we mean by "avoidance" is what ethnographers customarily mean: we will apply the term only to the relatively extreme customs that pertain only to special categories of persons (i.e., a man to his mother-in-law, a man to his sister, etc.). These avoidances are usually reported as formal rules or prohibitions: that is, it is reported to be "against the law" to eat with your mother-in-law, or talk to your sister, etc.

It is possible to curtail social interaction and intimacy without resort to this sort of formal prohibition. For example, in many primitive societies it is the custom for boys to leave their parents' house at adolescence, and start sleeping in a bachelors' house ("change of residence for adolescent boys"). This step must reduce interaction and intimacy between the boy and other family members. However, such arrangements, which may have the practical effect of avoidances but apparently do not involve formal prohibitions against certain types of behavior, will *not* be considered avoidances.

Kin-relationship is not the only reason for observing avoidance rules. A man may avoid a woman because she is menstruating, or because she has just washed a corpse, or for other reasons. But our discussion here focuses only on kin-avoidances: avoidance customs that are observed *because of* a particular kin-relationship—because she is your sister, your son's wife, your mother-in-law, etc.

To summarize, when we say "mother-in-law avoidance is reported to be present" in a particular society, we mean that in this society a man and his mother-in-law observe some of the extreme avoidance customs because of their particular kin-relationship. When we say that "a man and his mother-in-law are reported to observe no avoidance rules" we mean that the extreme avoidance customs are apparently absent; we do *not* mean that the mild, unnoticed or more or less universal avoidances are absent. The same applies for avoidances within other kin-relationships.

Kin-Avoidance Described

Extreme avoidances, similar to those described for the Araucanians and the Cheyenne, are fairly common in primitive societies. With some minor exceptions, avoidance of this sort is a cross-sex phenomenon: these prohibitions apply to interaction between men and women. Also, many of the avoidance rules have a very "sexy look." Here are some of the more common and widespread avoidance rules: can't look at each other, can't eat together, can't talk to each other, can't touch each other, can't sleep in the same room, can't be alone together, can't use each other's personal names, can't talk about sex (Appendix IV).

By far the most common (i.e., frequently reported) avoidance relationship is a man to his mother-in-law. Next in frequency are a man to his sister, and a man to his son's wife (Murdock, 1949: 277). Apparently, each of these avoidance relationships usually carries a number of "extensions." That is, if you avoid your real sister, you will also avoid your classificatory sisters (female cousins); if you avoid your mother-in-law, you will avoid some of her relatives; if you avoid your son's wife, you will avoid some of her relatives. Also, there appears to be a general avoidance syndrome. Primitive societies gravitate toward two poles: (1) societies with a great many extreme avoidance relationships; (2) societies with no kin-avoidances at all. Later in the chapter, we treat in detail this extension-pattern, and the avoidance syndrome.

In societies of this first type (many extreme avoidances), kin-avoidance must pose an extraordinary burden and complication to social intercourse. (For further illustration, refer to the examples of mother-in-law avoidance given in Chapter 3.) Note particularly the Eastern Timbira (Nimenaju) and the Chiricahua Apache (Opler). Among the Timbira, the young man and his mother-in-law live *in the same house.* Among the Chiricahua, they live in the same tiny band. In many societies, it seems, the avoiding parties are constantly "in each other's way"; the avoidance rules require more or less constant vigilance.

Apparently, some persons are never avoided. As far as we can tell, a man never observes extreme avoidance customs with his mother or his daughter, or with an aunt or niece (unless the aunt or niece is also an affinal relative).

Finally in one curious respect, kin-avoidances are different from menstrual taboos. We saw that menstrual taboos are frequently rationalized and sanctioned by superstitions about the danger of menstrual blood. There seem to be few "explanations" of this sort for kin-avoidances. At least, they rarely are reported.

The Incest-Phobia Hypothesis

The "meaning" we assign to kin-avoidances was suggested by Geza Roheim, when he wrote of the "phobic attitude of primitive people regarding incest" (Roheim, 1947: Vol. I, 10). The hypothesis we propose is that a major determinant of kin-avoidances is, in Roheim's words, a phobic attitude toward incest. The avoidances are motivated by fear of sexual contact between persons observing the incest taboo. The fear is characterized as "phobic" for a number of reasons. In the first place, many of the more extreme avoidance customs resemble sex-control precautions; that is, they look as if they reflect fear (an apprehensive expectation) of sexual contact between the avoiding parties. However, as sex-control precautions they certainly seem unnecessarily extreme; they have a superfluous quality. The customs' exaggerated nature suggests an exaggerated fear. Thus, we characterize the fear as "phobic."

A second reason for the term "phobic" stems from the first. It is an exaggerated fear of forbidden gratification; therefore, to some extent, it must be in response to some sort of active desire. The fear of gratification must somehow be connected with a desire to *get* gratification. We assume that the incest-fear is triggered by incestuous wishes.

Finally, we seriously doubt that (from the man's viewpoint) the mother-in-law is the most desirable of all tabooed sex objects, and that mother and aunt are completely undesirable; that daughter-in-law is often desirable, and daughter is not. We suspect that the original locus of the feared incestuous wish is not in the actual avoidance relationship: the fear is displaced.

From what we understand of clinical accounts of phobias, their most usual (but not only possible) genesis is thought to be this:

1. A desire to perform some act toward an object is
2. transformed into a fear of that object.
3. The fear is then displaced to another object (or situation) and motivates avoiding behavior toward this object (Fenichel, 1945: 196–203).

This formula for the genesis of phobias we would apply to the genesis and maintenance of kin-avoidances. We would add one qualification: unlike the phobia of a psychoanalytic patient, kin-avoidance represents "institutionalized phobia."

Left to his own devices, each phobic person would reach a more or less idiosyncratic solution with respect to the objects to be avoided and the manner of avoidance (Fenichel, 1945: 199). In the case of kin-avoidances, custom supplies a standardized, readymade phobic solution for all persons, regardless of their varying needs for such a phobic solution. We assume that, in an avoiding society, the avoidance rules coincide rather well with some persons' phobic tendencies. However, there are undoubtedly other persons in such a society who observe the kin-avoidances merely because they were taught to and because it is expected of them, and not because they have strong incestuous wishes and fears that require a phobic solution.

This evokes the question of the correspondence, within a tribe or society, between avoidance customs and phobic tendencies. Once installed in a society, would kin-avoidances continue more-or-less indefinitely, even if most people ceased to have phobic reactions to the idea of incest? How responsive are the institutionalized avoidance customs to population-changes, with respect to the fears that first generated them? To what extent are they characterized by "inertia"?

Of course, we have no way of knowing the answer. If superstition reigns, it rationalizes a great variety of fears and avoidances: of snakes, animals, insects, witches, menstruating women, the dead, ceremonial performers, and so on. We would suppose that at some time, and to some degree, each of these customs corresponded to a personality tendency. It is likely, however, that they are quite variable with respect to their correspondence with *current* personality tendencies. In lieu of factual knowledge, we propose the following rule because it seems reasonable: the more inconvenient, troublesome, and costly an avoidance custom appears to be, the more likely it is that the custom coincides (roughly) with current and pressing fears (i.e., personality trends) of a substantial proportion of the population; otherwise, the custom would be violated, neglected, and changed. Since, in the case of kin-avoidances, inconvenience seems fairly great, we would expect that the correspondence between "institutionalized phobia" and actual phobic tendencies is relatively high.

To summarize, we propose that kin-avoidance is an institutionalized or culturally standardized expression of a phobic attitude toward incest. No doubt the *severity* of avoidance depends on a number of factors or "antecedents." However, one important antecedent to severity of kin-avoidance is frequency and intensity, within a population, of phobic attitudes toward incest.

What, then, causes these phobic attitudes toward incest? We

propose that it is the Oedipal sex attraction (Fenichel, 1945: 168–170, 207). The original locus of the feared incestuous wishes is not in the actual avoidance relationship, but in the parent-child relationship. The formative events for the incest-phobic reaction do not occur at the stage of life when avoidance relationships are assumed—puberty and marriage—but instead in early childhood.

Quite possibly kin-avoidance reflects both the male (son-to-mother) and female (daughter-to-father) Oedipus complex. However, we shall follow my previous policy and concentrate on the male Oedipus complex. The antecedent we propose for severity of kin-avoidance is average intensity (within a tribe) of the son-to-mother sex attraction. As before, its index is the post partum sex taboo. Our assumptions are as follows:

1. The long post partum sex taboo intensifies the son-to-mother sex attraction.
2. This makes phobic attitudes toward incest more likely.
3. This contributes to the severity of kin-avoidances.

On the basis of these assumptions, we predicted a positive correlation between duration of the post partum sex taboo and severity of kin-avoidances.

The Kin-Avoidance Scale

At the time the prediction was made, we hoped to assign societies over-all scores on severity of kin-avoidance. As it turned out, this did not prove feasible. Instead, we assigned separate severity-scores for three avoidance relationships: a man to his mother-in-law, a man to his sister, and a man to his son's wife. These are the most frequently mentioned avoidance relationships; they are the only relationships reported often (and fully) enough to make cross-cultural rating practical. Also, we feel that they are the most "important" avoidance relationships: they appear to set limits on avoidance within other kin-relationships. This phenomenon will be described presently.

Once more the ethnographic data makes possible a Guttman scale. This scale measures severity of avoidance for each of the three avoidance relationships. Here is the scale (from "high" to "low"):

5. *Can't eat together, can't look eye-to-eye:* both these avoidance rules reported present (i.e., both these code-categories coded "present").
4. *Can't eat together, can't look eye-to-eye:* one of these avoidance rules "present."
3. *Can't talk directly.*
2. *Can't talk about sex.*
1. *No avoidance rules* (or *can't talk about sex* coded "absent").

Appendix IV gives coding rules, scaling procedures, and all individual scores on severity for mother-in-law avoidance, brother-sister avoidance, and son's wife avoidance.

A society's severity-score (for any of these avoidance relationships) is equal to the highest scale-point scored "present," or, if no points are scored "present," equal to the point immediately below the lowest point scored "absent."

Test of the Prediction

We were able to test our prediction by correlating duration of the post partum sex taboo with severity of each of the three

Table 22.
Duration of the Post Partum Sex Taboo Compared with Severity of Mother-in-Law Avoidance

Avoidance Scale (Applied to Mother-in-Law Avoidance)	DURATION OF THE POST PARTUM SEX TABOO	
	Long	*Short*
5	Arapaho	Lamba
	Araucania	Manus
	Bena	Murngia
	Cheyenne	Navaho
	Chiricahua	
	Ganda	
	Gesu	
	Kurtachi	
	Lango	
	Lesu	
	Lovedu	
	Thonga	
4	Fiji	Gros Ventre
	Kipsigi	
	Nuer	
	Tiv	
3	Dakota	Nama Hottentot
	Ojibwa	Timbira
		Warrau
2	Bassa	Ashanti
	Bulu	Baiga
	Ulithi	Gusii
		Lepcha
		Zapotec
1	Dahomey	Alor
	Hupa	Bella Coola
	Samoa	Chenchu
	Tallensi	Hopi
	Trobriands	Marquesas
		Papago
		Sanpoil
		Siriono
		Subanum
		Tarahumara

$P = 0.01$

Table 23.
Duration of the Post Partum Sex Taboo Compared with Severity of Son's Wife Avoidance

Avoidance Scale (Applied to Son's Wife Avoidance)	DURATION OF THE POST PARTUM SEX TABOO	
	Long	Short
5	Ganda	Manus
	Gesu	
	Nyakusa	
4	Arapaho	Zapotec
	Araucania	
	Chagga	
	Dakota	
	Fiji	
	Rajput	
3		Tungus
2	Bassa	Ashanti
	Bulu	Gusii
1	Bena	Alor
	Chiricahua	Baiga
	Dahomey	Bella Coola
	Hupa	Chenchu
	Kurtachi	Hopi
	Lango	Marquesas
	Ooldea	Navaho
	Tallensi	Papago
		Sanpoil
		Siriono
		Subanum
		Tarahumara

$$P = 0.05$$

avoidance relationships. These correlations are given in Tables 22, 23, and 24. They are all positive, strong, and statistically significant.

The correlations give emphatic support to the incest-phobia interpretation for kin-avoidance. They also give added sup-

Table 24.
Duration of the Post Partum Sex Taboo Compared with Severity of Brother-Sister Avoidance

Avoidance Scale (Applied to Brother-Sister Avoidance)	DURATION OF THE POST PARTUM SEX TABOO		
	Long		Short
5		(No Cases)	
4	Dakota Fiji Samoa Trobriands Ulithi		Ontong Java
3	Arapaho Cheyenne Chiricahua Ojibwa		Murngin Nama Hottentot
2	Chagga Kipsigi Kurtachi Rajput		Ashanti Manus Navaho Truk Zapotec
1	Arapesh Bassa Bulu Kwoma		Alor Chenchu Hopi Papago Siriono Subanum Tarahumara Tungus

$$P = 0.01$$

port to the general Oedipus complex hypothesis, and to the special assumption about the post partum sex taboo.

Focal Avoidances and Their Extensions

At this point we would like to make a brief excursion from our main subject and dally a while with kin-avoidance.

The kin-avoidance study brought some unexpected bonus-findings, which, though they have little to do with the Oedipus complex, are consistent, in a minimal way, with the incest-phobia interpretation. The interesting fact about kin-avoidances is that they exhibit numerous world-wide regularities. Sweeping generalizations can be made about them. Several of these generalizations were made by G. P. Murdock, in his previous survey of kin-avoidances (Murdock, 1949). We shall review these generalizations, and add several more.

All the statements to follow, except for the avoidance syndrome, are *not* based on standardized cross-cultural ratings; they are based on our ethnographic reading notes.

The three avoidance relationships we coded—mother-in-law, brother-sister, and son's wife—are *focal,* in the sense that they appear to set limits on other possible avoidance relationships. This is best illustrated by following an individual through two stages in his (or her) life cycle:

A boy ordinarily observes no kin-avoidances until he reaches sexual maturity. At this stage, if he assumes any avoidance relationships, he will avoid his real sister (provided she is also sexually mature). He may also avoid other persons, but these will include *only* other female consanguineal kin ("blood kin") of his own generation: female cousins, usually classificatory "sisters." If he does not avoid his sister, he will avoid no one. If he does avoid his sister, he may or may not avoid some female cousins, but will avoid no one else. We suspect (although evidence is scanty here) that he rarely observes more severe avoidance customs with his cousin than he does with his real sister. To summarize this stage in the life cycle: the real sister must be avoided if anyone else is avoided; female cousins are the only other persons who can be avoided; the avoidance of the real sister will be

the most extreme. We found three exceptions to this pattern—
Ganda, Lesu, and Malaita, where a cross-cousin is more
severely avoided than the real sister.

When the man marries he may assume more avoidance relationships—he may avoid some of his wife's kin. If he
avoids any of them, he will avoid his mother-in-law. The
mother-in-law avoidance will be equally or more severe than
the avoidance of other affines (the wife's kin). The only exception we found to this rule is the Baiga, who avoid the
wife's sister more severely than the wife's mother.

Finally, when a girl marries she may avoid some of her
husband's kin. If she avoids any of these, she will avoid her
husband's father (the man-to-son's wife avoidance). No other
affine (husband's blood-kin) will be more extremely avoided
than he. Again, the Baiga pose the lone exception to this
rule: there the husband's brother is more extremely avoided
than the husband's father.

The data on which these generalizations are based is summarized in Table 25. In the table we have termed these "other
persons," who may be avoided along with one of the focal
avoidance relationships (but who will *not* be avoided unless
there is a corresponding focal avoidance), "extensions."
Thus, female cousins are "extensions" of the real sister. The
wife's father, wife's mother's sister, wife's sister, etc., are
"extensions" of the wife's mother. The husband's mother,
husband's sister, etc., are (from the viewpoint of a married
woman) "extensions" of the husband's father.

Table 25 lists cases for two samples: the "world-wide
sample" and the "California sample." The California sample
represents trait-list notes, based on culture element distribution studies done among the California Indians. Each "case"

Table 25.
Severity Comparisons: Focal Avoidances and Their Extensions

Focal Avoidance Relationship	Focal Avoidance Mentioned; Extensions Not Mentioned	Both Focal Avoidance and Extensions Mentioned; No Severity-Comparisons	Focal Avoidance Is More Severe than Extensions	An Extension Is Equally Severe as the Focal Avoidance	An Extension Is More Severe than the Focal Avoidance	Extension Mentioned; Focal Avoidance Not Mentioned
Man and Mother-in-Law:						
World-Wide Sample	13*	17	10	0	0	1
California Sample	30	0	33	8	1	0
Woman and Father-in-Law:						
World-Wide Sample	8	8	4	0	0	1
California Sample	0	0	21	15	0	0
Brother and Sister:						
World-Wide Sample	10	16	4	0	2	1
California Sample	55	0	0	0	0	0

*In Tables 25 and 27, each numerical entry is a tally of cases. For example, there were thirteen cases (in the world-wide sample) of mother-in-law avoidance, with no mention made of extensions to the mother-in-law avoidance.

is usually a tiny band of people. Many of these bands are closely related to each other (linguistically almost identical, and/or geographically close). The California sample is described more fully in Appendix IV. The "world-wide sample" represents reading notes on all other primitive societies for which we could gather information.

We should mention two complications in the avoidance picture that are missed by following avoidance through the life cycle. In the first place, one person may become an extension to another person's focal avoidance relationship. For example, your brother's mother-in-law may avoid you. Secondly, it may be that in some societies "anticipatory affines" are avoided before marriage occurs. That is, there may be a large class of females who are potential mothers-in-law whom you will avoid after reaching puberty.

Finally, although the three focal avoidance relationships appear to predetermine other possible avoidance relationships, from what we know they do not predetermine each other. That is, they do not "scale." There is a tendency in this direction; the more frequent mother-in-law avoidance is usually present if either of the other two—brother-sister, or son's wife avoidance—is present. But there seem to be numerous exceptions. You may avoid your sister or son's wife and not avoid your mother-in-law. You may avoid your sister and not avoid your son's wife (and vice versa). See Table 41.

Is this pattern of focal-avoidance-with-extensions a near-universal rule, with almost no exceptions, or is it merely an extremely strong trend, with numerous exceptions? The data we have says it is a near-universal rule. However, as Table 25 suggests, there are many gaps in the data. Possibly, if all the facts were known, the percentage of exceptions would be much higher. But the incomplete picture we have allows a tentative conclusion:

Some sort of internal necessity, identical for nearly all primitive societies, dictates the above patterning phenomenon. If you avoid your cousin, you *must* avoid your sister. If a man avoids his father-in-law, he *must* avoid his mother-in-law. The widely varied primitive societies, scattered throughout the world, follow (with rare exceptions) the *same* general rule of patterning.

What is the internal necessity? Part of the answer may lie in a tendency among these primitive societies to group all persons into a few social categories, and to dictate similar behavior toward all individuals within any one social category. It looks as if the focal avoidance relationships are the "heart" of avoidance, and that extensions are avoided as a sort of "afterthought," that is, because of social similarity to the focal-avoided person vis-à-vis kin terms, age, sex, authority relations, etc. Perhaps a future study can shed more light on this question. However, the extensions are on the whole poorly reported.

It appears that extensions usually do occur. They are often unmentioned, but we found only three specific reports that they were absent: for the Lango and Navaho there are no extensions to mother-in-law avoidance; for the Zapotec there are no extensions to the son's wife avoidance.

Persons Who Are Not Avoided

One implication of the pattern of focal avoidances with extensions is that there are many persons who are rarely if ever avoided. The relatives who are excluded from avoidance relationships are primarily *different generation consanguineal kin:* mother, grandmother, aunt, daughter, niece, granddaughter, and male equivalents—in other words, parents and children, and *their* "extensions."

Neither Murdock nor we found any cases of avoidance between mother and son. Murdock lists two cases of father-daughter avoidance; we found two cases of mild avoidance between father and daughter—Gusii and Ulithi. Murdock reports one case of avoidance between a person and his grandchild; we found no cases of this sort. In our sample, the only avoidance between persons two generations removed was between affines, and these cases were extensions of one of the focal avoidances (mother-in-law or son's wife avoidance). Murdock gives a few instances in which a man avoids his aunt or niece (Murdock, 1949: 277). In our sample, the only time an aunt is avoided is when she is also an affine (a mother-in-law, or her extension). The same is true for nieces (with one possible exception—Ulithi). Since accounts are sometimes confusing on these points, we may be in error for a case or two; but we are confident that possible exceptions are rare.

Finally, we found little in the way of avoidance between consanguineal kin of the same sex. Apparently, a woman never avoids her mother, sister, aunt, daughter, niece, grandmother, granddaughter, or female cousin. In a few of the sample societies, a man does observe customs of respect-etiquette toward older male consanguines—toward his father, grandfathers, elder brothers, or uncles. This respect-etiquette usually has the appearance of demonstrations of obedience and submission; but occasionally it does have the flavor of sex-connected avoidance.

Table 26 gives a simplified graphic summary of this total effect. A condensed verbal summary would be as follows: you may avoid some same-generation consanguineal relatives, but never different-generation consanguineal relatives; for affinal relatives the reverse is true—you will frequently avoid different-generation affines, but rarely avoid same-generation affines (except as *extensions* to the mother-in-law or son's wife avoidance).

Table 26.
The Distribution of Avoidance among Possible Kin and Generation Relationships

	GENERATION RELATIONSHIP	
Kin Relationship	Same Generation	Different Generation
Consanguineal Kin	Yes	No
	Avoidance May Occur: Brother-Sister Avoidance and Its Extensions	Avoidance Almost Never Occurs
Affinal Kin	No	Yes
	Avoidance Seldom Occurs, and Then Only as an Extension of a Cross-Generation Affinal Avoidance (Exception: Baiga)	Avoidance Often Occurs: Mother-in-Law and Son's Wife Avoidance, and Their Extensions

Avoidance Is Primarily a Cross-Sex Phenomenon

Apparently, extreme same-sex avoidance relationships occure only between affines, and then only as (usually weaker) extensions of one of the focal avoidances. The most commonly cited same-sex avoidance relationship is between a man and his father-in-law. Also mentioned is avoidance between a man and his wife's brother, and between a woman and her husband's mother. There is only one case (in the California sample) in which same-sex avoidance is said to be more extreme than the focal cross-sex avoidance. Our data on same-sex avoidance relationships is summarized in Table 27.

The General Avoidance Syndrome

We now return to a consideration of the *severity* of the three focal avoidances, as measured by the Guttman scale. Although the three focal avoidance relationships do not pattern in relation to each other, they do *not* seem to be independent of each other. If one is present ("high") in a society, the others (when codable) are likely to be present too; when one is absent (or "low"), the others are usually absent. Severity scores on the three focal avoidances are rather strongly correlated:

	ρ	P
Mother-in-law avoidance—son's wife avoidance	+0.64	0.001
Mother-in-law avoidance—brother-sister avoidance	+0.46	0.02
Son's wife avoidance—brother-sister avoidance	+0.55	0.01

Table 41 also suggests that licentious joking relationships are a part of the general avoidance syndrome. Licentious joking relationships appear to occur in societies with a great many extreme avoidances; they are less likely in societies with no kin-avoidances.[2]

2. Presence or absence of licentious joking relationships, that is, kin-relationships within which sexual joking is expected, was judged informally on the basis of the ethnographic reading notes. They were not subjected to standardized rating. Some of these judgments were based on inference: the ethnographer does not clearly state that a "joking relationship" includes sexual joking. All cases of licentious joking involve a cross-sex relationship: a man to his sister, female cousin, brother's wife, or some other female relative. A few of these cases also include sexual joking between same-sex kin.

Table 27.

Severity Comparisons: Same-Sex Avoidances and Their Corresponding Focal (Cross-Sex) Avoidances

Same-Sex Avoidance Relationship	Corresponding Focal Avoidance	Focal Avoidance Mentioned; Same-Sex Avoidance Not Mentioned	Both Focal and Same-Sex Avoidance Mentioned; No Severity-Comparisons	Focal Avoidance Is More Severe Than Same-Sex Avoidance	Same-Sex Avoidance Is Equally Severe As Focal Avoidance	Same-Sex Avoidance Is More Severe Than Focal Avoidance
Man to Wife's Father	Man to Wife's Mother					
World-Wide Sample		18	14	4	0	0
California Sample		30	0	33	8	1
Man to Wife's Brother	Man to Wife's Mother (?)					
World-Wide Sample		27	6	3	0	0
California Sample		72	0	0	0	0
Woman to Husband's Mother	Woman to Husband's Father					
World-Wide Sample		14	4	1	0	0
California Sample		0	0	21	15	0

In other words, the world seems to be divided into "avoiding societies" and "non-avoiding societies." Apparently, most avoiding societies observe many severe avoidances, involving *several* of the focal avoidance relationships and numerous extensions to them and accompanied by licentious joking within other kin-relationships.

The Cumulative Pattern of Avoidance Customs

The last regularity applies not to avoidance relationships but to the patterning of avoidance rules. It is demonstrated by the Guttman scale of severity of avoidance (Appendix IV). This scale is composed of a few avoidance customs (or narrow custom-categories) that have a wide geographic distribution and—from what we know—observe the same cumulative pattern in almost all cases. Furthermore, the cumulative pattern seems to apply to any avoidance relationship.

This scale, and the similar scale for menstrual taboos, says that there are quasi-universal culture-patterning phenomena. In widely scattered societies, the same "problem" (the necessity to avoid certain kin, menstruating women, etc.) generates the same "solutions" (identical or near-identical avoidance customs). As the "problem" intensifies, the same customs are added in the same order.[3]

Avoidance and Social Structure

Other writers have proposed functionalist explanations for kin-avoidance: avoidance occurs because it serves to clarify

3. The "problem" also seems to generate some added "solutions" that are idiosyncratic: avoidance customs that are not widely distributed and/or do not pattern cumulatively.

role-relationships (implied in Radcliffe-Brown, 1940); it occurs because it serves to suppress conflict between kinsmen (Eggan, 1937); it occurs because it functions to prevent incestuous sexual relations (Murdock, 1949). We wanted to test these hypotheses; but we finally decided that, with the data at our disposal, they were untestable.

Instead, we merely report results of some additional correlations. These are correlations between severity of avoidance and certain "social structure variables"—presence of unilineal kin-groups, presence of exogamous communities, rules of descent and marriage, and propinquity of the avoiding parties. All these ratings but the last are drawn from Murdock's "World Ethnographic Sample" (1957). The propinquity ratings were made by Whiting and D'Andrade.

Kin-Groups and Rules of Descent. There is a positive correlation between severity of avoidance and presence of unilineal kin-groups (as defined by Murdock). For mother-in-law avoidance, the correlation is extremely strong. For brother-sister and son's wife avoidance, it is much weaker.

When the post partum sex taboo is held constant (i.e., when societies are divided into two groups—"long" and "short" on duration of the post partum sex taboo), presence of kin-groups is still positively correlated with severity of avoidance. The reverse is also true: with the presence of kin-groups held constant, the long post partum sex taboo still shows a positive correlation with severity of avoidance.

In only one instance does it appear to matter whether the kin-group is matrilineal or patrilineal. Severity of son's wife avoidance is closely associated with presence of *patrilineal* kin-groups.

Rules of Residence at Marriage. Son's wife avoidance is also closely associated with presence of a *patrilocal* rule of residence. This is the only discernible relationship between severity of avoidance and rules of residence. In our sample, it is *not* true that severe mother-in-law (or sister) avoidance characterizes matrilocal (as opposed to patrilocal) societies; neither does severe mother-in-law (or sister) avoidance characterize patrilocal (as opposed to matrilocal) societies. As stated above, an analogous statement may be applied to rules of descent: matrilineal and patrilineal societies do not seem to differ as to severity of mother-in-law or brother-sister avoidance.

Those few societies in our sample which are characterized by a *bilocal* rule of residence are uniformly "low" on severity of avoidance.

Finally, there is a weak positive correlation between presence of *exogamous communities* and severity of avoidance. It holds for all three focal avoidances.

We conclude from the above that some sort of formal structure factor is probably one of the determinants of kin-avoidance. Societies that are "highly structured," in the sense of having unilineal kin-groups, unilocal residence rules, and exogamous rules (applying to communities), are somewhat more prone to kin-avoidance. Societies with relatively "little formal structure"—no unilineal kin-groups, no unilocal rules of residence or community-exogamy rules—are less prone to kin-avoidance.

Avoidance and Propinquity. The Whiting-D'Andrade propinquity ratings estimate the distance between kinsmen. They "place" kinsmen in relation to each other according to customary sleeping places. They apply to residence after marriage. In other words, these ratings are similar to, but more detailed than, the Murdock rule-of-residence ratings. The scale is as follows: same bed; adjacent beds; same room; same house; adjacent houses; same neighborhood; same village; different villages (Whiting and D'Andrade).

Severity of avoidance is generally uncorrelated with propinquity of the avoiding parties. This is clear for mother-in-law avoidance and for brother-sister avoidance. It does not seem to matter (for avoidance) whether mother-in-law or sister are near you, or far away. For son's wife avoidance, it is hard to be sure; generally, for our sample, it is rare that a man and his son's wife live in different villages.

Summary

We draw the following conclusions from the evidence on kin-avoidance:

1. The distribution of avoidance relationships—i.e., who avoids whom—seems to follow a near-universal patterning regularity. There are three persons who, from the male ego's viewpoint, are "avoidable": his mother-in-law, his sister, and his son's wife. *If* male ego avoids one of these avoidable persons, he may also avoid, to an equal or lesser degree, other persons who are socially similar. Additional persons are "unavoidable"—parents and children, and other different-generation consanguineal kin.

2. Severity of avoidance does not seem to be affected by degree of propinquity of the avoiding parties. This at least seems clear for mother-in-law and brother-sister avoidance.

3. Severe avoidances are more frequent in societies characterized by a high degree of formal structure—i.e., unilineal kin-groups, etc.

4. There is a good reason to believe that one determinant of severity of avoidance is phobic attitudes toward incest, deriving from the Oedipus complex. The strongest evidence are the significant correlations between post partum sex taboo and severity of avoidance. There is added incidental evidence from other sources: the appearance of many avoidance customs suggests sexual concerns; avoidance is primarily between cross-sex persons; severity-scores on the various avoidance relationships are rather strongly intercorrelated, indicating a general causal factor (such as incest-phobia) that is not specific to individual avoidance relationships.

7

INITIATIONS, TOTEMISM, SORCERY, AND FEAR OF OTHERS

In THIS CHAPTER WE SHALL deal with customs of a different order. Up to now, we have been correlating the post partum sex taboo with avoidances. These avoidances seem to reflect various sorts of sexual fears, and, in the case of menstrual taboos and kin-avoidances, sometimes reach a grotesque level of inconvenience. The variables *initiations for boys, totemism,* and *sorcery* do not represent avoidance—at least, not in the same clear-cut way as do menstrual taboos and kin-avoidances. Neither do they clearly reflect sexual fears. Whether they represent the same kind of grotesque inconvenience is debatable.

Also, they fall beyond the boundaries of the Oedipus complex hypothesis, as narrowly defined in Chapter 2. I'm not sure I would have predicted a positive correlation between them and duration of the post partum sex taboo. One of the correlations we shall review (initiations) *was predicted,* on the basis of a different sort of Oedipus complex hypothesis. The second (totemism) was not predicted; however, totemism has been interpreted (by Freud) as reflecting the Oedipus complex. In other words, initiations and totemism appeared to other writers to have an "Oedipal flavor." I feel these variables add additional evidence that is consistent, in a loose way, with my Oedipus complex hypothesis. Sorcery also, perhaps, provides some supporting evidence for the hypothesis, but evidence that is even less direct.

Initiations for Adolescent Boys

This variable was measured by Whiting, Kluckhohn, and Anthony, and was reported in a paper entitled "The Function of Male Initiation Ceremonies at Puberty" (Whiting, Kluckhohn, and Anthony, 1958). The paper represented the "opening shot" in the cross-cultural attack on the Oedipus complex. I shall do little more here than review their findings.

An initiation is a rite of passage, a ceremonial recognition of a change in status. In primitive societies, initiations for boys usually involve one or several ordeals, imposed on the boys by older men. In some parts of the world the initiate is circumcised, or his penis is mutilated in other ways.[1] He may go through a period of isolation, or a period of strict seclusion from all females. In many ways, he may be frightened, intimidated, or discomfited. Usually the initiation is mandatory for all boys in the society.

Whiting, Kluckhohn, and Anthony define an initiation cere-

1. In the New World, I know of only one questionable case of genital operations—the Warrau of South America. Genital operations occur on all other continents, although they appear to be most popular in Africa and Australia. Presence of genital operations is only weakly correlated with duration of the post partum sex taboo.

mony for adolescent boys as a rite-of-passage ceremonial, occurring during the adolescent period, which has at least one of the following aspects: genital operations, seclusion from women, hazing, or tests of manliness (Whiting, Kluckhohn, and Anthony, 1958). Since I will be using their ratings, I shall abide by their definition.

However, the variable *initiations for boys* (as defined and rated by Whiting, Kluckhohn, and Anthony) does present some serious problems of definition. There are some marginal cases:

1. North American Indian societies, with the vision-quest (a solitary boy or young man fasts in the wilderness, to attract a supernatural helper). The vision-quest is counted as "seclusion from women." The following societies were rated "present" for *initiations for boys*, solely on the basis of the vision-quest: Ojibwa, Papago, Sanpoil.

2. Two societies, Dahomey and Samoa, have genital operations that do not seem to be a part of formal ceremonials. They are coded "present" for *initiations for boys*.

3. Two societies, Kazak and Tanala, circumcise boys in very early childhood. They are coded "absent."

4. One society, Ulithi, has a puberty ceremonial which, apparently, is not characterized by any of the defining ordeals (genital operations, seclusion from women, hazing, tests of manliness). It is coded "absent."

5. A number of societies have ordeals for the sake of adornment (tattooing or tooth-filing): Alor, Bali, Lakher, Maori, and Ontong Java. They are coded "absent."

These marginal cases will be starred in the table (Table 28).

Now a word about the interpretation of initiations. Whit-

ing, Kluckhohn, and Anthony hypothesize that the rites reflect, among other things, father-son rivalry (Whiting, Kluckhohn, and Anthony, 1958). Several psychoanalytic writers
have reached a similar conclusion (Fenichel, 1945: 79;
Balint, 1954: 72; Roheim, 1950: 75–97). This rivalry is
interpreted as *Oedipal* rivalry, that is, father-son rivalry
resulting from the son's more-or-less unconscious sex attraction toward his mother.[2] In other words, these interpretations
are based on a psychoanalytic formulation that I have deliberately excluded from my Oedipus complex hypothesis.
The formulation is: *as a result* of his sex attraction toward
his mother, the boy feels rivalrous toward his father (and
this rivalry generates further unconscious fantasies, death
wishes, etc., that have more or less continuing effects on the
male's relations with his father and other "father-figures,"
and affect his behavior in other ways); also, the sex-based
rivalrous feelings may be mutual (Fenichel, 1945: 78;
Freud, 1936: 81; Freud, 1950: 141; Mullahy, 1952: 25–29;
Sachs, 1934: 63–73).

Often, in initiations, older men appear to be "punishing"
the initiates in various ways; perhaps they are responding to
the boys' rivalrous feelings, or expressing their own jealousy
(or doing both). The frequent genital operations and seclusion from women suggest that sexual concerns probably, at
times, lie in the background.

Whiting, Kluckhohn, and Anthony also hypothesized that
the long post partum sex taboo intensifies the Oedipus com-

2. This characterization is only minimally true for the Whiting, Kluckhohn, Anthony interpretation. They speak of the son-to-father rivalry as
"the Oedipus complex," but they emphasize dependency-needs, instead
of sexual urges, as the main motive for the rivalry (Whiting, Kluckhohn,
and Anthony, 1958).

plex (meaning, primarily, father-son rivalry). Therefore,
they predicted a positive correlation between duration of the
post partum sex taboo and presence of initiations for boys.
In a moment we shall look at their test of this prediction.
First, to give the data a little more vividness, I shall give an
example of an initiation ceremony. It is the example that the
above three authors themselves use in their article: initiation
among the Thonga. The Thonga have an unusually severe
initiation. The example is probably a bit unrepresentative,
as regards elaboration and severity of ordeals. However, in
most cases the initiations do appear to be quite traumatic.

. . . Among the Thonga, a tribe in South Africa, every boy must
go through a very elaborate ceremony in order to become a man.
When a boy is somewhere between ten and sixteen years of age, he
is sent by his parents to a "circumcision school" which is held every
four or five years. Here in company with his agemates he undergoes
severe hazing by the adult males of the society. The initiation begins
for each boy by having to run the gauntlet between two rows of men
who beat him with clubs. At the end of this experience, he is stripped
of his clothes and his hair is cut. He is next met by a man covered
with lion manes and is seated upon a stone facing the "Lion man."
Someone then strikes him from behind and when he turns his head
to see who has struck him, his foreskin is seized and in two movements cut off by the "Lion man." Afterwards he is secluded for three
months in the "yards of mysteries," where he can be seen only by
the initiated. It is especially taboo for a woman to approach these
boys during their seclusion, and if a woman should glance at the
leaves with which the circumcised covers his wound, and which form
his only clothing, she must be killed.
During the course of his initiation, the boy undergoes six major
trials: beatings, exposure to cold, thirst, eating of unsavory foods,
punishment and the threat of death. On the slightest pretext he may
be severely beaten by one of the newly initiated men who is assigned

to the task by the older men of the tribe. He sleeps without covering and suffers bitterly from the winter cold. He is forbidden to drink a drop of water during the whole three months. Meals are often made nauseating by the half-digested grass from the stomach of an antelope poured over his food. If he is caught breaking any important rule governing the ceremony, he is severely punished. For example, in one of these punishments, sticks are placed between the fingers of the offender, then a strong man closes his hand around that of the novice practically crushing his fingers. He is frightened into submission by being told that in former times boys who had tried to escape or who revealed the secrets to women or to the uninitiated were hanged and their bodies burnt to ashes (Whiting, Kluckhohn, and Anthony, 1958).

Scale this description down somewhat, as to severity and elaboration of ordeals, and you have a fair picture of the variable *initiations for boys.*

In Table 28 is the significant positive correlation between duration of the post partum sex taboo and presence of initiations for adolescent boys.[3] This correlation provides evidence in favor of these authors' thesis that initiations reflect Oedipal (father-son) rivalry, and that the long post partum sex taboo intensifies this Oedipal rivalry. Also, I think, it gives some indirect support to my own Oedipus complex hypothesis.

3. Whiting, Kluckhohn, and Anthony rated two samples: an original sample selected by the "gold is where you find it" method and a second sample, drawn from the first, in which each of Murdock's culture areas is represented by no more than one society. In their article, the correlation is run on the second sample (Whiting, Kluckhohn, and Anthony, 1958). In this case I shall follow my usual convention, and use their first sample—all the cases they rated (Whiting and Kluckhohn; Whiting, Kluckhohn, and Anthony).

They also correlated initiations with a second variable—*presence of exclusive mother-infant sleeping arrangements.* I shall not consider that variable here; it corresponds fairly closely to the variable *percentage of mother-child households.*

Table 28.
Presence of Initiation Ceremonies for Adolescent Boys Compared with Duration of the Post Partum Sex Taboo

Duration of the Post Partum Sex Taboo	INITIATION CEREMONIES FOR ADOLESCENT BOYS			
	Present		Absent	
Long	Arapesh	Lesu	Arapaho	
	Azande	Lovedu	Araucania	
	Bena	Manam	Ganda	
	Chagga	Masai	Hausa	
	Cheyenne	Mende	Hupa	
	Chiricahua	Neur	Ifaluk	
	Dahomey*	Ojibwa*	Malaita	
	Dakota	Ooldea	Nyakusa	
	Fiji	Pondo	Pilaga	
	Gesu	Samoa*	Rajput	
	Jivaro	Thonga	Tallensi	
	Kipsigi	Tiv	Tepoztlan	
	Kiwai	Turkana	Trobriands	
	Kurtachi	Venda	Ulithi*	
	Kwakiutl	Wogeo	Yap	
	Kwoma	Yao		
	Lango	Yoruba		
Short	Chewa		Alor*	Lepcha
	Gusii		Ashanti	Manus
	Hopi		Bali*	Maori*
	Marquesas		Baiga	Maria Gond
	Mohave		Bella Coola	Mixtec
	Murngin		Chenchu	Navaho
	Nama Hettentot		Copper Esk.	Ontong Java*
	Nambicauru		Druz	Rwala Bedouin
	Papago*		Gros Ventre	Silwa
	Sanpoil*		Aymara	Siriono
	Timbira		Cagaba	Tanala*
	Truk		Igorot	Tarahumara
	Warrau		Kazak*	Tarasco
	Yaghan		Koryak	Yagua
			Lakher*	Yukaghir
			Lamba	Zapotec
			Lapp	

$$P = 0.01$$

* Marginal cases, viz., the initiation variable.

Before we move on, something more should be said about the Oedipal rivalry hypothesis. Traditionally, in psychoanalytic writings, the term "Oedipus complex" refers to *both* the mother-son sex attraction and father-son rivalry. If I may restate part of my paraphrasing of the traditional Oedipus complex formulation:

1. Young boys customarily become sexually attracted to their mothers.

2. As a result, they feel rivalrous toward their fathers.

As you will note, this formulation is in two parts; the two parts are analytically separable. Each part can be tested separately. For instance, it is possible that the first part is generally valid, and the second part is generally invalid, or is valid only under rather special conditions. I felt it would be easier to test only the first part. Therefore, to make hypothesis-testing more simple and direct (to exclude unnecessary assumptions) I deleted the father-son rivalry formulation from my limited Oedipus complex hypothesis.

I think it is still an open question whether all factors that intensify the mother-son sex attraction also necessarily intensify father-son rivalry. I am not too sure that the long post partum sex taboo intensifies Oedipal rivalry. A few cross-cultural findings (mainly the initiation findings) indicates that it does. Another piece of cross-cultural evidence raises some doubt about this. I rated the folktales and myths of primitive societies for frequency of father-son conflict: stated and, by rather conservative interpretations, disguised. These ratings are given in Appendix VII. There is a rather weak positive correlation between *frequency of father-son conflict in folklore* and *duration of the post partum sex taboo*. More interesting than this correlation is the fact that, for nearly all societies, father-son conflict (in folklore) is rare. Perhaps most father-son conflict was missed, because it was so extremely disguised that my conservative coding rules "missed" it. However, I can say that, for my sample, obvious preoccupation with father-son conflict does *not* characterize the folklore of societies having a long post partum sex taboo.

One more fact about initiation ceremonies: girls may also be initiated at puberty. The variable, *presence of girls' initiations*, was rated by Albert Anthony (1955). It is also positively correlated with the long post partum sex taboo, about as strongly as are boys' initiations. Perhaps this correlation is largely an artifact of the correlation between post partum sex taboo and menstrual taboos. It is my impression that, when menstrual taboos are at all extensive, they are usually accompanied by an elaborate puberty (first-menstruation) ceremony, rationalized as protection against the girl's new malignant power.

Totemism

Totemism is not easy to characterize; the term "totemism" has been applied to rather disparate sets of customs in different societies (Lessa and Vogt, 1958: 221). I suppose the "essence" of totemism is the belief in animal-ancestors. Usually, this belief is associated with food taboos (Fischer and Whiting). Often, too, it serves to rationalize exogamous rules (Lessa and Vogt, 1958: 222; Goldenweiser, 1912: 229). To explicate, I will describe an "ideal-type totemic society":

1. *Nonhuman ancestors.* The society is divided into a number of unilineal kin-groups. Each kin-group traces its descent to an original nonhuman ancestor. The kin-groups bear the names of these ancestors. There are the bears, the racoons, the flying squirrels, the eagles, the squashes, etc. Most of these nonhuman ancestors are animals; occasionally, the ancestor may be a plant, or a natural phenomenon (fire, wind, etc.).

2. *Food taboos.* There is a taboo against eating one's totem. For instance, if one is a raccoon (i.e., a member of a kin-group that traces its descent from a raccoon), one is not allowed to eat (or kill) raccoons.

3. *Rationale for exogamous rules.* Members of the same kin-group cannot intermarry, since they are "brothers and sisters" (descended from the same totem-ancestor).

There may be further elaborations. Freud, quoting Reinach, gives this list of totemic customs:

1. Certain animals may neither be killed nor eaten, but individual members of a species are reared by human beings and cared for by them.

2. An animal which has died an accidental death is mourned over and buried with the same honours as a member of the clan.

3. In some instances the eating prohibition extends only to one particular part of the animal's body.

4. When one of the animals which are usually spared has to be killed under the stress of necessity, apologies are offered to it and an attempt is made by means of various artifices and evasions to mitigate the violation of the taboo—that is to say, of the murder.

5. When the animal is made the victim of a ritual sacrifice, it is solemnly bewailed.

6. On particular solemn occasions and at religious ceremonies the skins of certain animals are worn. Where totemism is still in force, they are the totem animals.

7. Clans and individuals adopt the names of animals—viz. of the totem animals.

8. Many clans make use of representations of animals on their standards and weapons; the men have pictures of animals painted or tatooed on their bodies.

9. If the totem is a formidable and dangerous animal, it is supposed to spare members of the clan named after it.

10. The totem animal protects and gives warning to members of its clan.

11. The totem animal foretells the future to the loyal members of its clan and serves them as guide.

12. The members of the totemic clan often believe that they are related to the totem animal by the bond of a common ancestor (Freud, 1950: 101–102).

The ratings of totemism we shall use were made by Fischer and Whiting. These ratings consider two aspects of totemism: (1) belief in non-human ancestors, and (2) associated food taboos. Therefore, the variable we will deal with is *totemism with food taboos*. If societies have both these "totemic aspects," they are rated "present"; otherwise, they are rated "absent" (Fischer and Whiting).

According to Freud's famous interpretation, totemism reflects (is a projection of) the Oedipus complex (with the emphasis on father-son rivalry). He reached this interpretation by drawing parallels between totemic customs (in primitive societies) and the behavior of children. His discussion, "The Return of Totemism in Childhood," develops from two main clinical examples: the horse-phobia of Little Hans (one of his own cases) and the "chicken-totemism" of Little Arpad (a case first reported by Ferenczi). Let us review the case of Little Arpad:

When little Arpad was two and a half years old, he had once, while he was on a summer holiday, tried to micturate into the fowl-house and a fowl had bitten or snapped at his penis. A year later, when he was back in the same place, he himself turned into a fowl; his one interest was in the fowl-house and in what went on there and he abandoned human speech in favour of cackling and crowing. At the time at which the observation was made (when he was five years old) he had recovered his speech, but his interests and his talk were entirely concerned with chickens and other kinds of poultry. They were his only toys and he only sang songs that had some mention of fowls in them. His attitude towards his totem animal was superlatively ambivalent: he showed both hatred and love to an extravagant degree. His favorite game was playing slaughtering fowls. "The slaughtering of poultry was a regular festival for him. He would dance round the animals' bodies for hours at a time in a state of intense excitement." But afterwards he would kiss and stroke the slaughtered animal or would clean and caress the toy fowls that he had himself ill-treated.

Little Arpad himself saw to it that the meaning of his strange behavior should not remain hidden. From time to time he translated his wishes from the totemic language into that of everyday life. "My father's the cock," he said on one occasion, and another time: "Now I'm small, now I'm a chicken. When I get bigger I'll be a fowl. When I'm bigger still I'll be a cock." On another occasion he suddenly said he would like to eat some "fricassee of mother" (on the analogy of fricassee of chicken). He was very generous in threatening other people with castration, just as he himself had been threatened with it for his masturbatory activities.

There was no doubt, according to Ferenczi, as to the sources of Arpad's interest in events in the poultry-yard; "the continual sexual activity between the cock and hens, the laying of eggs and the hatching out of the young brood" gratified his sexual curiosity, the real object of which was *human* family-life. He showed that he had formed his own choice of sexual objects on the model of life in the hen-run, for he said one day to the neighbor's wife: "I'll marry you and your sister and my three cousins and the cook; no, not the cook, I'll marry my mother instead" (Freud, 1950: 130–131).

Now, Freud's conclusion, from this and other cases:

Later on we shall be able to assess the worth of this observation more completely. At the moment I will only emphasize two features in it which offer valuable points of agreement with totemism: the boy's complete identification with his totem animal and his ambivalent emotional attitude to it. These observations justify us, in my opinion, in substituting the father for the totem animal in the formula for totemism (in the case of males). It will be observed that there is nothing new or particularly daring in this step forward. Indeed, primitive men say the very same thing themselves, and, where the totemic system is still in force to-day, they describe the totem as their common ancestor and primal father. All we have done is to take at its literal value an expression used by these people, of which the anthropologists have been able to make very little and which they have therefore been glad to keep in the background. Psycho-analysis, on the contrary, leads us to put special stress upon this same point and to take it as the starting-point of our attempt at explaining totemism.

The first consequence of our substitution is most remarkable. If the totem animal is the father, then the two principal ordinances of totemism, the two taboo prohibitions which constitute its core—not to kill the totem and not to have sexual relations with a woman of the same totem—coincide in their context with the two crimes of Oedipus, who killed his father and married his mother, as well as with the two primal wishes of children, the insufficient repression or the reawakening of which forms the nucleus of perhaps every psychoneurosis. If this equation is anything more than a misleading trick of chance, it must enable us to throw a light upon the origin of totemism in the inconceivably remote past. In other words, it would enable us to make it probable that the totemic system—like little Hans's animal phobia and little Arpad's poultry perversion—was a product of the conditions involved in the Oedipus complex. In order to pursue this possibility, we shall have, in the following pages, to study a feature of the totemic system (or, as we might say, of the totemic religion) which I have hitherto scarcely found an opportunity of mentioning (Freud, 1950: 131–132).

At this point, Freud launches into his rather fanciful historical reconstruction of the origins of totemism.

Freud is interested in the historical origins of totemism. He does not state that the totemic customs are *maintained* by *current* Oedipal motives (in the population of the totemic society). If he actually did believe this, perhaps he would have "predicted" a positive correlation between totemism and the long post partum sex taboo (if he accepted our interpretation of the effects of the post partum sex taboo). At any rate, Table 29 presents the positive correlation between duration of the post partum sex taboo and the variable *totemism with food taboos*. The correlation falls slightly short of statistical significance.

Sorcery

I will define sorcery as the *belief* that some persons intentionally kill, sicken, or otherwise hurt other persons, by means of magic.[4] This is a very common sort of belief, which is probably current in nearly all societies. Sometimes the belief may be based partly on reality; in some societies there are real practicing sorcerers. Often, from all the ethnographer can tell, the sorcerers are completely imaginary. It is my impression that, generally, the number of imputed sorcerers far outstrips the number of practicing sorcerers.

4. The term "witchcraft" is usually used more or less synonymously with the term "sorcery."

magic (Evans-Pritchard, 1937). At times, the imagined sorcerer resides in a distant village (Kluckhohn, 1944). At other times (often, I believe) he is a near-neighbor (Evans-Pritchard, 1937). He may even be a family-member, a loved-one (Bowen, 1954). When sorcery is an important explanation for mysterious misfortunes, and community-members are believed to sorcerize each other, you can imagine the burden put on social living and general peace of mind, in terms of fear of magical-murder, suspicion of neighbors, and bitter recriminations (B. Whiting, 1950; Evans-Pritchard, 1937; Bowen, 1954).

Rampant sorcery does tend to characterize societies having the long post partum sex taboo. This fact is, I feel, also congenial to my Oedipus complex hypothesis. However, if it is supportive evidence, it is even less direct and less obvious than the evidence supplied by initiations and totemism. This is why I think it is supporting evidence, at least to some degree.

Lively sorcery-belief resembles a clinical phenomenon: paranoid delusions of persecution (Whiting and Child, 1953: 269, 272). We cannot say that all sorcery-fearing peoples "are paranoid." But I think we can say that they all "act like paranoids" (to some extent). I would apply the same argument I used for kin-avoidances. Sorcery looks like "institutionalized paranoia." Ethnographic accounts of sorcery-ridden societies do *not* describe people who spontaneously produce their own idiosyncratic paranoid delusions. Instead, the accounts describe people who "act paranoid" within the limits of approved social forms. It is the social forms, which dictate the nature of imputed sorcery, that have a paranoid appearance. I assume that there is some congruence between the paranoid-appearing social forms and actual paranoid personality trends in the population that observes those social forms. I assume the congruence is far from perfect: some persons "act paranoid" (as their culture dictates) who are not paranoid-type personalities.

What causes paranoia? The traditional psychoanalytic interpretation is that paranoia results from more or less unconscious homosexual urges; homosexuality, in turn, stems largely from Oedipal problems (Fenichel, 1945: 330). On this basis, we would expect the long post partum sex taboo to intensify (make more frequent and intense) paranoid personality trends. The cause-effect sequence would be as follows: (1) the long post partum sex taboo intensifies the son-to-mother sex attraction; (2) this intensifies Oedipal fears;[5] (3) this makes latent (and overt) homosexuality more likely; (4) this latent or unconscious homosexuality makes paranoid delusions of persecution more likely.

Now for the correlation. "Intensity" of sorcery was rated by Whiting and Child. The variable is *importance of sorcery as an explanation for illness* (or, as they term it, "fear of humans") (Whiting and Child, 1953: 263–264). The rating of this variable is not described in detail. I assume this is how it worked:

1. The coders assigned each society a score (on a 7-point scale) on importance of sorcery as an explanation for illness. The judgment was more or less intuitive, and, for each society, was based on two sorts of comparisons: (a) the importance of sorcerers as opposed to other sorts of agents (ghosts, animal spirits, etc.) as inflicters of illness; (b) how much sorcery seemed to be feared in the coded society, compared with other societies.

5. The psychoanalytic theorist would include here fears generated by son-to-father rivalry, as well as fears resulting from the son-to-mother sex attraction.

Table 30.
Duration of the Post Partum Sex Taboo Compared with Importance of Sorcery as an Explanation For Illness

Duration of the Post Partum Sex Taboo	Societies Rated at or above the Median on Importance of Sorcery as an Explanation for Illness	Societies Rated below the Median on Importance of Sorcery as an Explanation for Illness
Long	Arapesh	Bena
	Azande	Dahomey
	Chagga	Dakota
	Chiricahua	Masai
	Jivaro	Samoa
	Kiwai	Thonga
	Kurtachi	
	Kwoma	
	Lesu	
	Tiv	
	Trobriands	
	Venda	
	Witoto	
	Wogeo	
	Kwakiutl	
Short	Baiga	Ainu
	Chewa	Alor
	Hopi	Ashanti
	Lapp	Bali
	Maori	Chenchu
	Murngin	Copper Eskimo
	Sanpoil	Kazak
	Yagua	Lakher
		Lamba
		Lepcha
		Manus
		Marquesas
		Navaho
		Ontong Java
		Papago
		Rwala Bedouin
		Siriono
		Tanala
		Warrau
		Yukaghir

$P = 0.01$

2. The scores assigned by the various coders were combined, yielding scale-scores on intensity of sorcery-fear. Societies were then sorted (divided at the median score) into "highs" and "lows," on *importance of sorcery as an explanation for illness.*

In Table 30 is the significant positive correlation between duration of the post partum sex taboo and importance of sorcery as an explanation for illness.

Summary: Father-Son Rivalry

As you can see, I have not been completely successful in my effort to use a formulation of the Oedipus complex that excludes the father-son rivalry corollary. For the treatments of sex anxiety and kin-avoidances, this corollary could be excluded. But it has crept in, to a greater or lesser extent, when menstrual taboos, initiations, totemism, and sorcery were discussed. I did not set myself the task of documenting psychoanalytic hypotheses about Oedipal rivalry and its effects. I do think some of this data, in an indirect way, documents Oedipal (father-son) rivalry. But I feel the father-son rivalry corollary is much less impressively documented by the cross-cultural data than is the mother-son sex attraction and its hypothesized effects (sexual anxieties via unconscious fantasy).

Fear of Others

Perhaps, by this time, you suspect that the long post partum sex taboo would correlate positively with any other variable that reflected fearfulness or avoidance. I have some evidence

Table 31.
Duration of the Post Partum Sex Taboo
Compared With Over-All Fear of Others

Duration of the Post Partum Sex Taboo	Societies Rated at or above the Median on Intensity of Fear of Others	Societies Rated below the Median on Intensity of Fear of Others
Long	Arapesh	Azande
	Chagga	Bena
	Chiricahua	Dahomey
	Jivaro	Kurtachi
	Kiwai	Kwoma
	Kwakiutl	Lesu
	Tiv	Masai
	Trobriands	Dakota
	Venda	Samoa
	Witoto	Thonga
	Wogeo	
Short	Ainu	Alor
	Baiga	Ashanti
	Chewa	Bali
	Hopi	Chenchu
	Lakher	Copper Eskimo
	Maori	Kazak
	Marquesas	Lamba
	Murngin	Lepcha
	Navaho	Manus
	Ontong Java	Papago
	Sanpoil	Rwala Bedouin
	Tanala	Siriono
	Lapp	Warrau
		Yagua
		Yukaghir

that this is not so: that the pattern of correlations is specific to variables that have an "Oedipal-appearance." The evidence comes from a further Whiting and Child rating: *intensity of fear of others*. This is an over-all assessment of fearfulness of supernatural harm of all sorts, from agents human (sorcerers) or non-human ("spirits") (Whiting and Child, 1953: 263–265). This sort of intuitive estimate is difficult; it is probably rather inaccurate. Nevertheless, for whatever it is worth, the correlation between duration of the post partum sex taboo and intensity of fear of others is practically zero (Table 31). This finding suggests that the long post partum sex taboo societies are *not* characterized by a higher level of general fearfulness. These people do seem to be unusually fearful in some areas, particularly matters involving sex, but it may very well be that they are unusually secure and optimistic about other matters—for example, dependency.[6]

6. Whiting and Child attempted two indices of dependency-fears: *presence of dependency explanations for illness*, and *presence of dependency avoidance therapy* (Whiting and Child, 1953: 152–153, 208). The long post partum sex taboo is *negatively* correlated ($P < 0.05$) with *dependency explanations for illness*. It is uncorrelated with the other variable.

8

THE OEDIPUS
COMPLEX SYNDROME

TABLE 32 IS A CORRELATION matrix. It allows you to see the intercorrelations between most of the consequent variables, and compare them with the post partum sex taboo correlations. I have selected seven consequent variables, which I shall term hereafter the "Oedipus complex syndrome variables." Other consequent variables have been excluded from the matrix: brother-sister avoidance, son's wife avoidance, severity of sex training, breasts not sexual stimuli, and castration-suggestive incidents in folktales. If you wish you may add them to the matrix, since their scores are given in other parts of the book.

For comparison of relative strength of correlations, I have used contingency coefficients, based on two-by-two tables (McNemar, 1949: 203). To do this, the five- and nine-point scales had to be changed to two-point (high/low) scales. The cutting-points for these scales are as follows:

172

Table 32.
The Oedipus Complex Syndrome: Correlation Matrix

	Post Partum Sex Taboo	Change of Residence	Sex Anxiety	Menstrual Taboos	Mother-in-Law Avoidance	Initiations	Totemism	Sorcery
Part Partum Sex Taboo		0.37*	0.27	0.24	0.29	0.25	0.25	0.36
Change of Residence	(0.37)		0.03	0.13	0.14	0.33	0.47	0.13
Sex Anxiety	(0.27)	(0.03)		0.34	0.24	0.24	0.00	0.18
Menstrual Taboos	(0.24)	(0.13)	(0.34)		0.03	0.19	0.14	0.22
Mother-in-Law Avoidance	(0.29)	(0.14)	(0.24)	(0.03)		0.29	−0.04	0.02
Initiations	(0.25)	(0.33)	(0.24)	(0.19)	(0.29)		0.46	0.36
Totemism	(0.25)	(0.47)	(0.00)	(0.14)	(−0.04)	(0.46)		0.06
Sorcery	(0.36)	(0.13)	(0.18)	(0.22)	(0.02)	(0.36)	(0.06)	

* All numerical entries are contingency coefficients.

Menstrual taboos: societies rated 4 or 5 are scored "high" for Table 32; societies rated 3, 2, and 1 are "low."

Mother-in-law avoidances: societies rated 3, 4, or 5 are scored "high"; societies rated 2 or 1 are scored "low."

Sex anxiety: societies rated zero and above are scored "high"; societies rated −1 and lower are scored "low."

Reducing these scales to a high/low division tends, usually, to weaken correlations. This is particularly true for menstrual taboos.

Table 32 gives twenty-eight correlations, each represented by a C value (contingency coefficient). One is negative (−0.04), one is zero, and four others, while positive, are almost zero. Only two of the eight variables show pronounced positive correlations with every other variable: duration of the post partum sex taboo, and presence of initiation ceremonies for adolescent boys.

To summarize the correlation matrix:

The consequent variables are usually positively correlated with each other. However, these correlations among consequent variables are not *consistently* positive.

The post partum sex taboo (and also, perhaps, initiations) appear to represent the "center" of this network of relationships; that is, only it (and initiations) show pronounced correlations with *all* the other variables.

This pattern does seem congruent with my assumption that the long post partum sex taboo acts on the other variables as a partial "cause" or "antecedent."

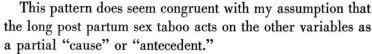

9

POLYGYNY AND MOTHER–CHILD HOUSEHOLDS

THROUGHOUT THE BOOK, great theoretical weight has been placed on the long post partum sex taboo. Many of the predictions have rested on a crucial assumption concerning the "meaning" of this sex taboo: that it makes maternal seduction more likely, thereby intensifying the young-son-to-mother sex attraction. This assumption was supported by various positive correlations between duration of the post partum sex taboo and extensiveness of menstrual taboos, severity of kin-avoidances, and other assumed consequent variables. Although predictions have been borne out by the data, a question remains: is it really the long post partum sex taboo which acts as a "cause" for menstrual taboos, etc? Or, is the crucial causative variable really one of the other "diluted marriage variables"—polygyny, or the mother-child household? Rephrased in terms that are answerable via cross-cultural data, the question is this: when the other two variables are held constant, does duration of the post partum sex taboo still correlate positively with the consequent variables?

The answer can be given in two parts:

1. Since the measures are crude, and the three diluted marriages variables are rather highly correlated with each other, there is little leeway for holding two of the variables constant, while examining the effects of the other.

2. Given this limitation, the answer is "yes." I performed two holding-constant operations. Both times, the duration of the post partum sex taboo still proved a fairly good (although not spectacularly good) predicter of the consequent variables.

As an introduction to these operations I refer you to Appendix VIII, which gives all individual scores on the three diluted marriage variables. Note that the ratings of frequency of mother-child households divide societies into two groups: "high" (40 per cent or more of the households in the society are estimated to be mother-child) and "low" (less than 40 per cent are estimated to be mother-child). The polygyny ratings make a three-way division: "high" (over 40 per cent of all wives in the society are estimated to be polygynous), "low" (less than 40 per cent), and "polygyny absent." Remember, too, what was said in Chapter 1: in most societies, the percentage of mother-child households seems to be approximately equal to the percentage of polygyny.

I performed two holding-constant operations. In the first, I held constant *frequency of mother-child households* while examining the effects of the long post partum sex taboo (and vice versa). In the second, I held constant *frequency of polygyny* while again examining the effects of the post partum sex taboo. I did not try to hold constant both polygyny and mother-child households simultaneously. Let us turn to the first holding-constant operation.

Post Partum Sex Taboo and Mother-Child Households

Table 33 divides societies into three groups: (1) societies rated "long" for post partum sex taboo and "high" for frequency of mother-child households; (2) societies rated "long" for post partum sex taboo and "low" for frequency of mother-child households; (3) societies rated "short" for post partum sex taboo and "low" for frequency of mother-child households. This sort of breakdown takes care of all but three cases—Ashanti, Gusii and Tanala—which are rated "high" for frequency of mother-child households and "short" for duration of the post partum sex taboo. I discarded these three leftover cases.

The numerical entries in Table 33 are average scores on each of the consequent variables (i.e., the "Oedipus complex syndrome variables," listed in Table 32) given for each of these three groups of societies: "long/high," "long/low," and "short/low." Table 33 says that *both* post partum sex taboo and mother-child household appear to "make a difference." Among societies rated "low" for frequency of mother-child households, those cases with "long" post partum sex taboo have consistently higher average scores on the consequent variables. The one near-exception is menstrual taboos. Among societies rated "long" for post partum sex taboo, those cases "high" on frequency of mother-child households also have higher average scores on the consequent-variables. There is one exception: sorcery.

Table 33.
The Partialed Effects of Duration of the Post Partum Sex Taboo and Frequency of Mother-Child Households

	Societies with "Long" Post Partum Sex Taboo and "High" Frequency of Mother-Child Households	Societies with "Long" Post Partum Sex Taboo and "Low" Frequency of Mother-Child Households	Societies with "Short" Post Partum Sex Taboo and "Low" Frequency of Mother-Child Households
1. Change of Residence for Adolescent Boys: Percentage "Present"	100%	42%	29%
2. Intensity of Sex Anxiety: Average Score	+1.5	+0.7	−1.8
3. Extensiveness of Menstrual Taboos: Average Score	4.0	2.6	2.5
4. Severity of Mother-in-Law Avoidance: Average Score	3.4	3.2	2.7
5. Initiations for Adolescent Boys: Percentage "Present"	63%	62%	30%
6. Totemism with Food Taboos: Percentage "Present"	77%	43%	22%
7. Importance of Sorcery as an Explanation for Illness: Percentage "High"	75%	86%	30%
Average Number of Cases	12	8	21

So the post partum sex taboo survives this first test fairly well. The surprise is that *both* post partum sex taboo and *mother-child household* appear to have about equal predictive power. I say "appear," but we should not draw any firm conclusions on this last point; the samples represented in Table 33 are very small.

Post Partum Sex Taboo and Polygyny

We can perform the same kind of holding-constant operation for polygyny. The sample societies may be divided into three groups: (1) "long" post partum sex taboo and "high" frequency of polygyny; (2) "long" post partum sex taboo and polygyny "low" or "absent"; (3) "short" post partum sex taboo and polygyny "low" or "absent." This sort of division leaves five cases which must be thrown out: Gusii, Murngin, Nambacauru, Siriono and Tanala, which are "high" on frequency of polygyny and "short" on duration of the post partum sex taboo.

When this is done, the results are similar to those given in Table 33. This is not surprising, since scores for frequency of polygyny and frequency of mother-child households are so highly correlated.

I then performed another kind of holding-constant operation on polygyny. The first one divided societies into three groups. This second procedure used a six-way division, as illustrated in the following table:

Frequency of Polygyny	Societies with "Long" Post Partum Sex Taboo	Societies with "Short" Post Partum Sex Taboo
High	11	3
Low	5	14
Polygyny Absent	2	7

This method yields six groups of societies. Average scores on the consequent variables can be computed for each of these six groups.[1] For example, we can see if the long post partum sex taboo leads to higher sex anxiety when polygyny

1. The numbers in the chart are the average number of cases in each cell.

is "high," when polygyny is "low," and when polygyny is "absent." We can make six comparisons as to the effect of polygyny, while "holding constant" the post partum sex taboo: (post partum sex taboo "long") high/low, high/absent, low/absent; (post partum sex taboo "short") high/low, high/absent, low/absent. Each of these comparisons is a correlation of sorts. No single correlation is very meaningful, since the number of cases in most cells is quite small. However, the correlations can be tallied, allowing an over-all comparison between post partum sex taboo and polygyny as to differential "strength."

If these comparisons are made, using the seven "consequent-variables" in Table 32, the results are as follows. For frequency of polygyny, twenty-one correlations are positive and seventeen are not. For duration of the post partum sex taboo, fourteen correlations are positive and five are not. On this "test," the post partum sex taboo does passably, although not exceptionally well, and polygyny does very poorly.

If this sort of breakdown could be applied to frequency of mother-child households, I assume the results would be similar.

Conclusion

These attempts at holding-constant are not very satisfactory. They do give some indication that the positive correlations between post partum sex taboo and the consequent variables were not merely an artifact of the effects of polygyny and/or mother-child households. It would be desirable to document this particular issue more thoroughly, but I know of no way to do it.

Are polygyny and mother-child household "antecedents" of the Oedipal syndrome in their own right? My guess is that they are, but the evidence on this point is weak and ambiguous.

10

CONCLUSION

THE MAIN JOB OF THIS BOOK
was to document the Oedipus complex hypothesis, as formulated in Chapter 2. Along the way there have been a good many incidental findings. The research also raises a number of implications, which could be speculated upon at great length. I shall not discuss incidental findings any further. Neither shall I draw implications; I leave this job to you, the reader. I shall devote this final chapter merely to a summary of the cross-cultural evidence bearing on the Oedipus complex hypothesis.

Here, once again, is the hypothesis of this volume: *Young boys, at least under optimal conditions (long post partum sex taboo), become sexually attracted to their mothers. This generates lasting sexual fears and avoidances. At least in one instance (castration anxiety), these fears are mediated by unconscious fantasy.*

182

The hypothesis is documented by correlational evidence. Most of these correlations were predicted in advance of the facts. The following are the added assumptions as to the "meaning" of cross-cultural variables, required for the predictions:

The long post partum sex taboo intensifies the son-to-mother sex attraction, thereby intensifying (and making more likely) castration anxiety, phobic attitudes toward incest, and (for initiations) Oedipal rivalry.

Extensiveness of menstrual taboos is partly caused by frequency and intensity, in a population, of castration anxiety.

The nine child rearing variables, correlated with menstrual taboos, reflect, rather indirectly, conditions that intensify castration anxiety.

Severity of kin-avoidance is caused to some degree by frequency and intensity, in a population, of phobic attitudes toward incest.

The occurrence of initiations for boys is partly determined by frequency and intensity of Oedipal (father-son) rivalry. (This prediction was made by Whiting, Kluckhohn, and Anthony.)

Table 34 lists all correlations that bear on the hypothesis: first all the correlations that were formally predicted, and then all the correlations that were not.

Once, out of a total of fourteen times, the direction of trend was not predicted. Nine of the sixteen predicted correlations are statistically significant. Six of the eight non-predicted correlations are significant.

These do not constitute twenty-four *independent* pieces of

Table 34.
Summary of Correlations Bearing on the Oedipus Complex Hypothesis

Variables Correlated		Direction of Correlation	Was Correlation in Predicted Direction?	P Value*
I. Correlations Formally Predicted				
Duration of Post Partum Sex Taboo	Presence of Initiations for Adolescent Boys	Positive	Yes	0.01
	Severity of Mother-in-Law Avoidance	Positive	Yes	0.01
	Severity of Son's Wife Avoidance	Positive	Yes	0.05
	Severity of Brother-Sister Avoidance	Positive	Yes	0.01
	Extensiveness of Menstrual Taboos	Positive	Yes	0.02
Extensiveness of Menstrual Taboos	Diffusion of Nurturance	Negative	Yes	0.28
	Severity of Punishment for Masturbation	Positive	Yes	0.01
	Over-All Severity of Sex Training	Positive	Yes	0.05
	Severity of Aggression Training	Positive	Yes	0.18
	Importance of Physical Punishment	Positive	Yes	0.07
	Pressure for Obedience	Negative	No	0.65
	Severity of Punishment for Disobedience	Positive	Yes	0.18
	Strictness of Father's Obedience Demands	Positive	Yes	0.20
	Whether or Not Father is the Main Disciplinarian	Positive	Yes	0.02
	Frequency of Severing In Folktales	Curvilinear	——	0.30
	Frequency of All Types of Physical Injury in Folktales	Curvilinear	——	0.001

Table 34 (cont.)

Variables Correlated		Direction of Correlation	Was Correlation in Predicted Direction?	P Value*
II. Correlations Not Formally Predicted				
Extensiveness of Menstrual Taboos	Composite Predicter of Castration Anxiety	Positive		0.000001
	Intensity of Sex Anxiety	Positive		0.01
Duration of the Post Partum Sex Taboo	Intensity of Sex Anxiety	Positive		0.03
	Severity of Sex Training	Positive		0.25
	Change of Residence for Adolescent Boys	Positive		0.002
	Breasts Not Considered Sexual Stimuli	Positive		0.04
	Totemism with Food Taboos	Positive		0.10
	Importance of Sorcery as an Explanation for Illness	Positive		0.01

* All P values are based on a two-tailed test of significance.

evidence, because some of the measures are contaminated by each other. The correlations have added limitations: the "variables" represent the Oedipus complex in only an indirect and far-fetched fashion; none of the correlations directly indicate the direction of causation.

Making allowance for this, I feel that the massive evidence leaves a rather small margin for doubt. The probability is high that this hypothesis, embodying several of the core-assumptions of psychoanalytic theory, is approximately valid.

APPENDIXES

I

INDEPENDENCE
OF CASES

T HE TEST OF SIGNIFICANCE
requires that the sample be composed of cases that are independent of each other. If some cases (i.e., societies) are influencing the scores of other cases, the P value is not strictly legitimate. I have no way of proving that all the cases in my samples actually are independent of each other. In fact, I suspect that a few cases are nonindependent. Therefore, the P values are suspect. Furthermore, the problem of independence of cases as it has just been stated is, for this research, at least, insoluble. I am unable to test my hypotheses on samples that I can prove are made up solely of independent cases.

If the problem is phrased in another way, it can be dealt with. We can ask: are the correlations—their direction and approximate strength—an artifact of the nonindependence of cases? This question can be answered. If we proceed in this way, we still cannot test the legitimacy of the *P* values. But we can see whether the evidence supporting the Oedipus complex hypothesis is merely an artifact of nonindependent cases. We can also "hold constant" the factor of possible nonindependence of cases and, while doing this, re-estimate the strength and impressiveness of the evidence. In this Appendix, we shall follow this second course.

To introduce the discussion, I shall give an example of independent cases, and then an example of nonindependent cases.

Independent Cases. You are flipping a coin. Each flip of the coin is an independent case. Your chance of getting "heads" on the next flip is in no way influenced by what came up on previous flips.

Nonindependent Cases. You and I are playing pool. You start the game, with fifteen balls on the table. In your first turn, you sink nine balls and then miss. It is now my turn. I do not have the opportunity to sink fifteen balls (as you had); the most I can sink is six. Your score (nine) has set a limit on my score. There are two cases here: your turn at the pool table, and my turn. The first case may influence the second case; your score may (if I sink all six balls) influence my score.

Now, let us try to imagine how nonindependence "works" in a sample of primitive societies.

Societies cluster into a number of geographically-bound culture areas. Tribes in one culture area are, to some extent, similar to each other. They share a certain number of cultural traits that are identical or only slightly modified. This sharing indicates that the peoples in the cultural area have been in contact (direct or indirect), and as a result have "borrowed" from each other certain customs and inventions.

Overlapping the culture areas are linguistic groupings. If two tribes have similar languages, we know that they are historically related. Some time in the distant past they diverged from the same tribe (i.e., the same language-group).

The overlap between culture areas and linguistic groupings is imperfect. For example, the Navaho are linguistically "distant" from their neighbors the Hopi, and linguistically "close" to the Kaska, several thousand miles north.

My samples usually contain several clusters of "close-together societies," (geographically and/or linguistically) and a larger number of widely dispersed "far-apart societies." The question is whether or not the "close-together societies" have influenced each other's scores on the variables, and whether this mutual influencing produces biased or spurious correlations.

How could they influence each other's scores? Let us take menstrual huts as an example. It may be that the menstrual hut is a culture trait that is hardly ever independently invented. Unless a tribe has a chance to borrow the menstrual hut from a neighboring tribe, or "inherit" the menstrual hut from an ancestral tribe, it will rarely have menstrual huts.

The Cheyenne and Dakota are neighboring tribes. They both have (had) menstrual huts. Are they affecting each other's scores on extensiveness of menstrual taboos? Quite likely they are. They are giving each other a good opportunity to borrow the culture trait menstrual huts (that is, perhaps in the recent past one tribe borrowed the use of menstrual huts from the other).

The Cheyenne and Ojibwa, although occupying different cultural areas, are linguistically quite similar. Both tribes have menstrual huts. Are they influencing each other's scores on menstrual taboos? Probably not. However, it is possible that both tribes have been influenced in parallel fashion by the "primal tribe" from which they both "descended"; they both "inherited" menstrual huts from this "primal tribe." Therefore, the menstrual taboo scores of these two tribes may also be nonindependent.

How could nonindependence of cases artificially produce strong correlations? Let us take a hypothetical example. Suppose we are correlating the presence of menstrual huts with the presence of the long post partum sex taboo, using a sample of thirty societies. In the sample there are four "clumps"; each clump contains five societies that are linguistically and/or geographically "close" to each other. Furthermore, in each clump all societies are *identical* in respect to the two variables. There are ten additional societies, each of which is not "close" to any other society in the sample. Suppose we got the correlation in Table 35.

Table 35.

	Both Menstrual Huts and Long Post Partum Sex Taboo Present	Both Menstrual Huts and Long Post Partum Sex Taboo Absent	Long Post Partum Sex Taboo Present, Menstrual Huts Absent	Menstrual Huts Present, Long Post Partum Sex Taboo Absent
Clump A	5	0	0	0
Clump B	0	5	0	0
Clump C	0	5	0	0
Clump D	0	0	5	0
Far-Apart Societies	3	2	3	2
Totals	8	12	8	2

This looks like a fairly pronounced trend. Menstrual huts and long post partum sex taboo do tend to accompany each other. It also looks as if nonindependence has affected the trend: in Clump A, all five societies have had a good chance to borrow or "inherit" both customs; in Clumps B and C, societies have had little chance to borrow or "inherit" either custom; in Clump D, societies could borrow or "inherit" one custom but not the other. If each clump is counted as only one case (and not as five cases) the trend virtually disappears.

Therefore, it is necessary to see whether the correlations are an artifact of this clumping effect. At the end of this Appendix, societies are listed by culture area (as designated in Murdock, 1957). In Table 36 duration of the post partum sex taboo has been re-correlated with the other "Oedipus complex syndrome" variables (given in Table 32); these correlations are based on new samples, in which each culture area is represented by no more than one society.

In other words, the new samples are composed of "independent cases" in the sense that no two cases come from the same culture area. All cases are geographically distant from each other. The samples also partially solve the problem of "linguistic nonindependence"; but they do not solve this problem completely. They still include a few cases that, while geographically distant, are not "linguistically distant." The most flagrant instance of this is the Ojibwa (in one culture area) and the Cheyenne and Arapaho (in another). Also, four African culture areas are represented by Bantu-speaking tribes which, although widely dispersed geographically, probably did, in the distant past, "descend" from the same "primal tribe."

The sampling procedure is as follows. For each culture area, tribes have been arranged in alphabetical order. The first sample I draw is composed of societies that are first, alphabetically, in their respective culture areas. That is, when correlating any two variables, I run down the alphabetized list for each culture area until I come to a society that is scored on both of these variables.

After the first sample is drawn and the correlation run, I draw a second sample; it is made up of societies that are second, alphabetically, in their respective culture areas. When a culture area is represented by only one society (scored on both variables being correlated), that society is counted in all samples, the first and the second (and the third). The same correlation is re-run on this second sample.

Finally, I draw a third sample, composed of societies that are third, alphabetically, in their respective culture areas. When a culture area is represented by only two societies (scored on both variables to be correlated) the second society (alphabetically) reappears in this third sample.

These samples are a good deal smaller than the original samples, given in the text. Giving P values for them would be rather meaningless; necessarily, the P value is usually considerably greater because of diminished sample-size. Instead, I present the direction and strength of correlations, in tabular form. Beside these "new tables" (based on the new samples) I again give the "old tables" (based on the larger original samples). We can make a visual comparison, and estimate how much strength-of-trend has been diminished by sampling relatively independent cases.

Strength-of-trend is affected, to some degree, by the "luck of the draw." That is the reason I have drawn three new samples for each pair of variables.

In Table 36 there are twenty-one "new correlations," based on the culture area samples. All the correlations are positive. Generally, they are about equal to the original correlations in regard to strength. Nine appear to be slightly stronger, ten appear to be slightly weaker, and two are much weaker. From this I conclude that nonindependence of cases, as represented by opportunity to borrow traits from neighboring tribes within a culture area, has little if any effect on the strength of the original correlations, and that it definitely does not determine the direction of these correlations.

Since there is considerable overlap between culture areas and linguistic groupings, I also conclude that nonindependence of cases as represented by opportunities to "inherit" common traits from a "primal tribe" also has no major effect on the original correlations.

It is possible that opportunity to borrow is not completely controlled by sampling from Murdock's culture areas. Probably larger geographic units, such as Africa or western North America, to some extent represent borrowing-pools. However, I think we can dismiss this as a possible reason for the correlations. If possible nonindependence shows little if any effect within the relatively small, concentrated borrowing-pools (Murdock's culture areas), there is no reason to believe that it becomes significant (vis-à-vis the strength of the correlations) within larger, more diffuse borrowing-pools (continents and subcontinents).

I do feel that some of these societies are nonindependent in regard to the variables being measured. Some societies are "close together" geographically and/or linguistically. There is a definite tendency for the "close together societies" to be similar, in respect to any single variable that is measured. It certainly appears that a society's chances to have such customs as menstrual huts, initiation ceremonies, long post partum sex taboo, totemism, etc., is influenced by its opportunities to borrow and/or inherit these customs. Opportunity to borrow and inherit is probably one of the contributing causes or antecedents for a society's score on any of the cross-cultural variables.

However, differential opportunity to borrow and/or inherit does *not* determine these strong positive correlations. At the very most, it inflates them slightly.

Societies Listed by Culture Areas: All Societies Scored on Duration of the Post Partum Sex Taboo and on at Least One Other Oedipus Complex Syndrome Variable

AFRICA

Khoisan. Nama Hottentot
Southern Bantu. Lovedu, Pondo, Thonga, Venda
Central Bantu. Chewa, Lamba, Yao
Northeast Bantu. Bena, Chagga, Gesu, Gusii, Kipsigis, Nya-kusa
Equatorial Bantu. Ganda
Guinea Coast. Ashanti, Dahomey, Mende, Yoruba
Western Sudan. Tallensi
Nigerian Plateau. Bassa, Bulu, Tiv
Eastern Sudan. Azande
Upper Nile. Lango, Masai, Nuer, Turkana
Moslem Sudan. Hausa
North Africa. Silwa
Near East. Rwala Bedouin

ASIA

Central Asia. Kazak
Arctic Asia. Ainu, Chukchee, Koryak, Tungus, Yukaghir

Himalaya. Lepcha
South India. Baiga, Chenchu, Gond (Hill Maria), Rajput
Indian Ocean. Tanala
Assam and Burma. Lakher

OCEANIA

Philippines and Formosa. Igorot, Subanum
Western Indonesia. Bali
Eastern Indonesia. Alor
Australia. Murngin, Ooldea
New Guinea. Arapesh, Kiwai, Kwoma, Manam, Wogeo
Micronesia. Ifaluk, Truk, Ulithi
Western Melanesia. Kurtachi, Lesu, Malaita, Manus, Trobriands
Eastern Melanesia. Fiji
Western Polynesia. Ontong Java, Samoa
Eastern Polynesia. Maori, Marquesas

NORTH AMERICA

Arctic. Copper Eskimo
Northwest Coast. Bella Coola, Kwakiutl
California. Hupa
Great Basin and Plateau. Sanpoil
Plains. Arapaho, Cheyenne, Dakota, Gros Ventre
Prairie. Ojibwa
Southwest. Chiricahua, Hopi, Mohave, Navaho
Northwest Mexico. Papago, Tarahumara
Central Mexico. Mixtec, Tarasco, Tepoztlan, Zapotec

SOUTH AMERICA

Caribbean. Cagaba
Guiana. Warrau
Interior Amazonia. Jivaro, Siriono, Witoto, Yagua

Andes. Aymara, Yaghan
Chile and Pategonia. Araucania
Gran Chaco. Pilaga
Mato Grosso. Nambicauru
Eastern Brazil. Eastern Timbara

Table 36.
Culture Area Samples: Duration of the Post Partum Sex Taboo Correlated with the Oedipus Complex Syndrome Variables

	ORIGINAL SAMPLE		FIRST CULTURE-AREA SAMPLE		SECOND CULTURE-AREA SAMPLE		THIRD CULTURE-AREA SAMPLE	
	Long Post Partum Sex Taboo	Short Post Partum Sex Taboo	Long Post Partum Sex Taboo	Short Post Partum Sex Taboo	Long Post Partum Sex Taboo	Short Post Partum Sex Taboo	Long Post Partum Sex Taboo	Short Post Partum Sex Taboo
Change of Residence for Adolescent Boys Is Customary								
Yes	25	11	12	10	16	7	14	7
No	7	20	3	11	3	12	5	12
Intensity of Sex Anxiety								
4	3	1			2	0	2	1
3	2	0	2	0	1	0	1	0
2	2	3	1	2	1	1	0	2
1	2	1	0	1	1	1	2	1
0	2	2	2	2	1	2	1	2
—1	0	3	0	2	0	3	0	2
—2	2	1	2	0	1	0	1	0
—3	1	1	1	1				
—4	2	8	1	6	1	8	1	7
Extensiveness of Menstrual Taboos								
5	11	5	5	4	6	2	8	3
4	6	4	2	4	3	3	2	3
3	8	8	4	6	3	6	4	6
2	5	9	4	5	1	4	2	3
1	5	10	2	3	3	6	2	6

Table 36 (cont.)

	ORIGINAL SAMPLE		FIRST CULTURE-AREA SAMPLE		SECOND CULTURE-AREA SAMPLE		THIRD CULTURE-AREA SAMPLE	
	Long Post Partum Sex Taboo	Short Post Partum Sex Taboo	Long Post Partum Sex Taboo	Short Post Partum Sex Taboo	Long Post Partum Sex Taboo	Short Post Partum Sex Taboo	Long Post Partum Sex Taboo	Short Post Partum Sex Taboo
Severity of Mother-in-Law Avoidances								
5	12	4	8	2	6	2	3	4
4	5	1	1	0	2	0	3	0
3	2	3	1	3	1	3	2	3
2	3	5	1	4	1	2	1	3
1	5	10	4	7	5	9	4	8
Initiation Ceremonies for Adolescent Boys								
Present	34	14	11	8	14	9	14	9
Absent	15	33	8	19	6	17	8	15
Totemism with Food Taboos								
Present	12	8	9	7	7	5	7	4
Absent	9	20	5	12	6	15	7	15
Importance of Sorcery as an Explanation for Illness								
High	15	8	7	5	7	3	7	2
Low	6	20	4	13	4	15	4	16

II

THE SEX
ANXIETY INDEX

T HIS COMPOSITE INDEX IS
made up of six other variables:

1. *Severity of sex training:* high (at or above the median
   score) or low (below the median score) (Whiting and
   Child, 1953: 77–78).
2. *Sexual intercourse before marriage prohibited:* yes or no
   (Ford and Beach, 1951: 182–190).
3. *Pregnancy sex taboo:* long (4½ months or more) or short
   (less than 4½ months) (Ayres, 1954).[1]
4. *Sexual explanations for illness:* present or absent (Whiting
   and Child, 1953: 152).
5. *Sexual avoidance therapy:* present or absent (Whiting and
   Child, 1953: 209).

1. Ayres' ratings were supplemented by a few extra judgments by
Ford and Beach (1951).

6. *Sexual intercourse usually punished in folklore:* yes or no (Stephens. see Appendix VII).[2]

These six variables were chosen by two criteria: (1) that they have some face-validity as reflections of sex-fear or sex-avoidance; (2) that they all positively correlate with each other, giving an empirical basis for assuming that they all reflect, to some degree, a single common factor.

All fulfill the second criterion except my ratings of *sexual intercourse usually punished in folklore.* This variable correlates positively with three of the others, but is uncorrelated with *severity of sex training* and *sexual intercourse before marriage prohibited.* Although it is "marginal," I decided to use it anyway. Table 37 shows the intercorrelations between the six variables. A further demonstration of their general interrelatedness can be made by correlating each variable with a composite score derived from the other five. When this is done, using the scoring conventions described below, each variable correlates strongly with the combined score on the other five.

As regards the first criterion, face-validity, several of these variables have previously been interpreted as reflecting sex-anxiety. Whiting and Child postulate that, to some degree, *sexual explanations for illness* and *sex avoidance therapy* are results of anxiety about sex (Whiting and Child, 1953: 149, 209). Ayres made a similar interpretation for *duration of the pregnancy sex taboo.* Whiting and Child (and myself) assume that *severity of sex training* is an *antecedent* or *cause* for sex anxiety; I assume it is both cause and effect—people who are

2. Societies were scored "yes" for *sexual intercourse usually punished in folklore* if frequency of punished sexual intercourse (in folktales) was equal to or greater than frequency of unpunished sexual intercourse.

Table 37.
Intercorrelations among the Component Variables in the Sex Anxiety Index

	PREGNANCY SEX TABOO		SEXUAL INTERCOURSE BEFORE MARRIAGE PROHIBITED		SEXUAL INTERCOURSE USUALLY PUNISHED IN FOLKLORE		SEXUAL AVOIDANCE THERAPY		SEXUAL EXPLANATIONS FOR ILLNESS	
	Long	Short	Yes	No	Yes	No	Present	Absent	Present	Absent
Severity of Sex Training										
High	9	4	9	2	5	7	6	14	12	11
Low	5	11	4	11	5	7	4	18	8	12
Pregnancy Sex Taboo										
Long			8	5	4	4	5	9	8	6
Short			2	7	3	8	3	13	6	10
Sexual Intercourse before Marriage Prohibited										
Yes					4	4	5	10	7	8
No					4	4	2	13	5	10
Sexual Intercourse Usually Punished in Folklore										
Yes							4	5	6	4
No							4	12	6	9
Sexual Avoidance Therapy										
Present									5	5
Absent									12	20

severe about their children's sexual activity are, to some extent, expressing their own anxiety about sex. A similar interpretation could be made for *sexual intercourse before marriage prohibited.* Finally, for *sexual intercourse usually punished in folklore,* I assume that folklore reflects, to some degree, view-of-the-world; people who tell stories about sex-connected punishment are more likely to expect sex-connected punishment in real life.

Whatever the virtues of these interpretations, all the variables have a minimal face-validity: they all have to do with sex; all but the folklore variable imply restriction or avoidance.

By these two criteria, two more variables could have been included in the sex anxiety index: duration of the post partum sex taboo, and extensiveness of menstrual taboos. Since I had other theoretical uses for them, and since I wanted to simplify my exposition, I decided to exclude these variables.

The assignment of the label, "sex anxiety," to the composite index is somewhat arbitrary. All the variables (but one) have to do with sex-connected restrictions and avoidances; all (but one) are positively correlated with all the rest. I have some right to assume that, to some degree, all variables reflect "the same thing." But what is the common characteristic—what should the label be? I chose "sex anxiety," assuming that anxiety underlies avoidance and restriction. A more conservative label might be "sex restriction index," "sex avoidance index," or "sexual problems index."

Deriving the Composite Scores

In Table 38 I give the individual scores on the six variables. Scores showing high sex anxiety are indicated by an "x": *high* severity of sex training; sexual intercourse before marriage prohibited—*yes*; pregnancy sex taboo—*long*; sexual explanations for illness—*present*; sexual avoidance therapy—*present*; sexual intercourse usually punished in folklore—*yes*. Scores showing low sex anxiety have been indicated with a "—": *low* severity of sex training, etc.

I chose this convention for giving over-all scores on sex anxiety: a society's "—" scores are subtracted from its "x" scores; the difference is its score on sex anxiety. For example, the Ashanti scored "x" on severity of sex training, pregnancy sex taboo and sexual intercourse before marriage prohibited, and "—" for sexual explanations for illness. Their one "—" score is subtracted from their three "x" scores; the resulting score for sex anxiety is 2 (or +2). The Balinese received four "—" scores and no "x" scores; their score on sex anxiety is —4.

Few societies are scored on all six variables. So another decision had to be made: how many scores must a society have, to get an over-all score on sex anxiety? I decided to give sex anxiety scores to societies that were scored on at least four of the six component variables. Then, to equalize opportunities to attain any given sex anxiety score, I set the maximum score at 4 (+4) and minimum score at —4. For example, the Siriono were "—" for five variables and "x" for none; they received the lowest possible sex anxiety score: —4. In the right-hand column of Table 38 are listed the final over-all scores on sex anxiety.

A composite index such as this has at least two advantages over any single rating as a means of estimating sex anxiety. In the first place, when scores are combined measurement error should tend to cancel out. Also, it has stronger face-validity. Each of the component variables has enhanced face-

Table 38.
Individual Sex Anxiety Scores*

Society	1	2	3	4	5	6	7
Africa							
Ashanti	x	x	x			—	2
Azande	x	—			—	x	0
Bena	—	—	x		—	—	−3
Chagga	x	x	x		—	—	1
Chewa	—		—	x			
Dahomey	x	x	x	—	x	x	4
Lamba	—		x	—	x		0
Masai	—	x	—	—	—	—	−4
Nama			x	x			
Rwala	x			x	x		
Thonga	—	—		—	x	x	−2
Tiv	x				x		
Asia							
Ainu	—	—	—		—	—	−4
Baiga	—	—			—	x	−3
Chenchu	—	—		—	—	—	−4
Chukchee	—		—				
Kazak		x		—	—		
Lakher	—	—		—	—	—	−4
Lepcha	—	—	—	—		x	−4
Maria Gond		x	—				
Oceania							
Alor	x	x			—	x	2
Arapesh	x	x		x	—	x	3
Bali	—		—		—	—	−4
Chamarro	x	—			—	—	−2
Ifugao	—	x	—		—	x	−1
Kiwai		x	x	x	x	x	4
Kurtachi	x	—	—	—		x	0
Kwoma	x	x	x		x	x	4
Lesu	—	x	—	x	x	x	2
Manus	x		x		x	x	4
Maori	—				—	x	
Marquesas	—		—	—	—	—	−4
Marshalls	—	—	—			x	−3
Murngin	—	x	x	—	—		−1
Ontong Java	x				—	—	
Pukapuka	—	—	—	x	—	x	−2
Samoa	x			—	—		
Tanala	x	x	—		—	—	−1
Trobriands	—	—	—	x	—	—	−4
Wogeo	x	x	—		—	—	−1
North America							
Chiricahua	x	x	x	—	—	x	2
Copper Eskimo			—	—	—	—	−4
Dakota	x			x			
Hopi	x	—		—	x	—	−1
Kwakiutl	x		x	x	—	x	3
Navaho	x		x	x		—	2
Paiute	x			—	—	—	−2
Papago	x			—	—	x	0
Sanpoil	x		x	x	—	—	1
South America							
Jivaro	—			—	x	—	−2
Siriono	—	—	—		—	—	−4
Timbira	x		x				
Warrau		x			—	—	
Witoto	—	x	x		x	—	1
Yagua	—	x		—	—		−2

* The column headings are as follows: (1) severity of sex training; (2) pregnancy sex taboo; (3) sexual intercourse before marriage prohibited; (4) sexual intercourse usually punished in folklore; (5) sexual avoidance therapy; (6) sexual explanations for illness; and (7) the final sex anxiety score.

validity because not only does it "look like" it might reflect sex anxiety but it is positively correlated with five other variables that also "look like" they might reflect sex anxiety.

III

CODING AND RATING
MENSTRUAL TABOOS

For MENSTRUAL TABOOS, THE coders made decisions on five code-categories. These are the coding instructions:

Menstrual Taboo Coding Instructions

1. Menstrual huts
   Code present
      If menstrual huts, or some special dwelling or room, is employed for menstruating women.
      If, in the absence of any mention of menstrual huts, and in the absence of any other account of where the menstruant stays, the menstruant is said to be "secluded," "sent away," etc.
      If there are exceptions to the rule of using menstrual

huts, or to the rule of seclusion, still code "present." Only if it is stated that menstrual huts are only used by some unusual category of women, such as queens, can menstrual huts be coded "absent."

Code absent

If menstrual huts are said to be absent.

If "seclusion," etc., is said to be absent.

If there are said to be "no serious restrictions," "no menstrual customs," etc., for the menstruating woman.

If menstrual huts are used only by some unusual category of persons (above).

If, in the absence of mention of menstrual huts or seclusion, some other account is given of where the woman stays: example, in the family house, or her husband moves out of the house, etc.

Code no information

If none of these rules can be applied, or if there are conflicting reports.

2. Cooking taboo

Code present

If there is a rule against a menstruating woman cooking all food for her husband (or for "men" or "others"), even though the rule is violated, or if the rule does not apply to some categories of women.

If, in the absence of any statement about a rule, there is a statement about behavior that seems equivalent. For example: "she doesn't cook," "someone else does the cooking," etc.

Code absent

> If there is no rule against a menstruating woman cooking for her husband.
>
> If, in the absence of any statement about a rule, the menstruant is said to cook for her husband, or for "others."
>
> If there is a rule against the woman cooking a few specific dishes, in the absence of any statement about an over-all cooking taboo.
>
> If there is said to be "no serious restrictions," "no menstrual customs," etc., for the menstruating woman.

Code no information

> If none of these rules can be applied, or if there are conflicting reports.

3. Menstrual sex taboo

Code present

> If there is a rule against the menstruant having sexual intercourse.
>
> If, in the absence of any statement about a rule, she is said to abstain from sexual intercourse, or if her husband (or "men") "can't sleep with her," "can't approach her," "can't touch her," etc.

Code absent

> If there is no rule against sexual intercourse.
>
> If, in the absence of any statement about a rule against sexual intercourse, there is mention of sexual intercourse during menstruation.

Code no information

> If none of these rules apply, or if there are conflicting reports.

Note: a statement of "no menstrual customs," etc., may
not be the basis for coding sex taboo "absent;" sex
must be specifically mentioned.

4. Belief that menstrual blood is dangerous to men

Code present

If the touch or presence of the menstruating woman or
her blood can hurt any men, physically or magi-
cally.

If the woman or her blood are "feared;" if she must
"warn" some man.

Code absent

If, in the absence of any mention of the menstruating
woman hurting men, she is said to be "not feared,"
"not contaminating," etc., or if there are "no
sanctions" to any menstrual customs.

Code no information

If none of these rules can be applied, or if there are
conflicting reports.

Note: a statement of "no menstrual customs," etc., may
not be the basis for coding danger to men "absent."

5. Other menstrual taboos

If the account of menstrual customs seems fairly complete, code whether other menstrual taboos, not
included in the above code-categories, are "many"
or "few" or "none." If the report seems not very
complete, or if you are unsure about a borderline
case, code "no information."

General

This code does not apply to special observance for girls
at first menstruation, but only to observances reg-
ularly followed by all mature women.

> If accounts of menstrual taboos are given for both before and after contact with Western culture, code for before contact.
>
> ("Danger to men") Danger to crops, hunting, fishing, religious articles, etc., should not be coded as danger to men.

The coding was done by three persons: Mr. John K. Harley, Mrs. Judith W. Stephens, and myself. Average agreement was as follows: menstrual huts 94 per cent; cooking taboo 88 per cent; danger to men 82 per cent; sex taboo 90 per cent; many other menstrual taboos 71 per cent.[1] The final code was decided by majority rule.

The Guttman Scale

One society, the Tikopia, was judged "no information" for all code categories. The final code for all other societies is entered in Table 39. This table shows the cumulative pattern these code-categories follow. *Menstrual huts, cooking taboo,* and *many other menstrual taboos* are, for all known cases, scalar in relation to each other. *Sex taboo* and *danger to men* also scale with the other code-categories, although they are not clearly scalar in relation to each other. Therefore, I designated the following Guttman scale of extensiveness of menstrual taboos (from high to low):

1. Average agreement is computed for each pair of coders, and then combined. For example, for the code-category *menstrual huts*, average agreement was computed three times: between J. Harley and J. Stephens, between J. Stephens and W. Stephens, and between J. Harley and W. Stephens. These three average agreement scores were then in turn averaged, giving an over-all average agreement of 94 per cent. The same procedure is followed for the other variables I code.

Table 39.
Menstrual Taboos: Final Code on the Code-Categories, Cumulative Scale Pattern, and Scale Scores*

Scale Score	Society	(1	2)	3	4	5
5	Arapesh				x	x
	Ashanti	x	x	x	x	x
	Cheyenne	x	x	x	x	x
	Dahomey				x	x
	Dakota					x
	Hupa					x
	Ifaluk	x	x	x		x
	Kwakiutl	x	x	x	x	x
	Malaita	x	x	x		x
	Maria Gond	x			x	x
	Ojibwa	x	x	x	x	x
	Paiute	x	x			x
	Papago	x	x	x	x	x
	Sanpoil	x	x	x	x	x
	Tiv	x	x		x	x
	Ulithi	x	x	x		x
	Warrau			x	x	x
4	Baiga	x	x	x	x	−
	Bali	x	x	x	x	−
	Ganda				x	
	Gesu				x	
	Kiwai	x	x	x	x	−
	Kurtachi	x		x	x	−
	Kwoma	x	x		x	−
	Lamba	x	x		x	
	Manam		x	x	x	
	Nama Hottentot		x	x	x	−
	Wogeo	x	x	x	x	
3	Araucania	x	x	x		−
	Aymara	x	x			−
	Azande	x	x			
	Bena	x	x			
	Chukchee	x				
	Copper Eskimo				−	−
	Flathead			x	x	
	Kazak			−	−	−
	Lakher	−	x	x		

Scale Score	Society	(1	2)	3	4	5
	Lesu	x	x			
	Maori		x	x	−	−
	Nyakusa	x	x	x	−	
	Ooldea	x	x			−
	Rwala Bedouin	x			−	−
	Tarasco	x	x		−	
	Thonga	x	x	x	−	−
	Timbira	x	x	x	−	−
	Tungus	x	x	x		
2	Ainu			−	−	−
	Arapaho	x	x	−	−	−
	Chiricahua	x	x	−	−	−
	Gros Ventre		x	−	−	−
	Jivaro	x		−	−	−
	Lepcha	x	x	−	−	−
	Murngin	x	x	−	−	−
	Navaho	x	x	−	−	−
	Siriono	x	x	−	−	−
	Tallensi			−	−	−
	Tarahumara			−	−	−
	Witoto			−	−	−
1	Alor	x	−	−	−	−
	Bassa	−		−	−	−
	Bulu	−		−	−	−
	Chenchu	−		−	−	−
	Gusii	−	−	−	−	−
	Hopi	−	−	−	−	−
	Manus	−				−
	Marquesas	−	x			
	Masai	x	−	−	−	−
	Mohave	−	x			
	Ontong Java	−			−	−
	Pukapuka	x	−	−	−	−
	Samoa	−		−	−	−
	Tanala	−		−	−	−
	Trobriands	x	−	−	−	−
	Zapotec	−	x	−	−	−

* Column-headings (code-categories) are as follows: (5) menstrual huts; (4) cooking taboo; (3) many other menstrual taboos; (2) belief that menstrual blood is dangerous to men; (1) menstrual sex taboo. Scale points coincide with column-headings, with this one exception: *sex taboo* and *danger to men*, since they did not scale with each other, were combined to form one scale point. If a society was scored "absent" for either *sex taboo* or *danger to men* (or for both), it received the lowest possible score on extensiveness of menstrual taboos—1. The only exception to this rule is the Lakher, who got a final score of 3 (highest point scored "present"). Entries are as follows: "x" indicates a final code of "present;"—" indicates a final code of "absent;" a blank indicates a final code of "no information."

5. Menstrual huts.
4. Cooking taboo.
3. Many other menstrual taboos.
2. Sex taboo and "danger to men" both present.
1. Either sex taboo or "danger to men" (or both) absent.

This scale does not meet all the ideal criteria for a Guttman scale (Green, 1954). However, it is the best scale that could be managed with this data. Cases of "no information" were handled in the following way: when scale points 2 or 3 were left blank because of no information, i.e., not assigned a final code, they were assigned "present" scores; when scale points 4 or 5 were left blank because of no information, they were scored "absent" (Samuel A. Stouffer: personal communication). When this convention is followed, the scale yields a coefficient of reproducibility of 0.965 (Green 1954).

Finally, each society was scored on extensiveness of menstrual taboos. Its score was equal to the highest scale point for which it received a final code of "present."

Two more cases—Bassa and Bulu—were added to the sample, some time after the coding had been done. They were supplied by Dr. George Horner, during an ethnographer-interview on kin-avoidances. He did the "coding" and I assigned the rating—point 1—for both these cases.

IV

CODING AND RATING
KIN–AVOIDANCE

THE SAMPLE WAS LIMITED TO (1) all societies coded by Whiting and Kluckhohn on duration of the post partum sex taboo; (2) all societies coded by Whiting and D'Andrade for propinquity of sleeping arrangements. A few more cases were added later; they will be listed presently.

For societies that fell within the Whiting-Kluckhohn sample, ethnographic page-references on kin-avoidance were gathered by myself. For additional societies, coded by Whiting and D'Andrade, page-references were gathered by Mrs. Emily McFarlin.

Cross-cultural coders were Mrs. Roberta Churchill, Mrs. Diane D'Andrade, and Mrs. Constance Pilz. They coded, separately, the three focal avoidance relationships: a man to his mother-in-law, a man to his sister, a man to his son's wife.

For each of these three avoidance relationships, they checked ten code-categories "present," "absent," or "no information." Here are the coding rules:

Avoidance Coding Rules

I. Avoidance customs
  1. Can't look eye-to-eye
    Code yes
      If there is this taboo, or if there is some other prohibition that implies this taboo. For example, the woman keeps her face covered, or looks at the ground.
      If the parties can't see each other at all (i.e., can't be together) (examples: "hides," "can't meet," "can't be together"), code *yes* for avoidance customs #1, 2, 3, 4, 5, and 6.
      If avoidance custom #1 is coded "yes," you can automatically code avoidance custom #2 as "yes."
  2. Can't talk directly
    Code yes
      If the parties can't talk while looking eye-to-eye.
      If they must converse through an intermediary.
      If they must converse at a distance, or out of sight of each other.
      If they can't look eye-to-eye.
      If the parties can't talk at all, code *yes* for avoidance customs #2 and 7.
  3. Can't eat together
    Code yes
      Can't eat together

Can't see each other
Code no
Can eat together
Description of eating together
4. Can't sleep in same room
Code yes
Can't sleep in same room or house
Can't be together in same room
Can't see each other
Code no
Can sleep in same room
Description of sleeping together in same room
5. Can't touch each other
Code yes
Can't touch each other
Can't pass (specific) articles
Specific touching taboos
Can't see each other
Code no
Can touch each other
Description of touching each other
6. Can't be alone together
Code yes
Can't be alone together
Can't be alone in same room or house
Can't see each other
Code no
Can be alone together
Description of being alone together
7. Can't speak or hear of sex (when in each other's presence)

Code yes

Can't speak or hear of sex

Various euphemisms such as "no lewd talk allowed between them"

Can't converse at all

Code no

Sexual intercourse allowed

Licentious joking allowed

Can speak or (together) hear of sex

Description of speaking of sex

II. Descriptive terms

1. "Avoids" (or "avoidance")

Code yes *only* if this word appears in the text, without qualification.

Code no if this word appears in the text *with* qualification. Examples: "some," "slight," "little," of "mild" avoidance.

2. "Restraint"

Code yes if the term "restraint" appears in the text, or if various terms appear that imply an unusually restrained relationship. Examples: "shy," "formal," "respectful," "ashamed," "reserved" (not "avoids").

Code no if a term or description appears in the text that implies that the relationship is *not* unusually restrained. Examples: "intimate," "free and easy," "may joke," "no formal respect relationship."

3. "No avoidance rules"

Code yes if there is some general statement implying that none of the avoidance customs listed in the beginning of these instructions are present. Example: "doesn't avoid," "no avoidance," "no taboos," "no

restrictions," "no obligatory etiquette." Do not code
this point "no."

III. Miscellaneous rules

This code should be applied separately to the relationship
between Male Ego and three categories of people: (1)
his Sister, (2) his Son's Wife (SoWi) (or daughter-in-
law), and (3) his Wife's Mother (WiMo) (or mother-
in-law).

Code "yes" if an avoidance custom applies both to Male
Ego and the Avoided Female, *or* if it applies only to one
but not the other. Example: SoWi lowers her eyes in
Male Ego's presence.

If there are conflicting reports about an avoidance custom, don't code for that custom.

If an avoidance relationship changes with the age of the
avoiding parties, code for the time of most extreme
avoidance.

If avoidance customs have changed since contact with
Europeans, code for pre-contact times.

If there are optional avoidance customs, code for most
extreme option.

The coders rarely coded "absent." Nearly always, the
coding-decision was either "present" or "no information."
This raises several serious problems. For one thing, we were
at a loss as to how to figure reliability. When two coders agree
that there is "no information" in respect to a code-category,
is this a case of "agreement"? If it is, average coder-agreement is very good, ranging between 85 per cent and 95 per
cent. However, another way of calculating average agreement
is to count as "agreement" *only* those times when two coders

agree on a "present" or (as rarely happened) an "absent" code. If this procedure is followed, average agreement is usually quite poor. Here is average-agreement, if we exclude agreements as to "no information": can't talk about sex 65 per cent; can't be alone together 57 per cent; can't touch each other 63 per cent; can't sleep in the same room 65 per cent; can't eat together 69 per cent; can't look eye-to-eye 86 per cent; can't talk directly 73 per cent; "avoids" 69 per cent; "restraint" 68 per cent; "no avoidance rules" 76 per cent.

We feel that the degree of standardization of coding is poorer than is represented by the first method of calculating agreement, and better than the second method (the figures above) indicates. In other words, it is rather mediocre. Frequently, avoidance is, in respect to the coding rules, vaguely decribed, leaving the coder in doubt as to whether to code "present" or "no information." Rarely did one coder enter "present" and another enter "absent"—twelve times out of approximately 2,000 chances.

As before, the final code was decided by majority rule. For most instances, this meant that if two or three coders judged "present" for a code-category, the final judgment was "present;" if two or three coders judged "no information," the final code was "no information."

The Guttman Scale

To demonstrate a Guttman scale-pattern, we had to show that some avoidance customs, i.e., code-categories, are frequently "absent" when others are "present," and rarely "present" when the "lower" customs are "absent." This is where the rarity of reported absences became really serious. To demonstrate a scale pattern properly, we needed many cases in which some customs were coded "present" and other customs were coded "absent." We did not have them.

As a poor substitute, we counted "no information" codes as "absent" codes. When, in describing an avoidance relationship, an ethnographer mentioned some avoidance customs and did not mention others, we assumed that the unmentioned avoidance customs were in fact absent: an assumption probably more often right than wrong, but frequently wrong.

When the data was treated in this way, five code-categories followed a pronounced cumulative scale-pattern. They were (from high to low): can't eat together; can't look eye-to-eye; can't talk directly; can't talk about sex; and "no avoidance rules." The other five code-categories didn't scale. After this treatment, we felt that a scale-pattern probably did exist, but that we had not yet clearly demonstrated it.

We took two steps to check on the scale. First, we interviewed ethnographers in the Boston area, to get more reported absences. We are indebted to the following people for providing, via interview, additional fully described cases: Dr. Cora DuBois (Alor), Dr. Charles Frake (Subanum), Dr. George Horner (Bassa, Bulu), Dr. Clyde Kluckhohn (Navaho), and Dr. Daniel McCall (Ashanti). These cases were scored by the interviewer (and not by the three coders) and entered into the sample.

Second, with the help of Dr. DuBois, we discovered "the California sample"—culture element distribution studies by Aginsky, Driver, Drucker, Essene, and Voegelin—in which specific avoidance customs were checked present *or absent* for a great many small bands and subtribes. Some avoidance customs in the California sample—paralleling our scalar code-categories—followed an extraordinary scale-pattern. This was not due to similarity (among California bands) in respect to severity of avoidance. There was considerable variability between rather widely separated bands; there was even a surprisingly large amount of variability within closely related clusters of bands.

One code-category in the California sample coincided with one of ours: "can't eat together." Another, "no obscenity allowed," seemed very close to our category "can't talk about sex." Their category "seldom speak" does not coincide with our category "can't talk directly"; but both imply a major limitation on conversation, and therefore appear to be similar. Finally, there appeared to be some similarity between their custom "the woman covers her head" and our category "can't look eye-to-eye." These customs in the California sample followed the same scalar relationships as the analogous customs in our "world-wide sample," with one exception: "the woman covers her head" was a higher scale point than "can't eat together." Table 40 summarizes the scalar relationships among these customs in the California sample.

One case from the California sample (Hupa, scored by myself, previously in the Whiting-Kluckhohn sample) was added to the world-wide sample.

These treatments convinced us we had a right to designate the following Guttman scale of severity of avoidance (from high to low):

5. Both customs present: *can't look eye-to-eye* and *can't eat together*.

4. One of these customs present: *can't look eye-to-eye* or *can't eat together*.

3. *Can't talk directly*.

Table 40.
Scalar Relationships between Selected Avoidance Customs in the California Sample

Avoidance Customs	Tally of Cases in Which, for a Given Pair of Avoidance Customs: Both Customs Are Present; Both Are Absent; One Is Present and the Other Is Absent			
No Obscenity	Present	Absent	Present	Absent
Seldom Speak	Present	Absent	Absent	Present
	112	77	20	3
No Obscenity	Present	Absent	Present	Absent
Woman Keeps Head Covered	Present	Absent	Absent	Present
	18	9	63	0
No Obscenity	Present	Absent	Present	Absent
Can't Eat Together	Present	Absent	Absent	Present
	65	38	22	0
Seldom Speak	Present	Absent	Present	Absent
Woman Keeps Head Covered	Present	Absent	Absent	Present
	18	37	60	0
Seldom Speak	Present	Absent	Present	Absent
Can't Eat Together	Present	Absent	Absent	Present
	34	43	49	0
Woman Keeps Head Covered	Present	Absent	Present	Absent
Can't Eat Together	Present	Absent	Absent	Present
	16	59	2	16

2. *Can't talk about sex.*
1. *"No avoidance rules."*

This scale was not applied to the California sample; it only applies to the world-wide sample—the coded cases, plus the added cases we mentioned. Table 41 gives all scale-scores and illustrates the scale-pattern. The scale yielded the following coefficients of reproducibility (with "no information" counted as "absent"): 97 per cent when applied to mother-in-law avoidance; 98 per cent, when applied to son's wife avoidance; 97 per cent, when applied to brother-sister avoidance.

Table 41. Final Ratings: Avoidance and Licentious Joking

Society	MOTHER-IN-LAW						SON'S WIFE						SISTER						Licentious Joking Relationship
	1	2	3	4	5	Score	1	2	3	4	5	Score	1	2	3	4	5	Score	
Arapaho		x	x	(x)	x	5		x	x	x	-	4		x	x			3	x
Araucania		x	x	(x)	x	5		x	x	x		4							
Bena		x	x	(x)	x	5	x					1							
Cheyenne		x	x	(x)	x	5								x	x			3	x
Chiricahua		x	x	(x)	x	5	x					1		x	x			3	
Callingo		x	x	(x)	x	5		x	x	(x)	x	5							
Ganda		x	x	(x)	x	5		x	x	(x)	x	5							
Gesu		x	x	(x)	x	5		x	x	(x)	x	5							
Kurtachi		x	x	(x)	x	5	x					1		x				2	
Lamba		x	x	(x)	x	5													
Lango		x	x	(x)	x	5	x					1							
Lesu		x	x	(x)	x	5													
Lovedu		x	x	(x)	x	5							x	x				2	x
Manus		x	x	(x)	x	5			x	(x)	x	5		x				2	x
Murngin		x	x	(x)	x	5								x	x			3	x
Navaho*		x	x	(x)	x	5		x	-	-	(-)	2		x	-	-	(-)	2	x
Thonga		x	x	(x)	x	5													x
Bemba				x	x	4													
Crow		x	x	x	-	4													x
Fiji		x	x	x		4		x	x	x	-	4		x	x	x		4	x
Gros Ventre		x	x	x		4											-		
Kipsigi		x	x	x		4								x				2	
Nuer		x		x		4													
Omaha		x		x		4		x	x			3							x
Tiv		x		x		4													

Table 41 (cont.)

Society	MOTHER-IN-LAW						SON'S WIFE						SISTER						Licentious Joking Relationship	
	1	2	3	4	5	Score	1	2	3	4	5	Score	1	2	3	4	5	Score	Score	
Dakota		x	x			3		x	x	x		4		x	x	x		4	4	
Nama Hottentot		x	x			3								x	x			3	3	x
Ojibwa		x	x			3		x	x	x		4		x	x			3	3	x
Semang		x	x			3		x	x			3								
Timbira		x	x			3														
Warrau		x	x			3														
Ashanti*		x	−	−	(1)	2		x	−	−	(1)	2		x			(1)	2	2	
Baiga	x					2														
Bassa*			−	−	(1)(1)	2			−	−	(1)(1)	2		−	−	−	(1)(1)	1	1	−
Bulu*			−	−	(1)	2			−	−		2		−	−	−		1	1	x
Gusii		x				2		x				2								
Iban		x				2								x				2		
Ifugao		x				2		x				2		x				2	2	
Lepcha		x				2														
Tikopia		x				2		x				2		x						
Ulithi		x			(1)	2		x		x	−	4		x	−	x	(1)	4	4	−
Zapotec	x	x	−	−	(1)	2	x	x		x	−	4	x	x	−	−	(1)	2	2	−
Alor*	x	−	−	−	(1)	1	x	−			(1)	1	x	−	−	−	(1)	1	1	−
Bella Coola	x					1	x					1	x						1	
Chenchu	x					1	x					1	x						1	
Comanche	x					1	x					1		x					2	
Dahomey	x					1	x					1								x
Hopi	x					1	x					1	x						1	

Table 41 (cont.)

Society	MOTHER-IN-LAW						SON'S WIFE						SISTER						Licentious Joking Relationship
	1	2	3	4	5	Score	1	2	3	4	5	Score	1	2	3	4	5	Score	Score
Hupa*		−	−	−	(−)	1		−	−	−	(−)	1							
Marquesas		−				1		−				1							
Marshalls	x					1	x					1		x				2	
Paiute	x					1	x					1							
Papago	x					1	x					1	x					1	−
Samoa	x					1	x					1		x	x	x		4	−
Sanpoil	x					1	x					1							
Siriono	x					1	x					1	x					1	
Subanum*		−		−	(−)	1		−	−	−	(−)	1		−	−	−	(−)	1	−
Tallensi	x	−				1	x					1	x					1	x
Tarahumara	x					1	x					1		x				1	x
Trobriands		−				1	x					1		x		x		4	x
Arapesh													x					1	
Chagga								x	x	x		4	x	x				2	
Kwoma													x	−				1	x
Nyakusa								x	x	(x)	x	5							
Ontong Java							x							x	−	x		4	
Ooldea							x					1							
Pukapuka														x	x	x	−	4	
Rajput									x	x		4		x	x	x		4	
Truk														x				2	
Tungus									x			3	x					1	

* Societies marked with an asterisk were not scored by the cross-cultural coders. Information on them was gathered after the coding had been completed. Hupa was scored on the basis of the California sample data. The others—Alor, Ashanti, Bassa, Bulu, Navaho, and Subanum—were scored on the basis of ethnographer-interviews.

Column headings are as follows: (1) "no avoidance rules"; (2) can't talk about sex; (3) can't talk directly; (4) either "can't eat together" or "can't look eye-to-eye"; (5) both "can't eat together" and "can't look eye-to-eye."

Entries are as follows: "x" indicates "present"; "−" indicates "absent"; a blank indicates no rating.

Evaluation of the Scale

Like the menstrual taboo scale, the scale of severity of avoidance does not meet all the idea requirements for a Guttman scale (Green, 1954). Unlike the menstrual taboo scale, it is based on a code with mediocre reliability. In these added ways the scale is no doubt rather crude:

1. We suspect that the intervals between the scale points are quite unequal. In particular, the "distance" (in relative severity of avoidance) between points 2 and 3 is probably much greater than the other scale intervals.

2. There are probably some minor discrepancies between scale-scores and "real" scores. These appear to be of two types. The first consists of "high" cases that should be even higher: cases given scores of 3 or 4 which, if they had been more fully reported, would have been scored a point or two higher. The second type consists of cases assigned the lowest possible scale-score ("no avoidance rules") that should have been scored at point 2 ("can't talk about sex"). Whereas the "high" customs—can't eat together, can't look eye-to-eye, and can't talk directly—seem to be relatively extreme and noticeable, "can't talk about sex" comes dangerously close to the level of mild, usual, taken-for-granted avoidance customs. We suspect that some cases characterized as having "no avoidance rules" actually had the rule against talking about sex, but that it either went unnoticed or was taken for granted and therefore not reported. In fact, there are five cases in our sample which were checked "yes" for both "no avoidance rules" and "can't talk about sex."

We do feel that the scale separates "high" from "low"

cases with a good deal of precision; cases scored 1 or 2 that should have been scored 3 or higher, and cases scored 3 or higher that should have been scored 1 or 2, are probably rare or nonexistent.

3. There is one dimension of avoidance that is not represented by this scale: how long does it last? Do a man and woman avoid each other for life, or until they are very old, or only for a few years? We know of the following cases of "temporary avoidance" (where after a few years avoidance customs are laid aside or substantially reduced): brother-sister avoidance—possibly Ojibwa; son's wife avoidance—Chagga, Manus, Ojibwa, Zapotec; mother-in-law avoidance—Bena, Cheyenne, Lovedu, Nuer, Thonga. Three avoidance cases are said to last a lifetime: Lango and Navaho (mother-in-law avoidance); and Nyakusa (son's wife avoidance). Usually, the ethnographer makes no statement about duration of avoidance. There did not seem to be much we could do about this duration-dimension, so we simply ignored it in our ratings.

Given these limitations, we still think this measure is very good, as cross-cultural measures go. Like the menstrual taboo scale, it empirically demonstrates a continuum (severity of avoidance), and it gives an empirical basis for placing cases on this continuum.

V

CODING THE VARIABLE "BREASTS NOT SEXUAL STIMULI"

This is a variable that was rated directly by the cross-cultural coders. Here are the coding instructions (i.e., rating procedures):

Code "x" (breasts *not* sexual stimuli) if
  Breast-feeling, by hand or mouth, is rarely or never a form of sex-play. (Sex-play defined: body-contact for sexual pleasure, whether or not it leads to coitus. Adults only.)
  It is stated that breasts are not considered sexual stimuli (any more than elbows, toes, etc.).
Code "—" (breasts *are* sexual stimuli) if
  There is mention of breast-feeling, by hand or mouth, during sex-play.
  There is a statement to the effect that breasts are considered a special sexual stimulus (more so than toes, elbows, etc.).

Rules for Inference. Some of these reports will be vague and sketchy, so you will have to infer. However, do not feel you have to code every case. If you don't think there is enough information, code "no information." Follow these rules for inferences:

1. Infer—if it involves guessing what the ethnographer means by a vague statement.
2. Don't infer when you feel nothing has been said in respect to the code-category, i.e., when, on the basis of the report, it looks as if the ethnographer couldn't code this case himself.

The coders were Mrs. Diane D'Andrade, Mrs. Constance Pilz, and Mrs. Judith W. Stephens. Average agreement was 92 per cent. Final ratings were decided by majority rule. In Table 42 are given all the final ratings, except for Ifaluk, which received a final rating of "no information."

These ratings were supplemented by three more cases, drawn from Ford and Beach. Although I scanned these ethnographies, I could find no mention of breasts or breast-feeling. I assume that two of these cases (Kwoma and Tarahumara) were judged on the basis of ethnographer-interviews, and the third (Kwakiutl) was judged on the basis of Ford's own field-work experience. Ford and Beach designated the Tarahumara as one of the societies where "Stimulation of the woman's breast by her partner is a common precursor or accompaniment of intercourse . . ." (Ford and Beach, 1951: 46). On this basis, I have rated the Tarahumara "—" on *breasts not sexual stimuli.* They designated the Kwakiutl and Kwoma as among the societies "in which breast stimulation is reported to be completely lacking" (Ford and Beach, 1951:

47). On this basis, I rated Kwoma and Kwakiutl "x" on the variable *breasts not sexual stimuli*.

Table 42.
Final Ratings: Breasts Not Sexual Stimuli

Breasts Are Considered Sexual Stimuli	Breasts Are Not Considered Sexual Stimuli
Alor	Kurtachi
Baiga	Kwakiutl*
Chukchee	Kwoma*
Gusii	Navaho
Lakher	Siriono
Lepcha	Ulith
Lesu	
Manus	
Marquesas	
Mohave	
Rwala Bedouin	
Tarahumara*	
Trobriands	
Truk	

* Societies rated by Ford and Beach (1951).

VI

CODING THE
VARIABLES RELATED
TO FATHER'S ROLE

For the variables "severity of the Father's Obedience Demands" and "Whether or Not the Father Is the Main Disciplinarian," ratings were assigned directly by the coders. Here are the coding rules (i.e. rating procedures):

The Father's Role: Coding Instructions

This code applies to interaction between *father* and *son*. There will be cases in which "sons" are not specifically mentioned, but only "children." In these cases you may assume that the treatment of boys and girls is similar. There will be other cases in which "father" is not mentioned, but only "parents" or "elders." In such cases you may assume that the *obedience demands* of father and mother are similar. If the son does not live with his real parents, the male head of the household in which he lives may be coded as "father." Code for this age period: the first six years of the boy's life.

230

1. *Father Demands Strict Obedience.* When father and son are in face-to-face interaction, the son's behavior may be more or less restrained in accord with the father's wishes. Extreme restraint would perhaps be a case in which the son did everything his father told him to do without argument, addressed him in a humble voice, using special respectful language, and in general did not express his own wishes or impulses. The other extreme might be a case in which the father "spoils" the son; not only does he allow the son to do practically anything he wishes when they are together, but he even restrains his own behavior in order to please his son; he indulges his son's whims, puts up with discomfort and irritations without complaint, and so forth. Between these two extremes would be cases of father-son interaction which were characterized by informal give-and-take. The son must meet some demands of the father, and cannot "get away with murder," but the father allows the son some latitude to express himself and disagree. This code is designed to separate the cases of fairly extreme restraint (exercised on the son) from all other cases ("informal give-and-take," and "spoiling").

Code "yes"
> If it is directly stated that the father demands strict obedience.
> If a demand for strict obedience can be inferred, from mention of the father's behavior or other demands. For example, if fairly strict respect etiquette is demanded, "strict obedience" may be inferred.

Code "no"
If it is specifically stated that the father's obedience demands are less than strict.

If absence can be inferred, from descriptions of father-son interaction in which strict obedience, or deference, or respect etiquette, is lacking: "free and easy," "informal," "permissive," "indulgent," etc.

Code "no information"

If the ethnographer gives you no basis for making a judgment about whether the father's obedience demands are "strict" or less than strict, or if there are conflicting reports about his obedience demands.

2. *Father Is the Main Disciplinarian.* The question to ask yourself here is: if the child does something in the presence of both the father and the mother which requires punishment, who is most likely to punish him, the father or the mother (or someone else)?

Code "yes"

If the father is said to be the "disciplinarian"; if he is said to be "more strict" than the mother; if most of the training which requires punishment—*at some time* in the first six years—is the responsibility of the father.

Code "no"

If the father is said to be the "disciplinarian"; if he is said not to be more strict than the mother; if, during the whole first six years, the father is never mainly responsible for that part of the training of the child which requires punishment; if the father has some sort of immunity from punishing his son, because of kinship regulations.

Code "no information"

If the ethnographer gives you no basis for deciding, or if there is conflicting information.

The coders were Mrs. Roberta Churchill, Mrs. Cynthia Landauer, and Mrs. Katherine Wilson. The final ratings on the *strictness of the father's obedience demands* are given in Table 43; average agreement was 63 per cent. The final ratings on *whether or not the father is the main disciplinarian* are also given in Table 43; average agreement was 67 per cent. As always, final scores were decided by majority rule.

These are poor ratings. Reliability is low. Also, I suspect, is validity. Usually the ratings are based on sketchy, impressionistic ethnographic accounts, i.e., impressions and evaluations of behavior.

Table 43.
Father's Role Ratings

Societies	1	2	Societies	1	2
Alor	–	–	Maori	–	
Araucania	–		Murngin		–
Ashanti	x	x	Navaho	–	–
Bali	–	–	Ontong Java	–	
Bena	x		Ooldea	–	
Chenchu	–		Papago	–	x
Cheyenne		–	Pukapuka		–
Dahomey	x	–	Samoa	–	–
Gusii	x	x	Siriono	–	–
Hopi	x	–	Tallensi	–	x
Kiwai	x	x	Tanala	x	–
Kwakiutl	x		Tarasco		–
Kwoma	x		Thonga	x	x
Lamba	x		Timbira	–	–
Lesu	x	–	Trobriands	–	–
Lepcha	–	–	Ulithi	–	x
Malaita	–	x	Wogeo	–	–
Manam	–		Zapotec	–	–
Manus	–	–			

Column headings are as follows: (1) father demands strict obedience; (2) father is the main disciplinarian.

Entries are as follows: "x" indicates a final rating of "yes"; "–" indicates a final rating of "no."

VII

CODING FOLKLORE

FOLKLORE WAS MUCH MORE difficult to code than were the other variables. The coding rules evolved over a long period of time and with much trial and error. Several sets of rules were tried and rejected, due to low coder-agreement. The final rules were quite conservative as to latitude for inference and interpretation. They were very formalized; many an incident is "missed" because the wording of the story does not allow it to be coded. This seemed to be the only way in which folklore variables could be measured in an acceptably standardized manner.

We coded all societies that had been in the menstrual taboo sample, and that had at least 4000 words (about ten pages) of literary text. By these criteria, 42 cases were included in the folklore sample.

Songs and verse were not coded. All prose text was, except

for a few societies with particularly voluminous literature. If a society had less than 200 pages of recorded folktales, this was all coded. If the text was between 200 and 300 pages in length, every other story (alternate stories) was coded. If the text was between 300 and 400 pages, every third story was coded. And so forth. The range was from 4500 words (Lesu) to 98,000 words (Navaho).

Below, the coding rules are given. Let me preview them by saying that the coder had three main tasks. First, she had to note "incidents" of *physical injury* (genital injury, biting, severing, or other types of physical injury) and *fighting*. Second, when coding an incident, she noted who the actors were: father and son, mother and son, etc. Third, she noted incidents of *sexual intercourse: punished or unpunished.* Here are the coding rules:

Folklore: Coding Instructions

I. Incidents of physical injury

An incident of physical injury is:

1. A subject-verb-predicate statement, containing an active verb (describing something which one person does to another). Examples: (Code) "he *killed* her," "the boy whom he *killed*," "he *cut* his arm." (Don't Code) "he went about killing," "the slain warrior."

2. Implying physical change accompanied by bleeding or death.

3. As a result of physical contact. Either the bodies of both parties must touch, or an implement is used. Examples: "he *speared* him," "he *shot* them."

Such verbs are: hurt, killed, crushed, castrated, decapitated, cut, bit, eaten, etc. A list of physical injury verbs is given below. Here are some examples of physical injury instances, with the crucial verbs underlined: "he *killed* her"; "all the men she had *speared*"; "he *scalped* them"; "she *ate* one and then the other"; "she *ate* one and then *ate* the other" (Code Twice).

Here are some examples that do *not* qualify as instances of physical injury, because they contain no active verbs which imply action by one person to another: "he was killed"; "he went about slaying them"; "the wound was bad"; "the man who was killed returned to life"; "the people he ate were delicious"; "she picked him up and his back broke."

Here are some examples that do *not* qualify as instances of physical injury, because they do not contain verbs which imply physical change (with bleeding or death): "they fought." Also verbs like poked, wrestled, hit, threw, etc. Verbs that imply physical contact with aggressive intent, but do not imply physical change with bleeding or death, will be coded as *fighting*, not as physical injury. The rules for coding the category *fighting* are given below, along with a list of *fighting* verbs.

Here are some examples which do *not* qualify as instances of physical injury, since the verbs do not imply physical contact followed by bleeding or death: "she changed him into a toad"; "he poisoned him."

The crucial factor in making your judgment about whether or not an incident of physical injury has occurred is the meaning implied by the *verb*, not the meaning implied by the whole sentence or episode.

The *category* of physical injury (genital injury, severing, biting or other) *may* be inferred from the wider context of the episode. For example, "she *cut* him with her teeth" would be coded as "biting"; the phrase "she cut him" allows you to code an incident of physical injury; the phrase "with her teeth" allows you to assign this incident to the category "biting."

To be coded, a phrase must apply to an actual happening, and not to imagined, supposed, or future happenings.

Code self-injury by same rules. Example: "He *cut* himself on the coral."

II. Categories of physical injury

Each incident of physical injury should be coded in one of four categories:

G—Genital injury: physical injury to the genital organs

S—Severing: cutting off or detaching part of the body

B—Biting or eating

O—Other types of physical injury (including "kill" and "hurt")

Code only when the object is living.

Code when both characters are animate: humans or animals. Do not code when one of the characters is inanimate (examples: hail, a rock, the water, a tree) unless the inanimate object is personalized (speaks, thinks, or has a will).

An additional category is

F—*Fighting:* physical contact with intent to do physical injury. Below (V) is a list of automatic fighting verbs— if intent to hurt can be inferred.

III. Coding relationships between characters in physical injury incidents.

Each incident of physical injury or fighting should be coded in one of the first nine columns on the coding sheet, depending on the relationship between the persons who interact in the incident. If a son injures his father, code under the column headed "son-father." If the father injures the son, code under "father-son." If one man injures another but relationship between father and son cannot be coded, enter under the column headed "male-male." And so forth. You must decide two points in order to code relationship: (1) the sex of the characters; (2) whether interaction between a son and a parent is involved.

1. *Coding for sex.* A character may be coded as a man if he is directly designated male. For example, if he is referred to as "he," "a man," "the father," "the nephew." The same rule applies to coding for females. Indirect sex designations (examples: "the warrior," "the cook") are *not* sufficient.

Code in the column headed Sex Unknown if the sex of one or both characters is not directly stated.

Also code "Sex Unknown" in all cases where one party to the incident is a *group,* that is not clearly designated as a group made up only of men or only of women. Examples: "them," "the people," "the children," "the warriors."

2. *Coding for son-parent relationship* (father-son, son-father, mother-son, son-mother).

   a. Stated. Sometimes the family relationship will be directly stated. Example: "She ate her son." In these cases, prefix your code with "S-" (indicating *S*tated relationship). For example, in the above case you would enter, under the "mother-son" heading, "S-B" (stated mother-son interaction: biting).

   b. Inferred. If the sex of both parties is known, you can *infer* disguised son-parent interaction, if one party is stated to be (in priority order): (1) Of a different generation—grandfather, uncle, father-in-law, parent of a real or anticipated sex partner, aunt, "boy" to "man," etc.; (2) A political (or economic) ruler. Examples: queen, chief, landlord, slave-owner (that is, one character is a ruler and the other character is not).

IV. Automatic physical injury verbs

(If phrase form is correct): kill, hurt, injure, bite, eat, swallow, devour, cut, pierce, scratch, chop, tear, crush, circumcise, castrate, scalp, remove (from body), shoot, burn, stab, drown, sting, break. Also, compound verbs of this type: succeeded in killing, was killing, was able to kill, used to kill.

V. Automatic fighting verbs

(If intent to do physical injury is implied): hit, strike, wrestle, kick, pinch, attack, push, throw, jumped on, grab, catch, beat, squeeze, slap, set upon, fell upon, stamped on, knocked (down or over), whip.

VI. Sexual Intercourse (code)

P—Punished. Anything unpleasant (injury, abandonment, ostracism, shame, ridicule, disgrace, etc.) comes to a person as a (causally connected) result of participating in sexual intercourse.

U—Unpunished. Sexual intercourse takes place with no mention of resulting unpleasantness to either of the parties.

The unit for coding sexual intercourse is a verb: "copulate," "had intercourse," etc. Code obvious euphemisms: "slept with," "had her." Do not code "marry" or terms for marriage. Example: "took her for his wife." Do not code terms for courtship which do not specifically apply to intercourse. Example: "they were going together."

If it is clear that several references refer to only one act of coitus, code only once. Otherwise, code every sexual intercourse verb.

Examples of incidents of sexual intercourse punished (P):

"They *slept together* that night." As a result her father ran him out of camp.

"They *copulated* three times" (Code once). As a result she couldn't walk properly.

"He *went around making love* to all the girls." People laughed at him.

Examples of sexual intercourse unpunished (U):

These are merely quotations like the above, with no resulting unpleasantness to either party.

Miscellaneous. Code only narrative material. Do not code verse, songs, titles, the author's discussion in the text, or footnotes.

Two coders—Mrs. Diane D'Andrade and Mrs. Constance Pilz—divided the sample between them. In other words, scores were assigned on the basis of only one coder's judgment; for half the sample it was Mrs. D'Andrade, and for the other half it was Mrs. Pilz. I coded about 20 per cent of the sample, to enable a reliability spot-check (my coding judgments do not figure in the final scores). For the folklore variables we shall refer to, coder-agreement was as follows:

Incidents of genital injury—50 per cent.
Incidents of severing—72 per cent.
Incidents of physical injury of all types—78 per cent.
Identity of the actors in conflict-incidents (includes the "fighting" category)—62 per cent.
Sexual intercourse: punished or unpunished—65 per cent.

Compared with some of the other variables, folklore yielded low average agreement. However, for the folklore coding, the likelihood of chance agreement was virtually zero. On the other coding jobs, likelihood of chance agreement ranged between 0.35 and 0.55.

Table 44 gives individual scores. For *sexual intercourse: punished or unpunished,* number of incidents is given. For the other variables a decimal score is entered. These decimal scores represent frequency per 1,000 words of literary text. For example, the Arapesh had four genital injury incidents and 26,900 words of text; their score on genital injury is 0.15. The Chukchee had eight severing incidents and 36,000 words of text; their severing score is 0.22.

Scores on the variable, *all types of physical injury,* are derived by combining frequencies of genital injury, severing, biting, and "other" types of physical injury.

Table 44.
Individual Scores on Folklore Variables

Society	Frequency of Genital Injury	Frequency of Severing	Frequency of All Types of Physical Injury	Frequency of Father-Son Conflict	SEXUAL INTERCOURSE: Punished	Unpunished
Arapesh	0.15	0.26	3.16	0.26	20	15
Cheyenne	0.00	0.05	1.17	0.16		
Dahomey	0.00	0.47	1.79	0.12	5	8
Dakota	0.00	0.10	1.73	0.22	3	0
Hupa	0.00	0.00	0.71	0.16	0	3
Ifaluk	0.00	0.30	2.35	0.68	4	3
Kwakiutl	0.05	0.15	1.52	0.37	6	2
Malaita	0.00	0.14	1.52	0.09		
Ojibwa	0.11	0.20	1.78	0.00		
Paiute	0.25	0.21	2.53	0.35	3	8
Papago	0.00	0.19	1.65	0.12	1	2
Sanpoil	0.00	0.11	1.33	0.02	9	4
Tiv	0.18	0.09	1.65	0.22		
Baiga	0.04	0.19	1.51	0.20	3	13
Ganda	0.00	0.09	1.82	0.00		
Kiwai	0.06	0.23	3.04	0.19	21	20
Kurtachi	0.00	0.27	1.62	0.14	2	4
Lamba	0.00	0.26	2.51	0.09	1	1
Nama Hottentot	0.00	0.24	3.19	0.05	2	2
Azande	0.00	0.00	1.67	0.21		
Chukchee	0.14	0.22	3.61	0.08	3	8
Copper Eskimo	0.00	0.53	4.27	0.93	1	2
Lakher	0.29	0.38	4.19	0.57	0	2
Lesu	0.00	0.22	3.33	0.00	5	4
Thonga	0.00	0.54	2.38	0.04	1	0
Timbira	0.13	0.40	2.93	1.20	3	0
Ainu	0.00	0.26	1.23	0.06		
Arapaho	0.00	0.11	1.40	0.26	2	4
Chiricahua	0.02	0.13	1.91	0.11	3	5
Jivaro	0.00	0.08	2.00	0.58	1	4
Lepcha	0.00	0.59	3.43	0.00	1	5
Murngin	0.04	0.00	0.94	0.36	2	10
Navaho	0.00	0.34	1.21	0.06	9	2
Chenchu	0.00	0.18	2.02	0.00	0	3
Hopi	0.07	0.11	1.07	0.02	6	10
Marquesas	0.00	0.48	1.58	0.38	13	17
Masai	0.00	0.23	2.86	0.06	0	3
Pukapuka	0.03	0.23	2.10	0.08	10	7
Samoa	0.00	0.06	0.51	0.22	1	3
Tanala	0.00	0.00	0.78	0.00		
Trobriands	1.07	0.11	1.60	0.21	12	9
Zapotec	0.00	0.32	1.16	0.00		

Scores on *father-son conflict* combine two categories— father-son conflict (stated), and father-son conflict (inferred). "Conflict" includes (1) all physical injury incidents, and (2) all "fighting" incidents. The scores combine all incidents in which father attacks son, and all incidents in which son attacks father.

VIII

RATINGS OF DILUTED
MARRIAGE VARIABLES

T<small>HIS APPENDIX IS DEVOTED TO</small>
listing individual scores on the three "diluted marriage variables."

Percentage of polygyny and percentage of mother-child
households was coded by Whiting and D'Andrade; I decided
on the high/low cutting points. Percentage of polygyny is
rated "high" (40 per cent or more wives are estimated to be
polygynous), "low" (less than 40 per cent of all wives are
estimated to be polygynous), and "absent" (strict monogamy). Societies are listed in four columns, according to their
scores on polygyny: "high," "low," "absent," and unrated.

Percentage of mother-child households (father sleeping
outside the house at least half the time) is rated "high" (at
least 40 per cent of all households are estimated to be
mother-child) or "low" (less than 40 per cent of all house-

Table 45.
Scores on Frequency of Polygyny, Frequency of Mother-Child Households, and Duration of the Post Partum Sex Taboo

High Polygyny	1	2
Arapesh	x	x
Araucania	–	x
Arunta	–	
Azande	x	x
Bemba	x	
Bhil	–	
Dahomey	x	x
Ganda	x	x
Gusii	x	–
Hausa	x	x
Jivaro	–	x
Kapauka	x	
Kurtachi	x	x
Kwoma	–	x
Lovedu	x	x
Mende	x	x
Murngin	–	–
Nambicauru	–	–
Nuer	x	x
Nyakusa	x	x
Riff	–	
Siriono	–	–
Tallensi	x	x
Tanala	x	–
Thonga	x	x
Tiv	x	x
Venda	x	x
Wogeo		x

Low Polygyny	1	2
Aleut	–	
Alor	–	–
Ashanti	x	–
Baiga	–	–
Bali	–	–
Bena		x
Cagaba	–	–
Camayura	–	
Carib	–	–
Chiricahua	–	x
Copper Esk.	–	–
Comanche	–	
Fiji		x
Gilyak	–	
Igorot	–	–
Kazak	–	–
Koryak	–	–
Kutenai	–	
Lamba	–	–
Lepcha	–	–
Malekula	–	
Manus	–	–
Montana	–	
Maori	–	–
Munducuru	x	
Nama Hott.	–	–
Navaho	–	–
Oijbwa	–	x
Ooldea	–	x
Paiute	–	
Papago	–	–
Pomo	x	
Pondo	–	x
Pilaga	–	x
Samoa	–	x
Silwa	–	
Siwai	–	
Tarahumara	–	
Thai	–	
Tikopia	–	
Tlingit	–	
Toda	–	
Trobriands	–	x
Truk	–	–
Tupinamba	–	–
Yagua	–	–
Yurok	x	

Polygyny Absent	1	2
Ainu	–	–
Andamans	–	
Aymara	–	–
Chenchu	–	–
Cuna	–	
Dobu	–	
Hopi	–	–
Iban	–	
Ifaluk	–	x
Ifugao	–	
Iroquois	–	
Kaska	–	
Kwakiutl	–	x
Lakher	–	–
Lapp	–	–
Marquesas	–	–
Omaha	–	
Pukapuka	–	
Rajput	x	x
Semang	–	
Tepoztlan	–	x
Timbira	–	–
Tubatulabal	–	
Tzeltal	–	
Witoto	–	x
Yuchi	–	
Zapotec	–	
Zuni	–	

Polygyny Unrated	1	2
Arapaho		x
Bassa		x
Bella Coola		–
Bulu		x
Chagga		x
Chewa		–
Cheyenne		x
Chukchee		–
Dakota		x
Gesu		x
Gros Ventre		–
Hupa	x	x
Kipsigi	x	x
Kiwai	x	x
Lango		x
Lesu		x
Malaita	x	x
Manam		x
Maria Gond		–
Masai		x
Mixtec		–
Mohave		–
Ontong Java		–
Rwala Bedouin		–
Sanpoil		–
Subanum		–
Tarasco		–
Tungus		–
Turkana		x
Ulithi		x
Warrau		–
Yaghan		–
Yao		x
Yoruba		x
Yukaghir		–

holds are estimated to be mother-child). Mother-child household ratings are entered in Column *1* of Table 45. The entry "x" stands for "high"; the entry "—" indicates "low."

Duration of the post partum sex taboo was rated by Whiting and Kluckhohn. They decided on the high/low cutting point (Whiting, Kluckhohn, and Anthony, 1958). These scores are listed in Column 2 of Table 45. The entry "x" indicates a "long" post partum sex taboo (customarily lasting a year or more); "—" indicates a "short" post partum sex taboo (customarily lasting less than a year).

BIBLIOGRAPHIES

ETHNOGRAPHIC
BIBLIOGRAPHY

Ainu

Batchelor, J. *Ainu Life and Lore*. Tokyo: Kyobunkwan, 1927.
Murdock, G. P. *Our Primitive Contemporaries*. New York: Macmillan, 1934.

Alor

DuBois, C. *The People of Alor*. Minneapolis: University of Minnesota Press, 1944.
———. Personal communication.

Arapaho

Dorsey, G. A., and A. L. Kroeber. "Traditions of the Arapaho." *Field Columbian Museum Anthropological Series*, Vol. 5, Publication 81, 1903.
Eggan, F. A. *Social Anthropology of North American Tribes*. Chicago: University of Chicago Press, 1937.
Hilger, M. I. *Arapaho Child Life and Its Cultural Background*. Washington: U.S. Government Printing Office, 1952.

Arapesh

Mead, M. "The Mountain Arapesh. II. Supernaturalism." *Anthropological Papers of the American Museum of Natural History*, Vol. 37, Part 3, 1940.

Mead, M. "The Mountain Arapesh. III. Socio-Economic Life." *Ibid.*, Vol. 40, Part 3, 1947.

———. *Sex and Temperament in Three Primitive Societies.* New York: New American Library of World Literature, 1950.

*Araucania**

Titiev, M. *Araucanian Culture in Transition.* Ann Arbor: University of Michigan Press, 1951.

*Ashanti**

Fortes, M. "Kinship and Marriage among the Ashanti," in A. R. Radcliffe-Brown and D. Forde (eds.), *African Systems of Kinship and Marriage.* London: Oxford University Press, 1950.

Rattray, R. S. *Ashanti Law and Constitution.* Oxford: Clarendon Press, 1929.

———. *Religion and Art in Ashanti.* Oxford: Clarendon Press, 1927.

McCall, D. Personal communication.

*Aymara**

Steward, J. H. *Handbook of South American Indians,* Vol. 2. Washington: U.S. Government Printing Office, 1947.

*Azande**

Evans-Pritchard, E. E. "Social Character of Bride-Wealth, with Special Reference to the Azande." *Man,* Vol. 34, 1934.

———. *Witchcraft, Oracles and Magic among the Azande.* Oxford: Clarendon Press, 1937.

Larken, P. M. "An Account of the Zande." *Sudan Notes and Records,* Vols. 9 and 10, 1926 and 1927.

Seligman, C. G., and B. Z. Seligman. *Pagan Tribes of the Nilotic Sudan.* London: George Routledge, 1932.

Baiga

Elwin, V. *The Baiga.* London: Murray, 1939.

Bali

Covarrubias, M. *Island of Bali.* New York: Alfred A. Knopf, 1937.

* Societies marked with an asterisk are, at the time of this writing, included in the Human Relations Area Files (Yale University).

Bassa

Horner, G. Personal communication.

Bella Coola

McIlwraith, T. F. *The Bella Coola Indians*. Toronto: University of Toronto Press, 1948.

Bena

Culwick, A. T., and G. M. Culwick. *Ubena of the River*. London: Allen and Unwin, 1936.

Bulu

Horner, G. Personal communication.

California Sample (*in University of California Anthropological Records*)

Aginsky, B. W. "Culture Element Distributions: XXIV—Central Sierra," Volume 7, 1942.
Driver, H. "Culture Element Distributions: X—Northwest California," Volume 1, 1937–39.
———. *Ibid.*: VI—Southern Sierra Nevada," Volume 1, 1937–39.
Drucker, P. "Culture Element Distributions: V—Southern California," Volume 1, 1937–39.
Essene, F. "Culture Element Distributions: XXI—Round Valley," Volume 7, 1942.
Voegelin, E. W. "Culture Element Distributions: XX—Northeast California," Volume 7, 1942.

Chagga*

Gutmann, B. *The Tribal Teachings of the Chagga*, tr. by W. Goodenough and D. Crawford. Munchen: C. H. Beck'sche Verlagsbuchhandlung, 1932.
Raum, O. F. *Chaga Childhood*. London: Oxford University Press, 1940.

Chenchu

Furer-Haimendorf, C. *The Chenchus*. London: Macmillan, 1943.

Cheyenne

Eggan, F. A. *Social Anthropology of North American Tribes.* Chicago: University of Chicago Press, 1937.

Grinnell, G. B. *The Cheyenne Indians.* New Haven: Yale University Press, 1923.

Chiricahua Apache

Eggan, F. A. *Social Anthropology of North American Tribes.* Chicago: University of Chicago Press, 1937.

Opler, M. E. *An Apache Life Way.* Chicago: University of Chicago Press, 1941.

———. "Myths and Tales of the Chiricahua Apache Indians." *Memoirs of the American Folklore Society,* Vol. 37, 1942.

Chukchee (Reindeer)*

Bogoras, V. G. "The Chukchee." *Memoirs of the American Museum of Natural History,* Vol. 2, 1904.

———. "Chukchee Mythology." *Ibid.,* Vol. 8, 1910.

Comanche*

Wallace, E., and E. A. Hoebel. *The Comanches: Lords of the South Plains.* Norman: University of Oklahoma Press, 1952.

Copper Eskimo*

Jenness, D. "The Life of the Copper Eskimos." *Report of the Canadian Arctic Expedition, 1913–1918,* Vol. 12. Ottawa: Acland, 1922.

Crow*

Lowie, R. H. *The Crow Indians.* New York: Holt, Rinehart and Winston, 1935.

Dahomey

Herskovits, M. J. *Dahomey: An Ancient West African Kingdom.* New York: Augustin, 1938.

——— and F. S. Herskovits. *Dahomean Narrative.* Evanston, Ill.: Northwestern University Press, 1958.

Dakota (*Teton*)

Deloria, E. "Dakota Texts." *Publications of the American Ethnological Society*, Vol. 14, 1932.

Neihardt, J. G. *When the Tree Flowered*. New York: Macmillan, 1951.

Spier, L. *Klamath Ethnography*. Berkeley: University of California Press, 1930 (pp. 313–316).

*Eastern Timbira**

Nimenaju, C. "The Eastern Timbira," tr. and ed. by R. H. Lowie. *University of California Publications in American Archeology and Ethnology*, Vol. 16, 1946.

Fiji (*Lau*)*

Hocart, A. M. "Lau Islands, Fiji." *Bernice P. Bishop Museum Bulletin*, No. 62, 1929.

Thompson, L. "Southern Lau, Fiji: an Ethnography." *Ibid.*, No. 162, 1940.

Flathead

Turney-High, H. H. "The Flathead Indians of Montana." *Memoirs of the American Anthropological Association*, No. 47, 1937.

*Ganda**

Mair, L. P. *An African People in the Twentieth Century*. London: George Routledge, 1934.

Roscoe, J. *The Baganda*. London: Macmillan, 1911.

Gesu

Roscoe, J. *The Bagesu and Other Tribes of the Uganda Protectorate*. Cambridge: Cambridge University Press, 1924.

Gros Ventre

Kroeber, A. L. "Ethnology of the Gros Ventre." *Anthropological Papers of the American Museum of Natural History*, Vol. 1, 1908.

*Gusii**

LeVine, R. "Social Control and Socialization among the Gusii." Doctoral thesis, Harvard University, 1958.

———. Personal communication.

Hopi

Dennis, W. *The Hopi Child.* New York: Appleton-Century-Crofts, 1940.
Kluckhohn, R. Personal communication.
Simmons, L. W. *Sun Chief.* New Haven: Yale University Press, 1942.
Stephen, A. "Hopi Tales." *Journal of American Folklore,* Vol. 42, 1929.
Titiev, M. "Old Oraibi." *Papers of the Peabody Museum of American Archeology and Ethnology,* Harvard University, Vol. 22, No. 1, 1944.

Hupa

Driver, H. E. "Culture Element Distributions: X—Northwest California." *University of California Anthropological Records,* Vol. 1, 1937–39.
Goddard, P. E. "Life and Culture of the Hupa." *University of California Publications in American Archeology and Ethnology,* Vol. 1, 1903.

Iban*

Freeman, J. D. *The Iban.* Canberra: The Australian National University, 1958.

Ifaluk*

Burrows, E. S. "The People of Ifaluk," 1948, and Spiro, M. "Ifaluk: a South Sea Culture," 1947. Unpublished manuscripts: Coordinated Investigation of Micronesian Anthropology, Pacific Science Board, National Research Council, Washington, D.C.

Jivaro*

Karsten, R. *The Head-Hunters of Western Amazonas.* Helsingfors: Centraltrycheriet, 1935.

Kazak

Hudson, A. E. *Kazak Social Structure.* New Haven: Yale University Press, 1938.

Kipsigis

Peristiany, J. G. *The Social Institutions of the Kipsigis.* London: George Routledge, 1939.

Kiwai

Landtman, G. "The Folk-Tales of the Kiwai Papuans." *Acta Societas Fennicae,* Tome 47, Helsingfors, 1917.

———. *The Kiwai Papuans of British New Guinea.* London: Macmillan, 1927.

Kurtachi*

Blackwood, B. M. *Both Sides of Buka Passage.* Oxford: Clarendon Press, 1935.
———. "Folk Stories from the Northern Solomons." *Folk-Lore,* Vol. 43, 1932.

Kwakiutl

Boas, F. *Kwakiutl Tales.* New York: Columbia University Press, 1910.
Ford, C. S. *Smoke from Their Fires.* New Haven: Yale University Press, 1941.

Kwoma

Whiting, J. W. M. *Becoming a Kwoma.* New Haven: Yale University Press, 1941.
———. Personal communication.

Lakher

Parry, N. E. *The Lakhers.* London: Macmillan, 1932.

Lamba

Doke, C. M. "Lamba Folk-Lore." *Memoirs of the American Folk-Lore Society,* Vol. 20, 1927.
———. *The Lambas of Northern Rhodesia.* London: Harrap, 1931.

Lango

Driberg, J. H. *The Lango.* London: Fisher and Unwin, 1923.

Lepcha*

Gorer, G. *Himalayan Village.* London: Michael Joseph, 1938.
Morris, J. *Living with Lepchas.* London: William Heinemann, 1938.

Lesu

Powdermaker, H. *Life in Lesu.* New York: W. W. Norton, 1933.

Lovedu*

Krige, E. J., and J. D. Krige. *The Realm of a Rain Queen*. London: Oxford University Press, 1943.

Malaita

Hogbin, H. I. *Experiments in Civilization*. London: George Routledge, 1939.

Ivens, W. G. *Melanesians of the South-East Solomon Islands*. London: Kegan, Paul, Trench, Trubner & Co., 1927.

Manam

Wedgewood, C. H. "Women in Manam." *Oceania*, Vol. 8, 1937.

Manus

Mead, M. *Growing Up in New Guinea*. New York: William Morrow, 1930.

————. "Kinship in the Admiralty Islands." *Anthropological Papers of the American Museum of Natural History*, Vol. 34, Part 2, 1934.

Maria Gond (Hill Maria)

Grigson, W. V. *The Maria Gonds of Bastar*. London: Oxford University Press, 1938.

Marquesas*

Handy, E. S. C. "Marquesan Legends." *Bernice P. Bishop Museum Bulletin*, No. 69, 1930.

————. "The Native Culture of the Marquesas." *Ibid.*, No. 9, 1923.

Linton, R. "Marquesan Culture," in A. Kardiner. *The Individual and His Society*. New York: Columbia University Press, 1939.

Marshalls*

Spoehr, A. "Majuro: a Village in the Marshall Islands." *Fieldiana: Anthropology*, Vol. 39. Chicago: Natural History Museum, 1949.

Masai

Hollis, A. C. *The Masai: Their Language and Folklore*. Oxford: Clarendon Press, 1905.

Leakey, L. S. B. "Some Notes on the Masai of Kenya Colony." *Journal of the Royal Anthropological Institute*, Vol. 60, 1930.

Mende*

Little, K. L. *The Mende of Sierra Leone.* London: Routledge and Kegan Paul, 1951.

Mohave

Devereux, G. "Heterosexual Behavior of the Mohave Indians," in G. Roheim (ed.), *Psychoanalysis and the Social Sciences,* Vol. II. New York: International Universities Press, 1950.

Murngin

Warner, W. L. *A Black Civilization.* New York: Harper & Brothers, 1937.

Nama Hottentot*

Hoernle, W. "The Social Organization of the Nama Hottentots of South Africa." *American Anthropologist,* Vol. 27, 1925.
Schapera, I. *The Khoisan Peoples of South Africa.* London: George Routledge, 1930.
Schultz, L. *Aus Namaland und Kalahari.* Jena: Gustav Fischer, 1907.

Navaho*

Evans, W., "The White Haired One Wrestles with Hosteen Bear." *Southwestern Lore,* Vol. 13, No. 4, 1948.
———. "Hosteen Bear Loses the Second Fall." *Ibid.,* Vol. 14, No. 1, 1948.
———. "Navajo Folk Lore." *Ibid.,* Vol. 14, No. 3, 1948.
Hill, W. W., and D. W. Hill. "Navaho Coyote Tales and Their Position in the Southern Athabascan Group." *Journal of American Folklore,* Vol. 58, 1945.
Kluckhohn, C. "Navaho Witchcraft." *Papers of the Peabody Museum of American Archeology and Ethnology,* Harvard University, Vol. 22, 1944.
———. "Some Aspects of Navaho Infancy and Childhood," in G. Roheim (ed.), *Psychoanalysis and the Social Sciences,* Vol. 1, 1947.
———. Personal communication.
Leighton, D., and C. Kluckhohn. *Children of the People.* Cambridge: Harvard University Press, 1947.
Matthews, W. "Navaho Legends." *Memoirs of the American Folklore Society,* Vol. 5, 1897.

*Nuer**

Evans-Pritchard, E. E. *Kinship and Marriage among the Nuer.* Oxford: Clarendon Press, 1951.

*Nyakusa**

Wilson, M. "Nyakusa Kinship," in A. R. Radcliffe-Brown and D. Forde (eds.), *African Systems of Kinship and Marriage.* London: Oxford University Press, 1950.
———. *Rituals of Kinship among the Nyakusa.* London: Oxford University Press, 1957.

*Ojibwa**

Jones, W. "Ojibwa Texts." *Publications of the American Ethnological Society,* Vol. 7, 1917.
Landes, R. "Ojibwa Sociology." *Columbia University Contributions to Anthropology,* Vol. 29, 1937.
Radin, P. *Some Myths and Tales of the Ojibwa of Southeastern Ontario.* Ottawa: Government Printing Bureau, 1914.

Ontong Java

Hogbin, H. I. "Education at Ontong Java, Solomon Islands." *American Anthropologist,* Vol. 33, 1931.
———. "The Sexual Life of the Natives of Ontong Java." *Journal of the Polynesian Society,* Vol. 40, 1931.
———. "The Social Organization of Ontong Java." *Oceania,* Vol. 1, 1930–31.

Ooldea

Berndt, R. M., and C. H. Berndt. "A Preliminary Report of Field Work in the Ooldea Region, Western South Australia." *Oceania,* Vols. 13 and 14, 1942, 1943.

*Paiute**

Kelly, I. T. "Ethnography of the Surprise Valley Paiute." *University of California Publications in American Archeology and Ethnology,* Vol. 31, No. 3, 1932.
Sapir, E. "The Southern Paiute Language." *Proceedings of the American Academy of Arts and Sciences,* Vol. 65, No. 1, 1930.
Whiting, B. "Paiute Sorcery." *Viking Fund Publications in Anthropology,* No. 15, 1950.

Papago*

Densmore, F. "Papago Music." *Bureau of American Ethnology Bulletin,* No. 90. Washington: Smithsonian Institute, 1929.
Underhill, R. M. *Social Organization of the Papago Indians.* New York: Columbia University Press, 1939.
Williams, T. R. "Papago Socialization." Unpublished manuscript.

Pukapuka*

Beaglehole, H., and P. Beaglehole. "Ethnology of Pukapuka." *Bernice P. Bishop Museum Bulletin,* No. 130, 1938.

Rajput

Triandis, L. M., and J. Hitchcock. "An Indian Village," in B. B. Whiting (ed.), *Child-Rearing in Six Societies.* New York: John Wiley & Sons, 1962.

Rwala Bedouin*

Musil, A. *The Manners and Customs of the Rwala Bedouin.* New York: Czech Academy of Sciences and Arts, Charles A. Crane, 1928.

Samoa*

Buck, P. H. "Samoan Material Culture." *Bernice P. Bishop Museum Bulletin,* No. 75, 1930.
Fraser, J. "Folk Songs and Myths from Samoa." *Journal of the Polynesian Society,* Vol. 5, 1896; Vol. 6, 1897.
———. "Folk Songs and Myths from Samoa." *Proceedings of the Royal Society of New South Wales,* Vols. 24, 25, and 26, 1892.
Mead, M. *Coming of Age in Samoa.* New York: New American Library for World Literature, 1949.
———. "Social Organization of Manua." *Bernice P. Bishop Museum Bulletin,* No. 76, 1930.
Stair, J. B. *Old Samoa.* London: The Religious Tract Society, 1897.
Turner, G. *Samoa: a Hundred Years Ago and Long Before.* London: Macmillan, 1884.

Sanpoil

Boas, F. *Folk-Tales of Salishan and Sahaptan Tribes.* New York: G. E. Stechert and Company, 1917.
Ray, V. F. "The Sanpoil and the Nespelem." *University of Washington Publications in Anthropology,* Vol. 5, 1932.

Ray, V. F. "Sanpoil Folk Tales." *Journal of American Folklore*, Vol. 46, 1933.

Siriono*

Holmberg, A. R. *Nomads of the Long Bow*. Washington: U.S. Government Printing Office, 1950.

Subanum*

Frake, C. Personal communication.

Tallensi*

Fortes, M. *The Web of Kinship among the Tallensi*. London: Oxford University Press, 1949.

Tanala*

Linton, R. "The Tanala: a Hill Tribe in Madagascar." *Publications of the Field Museum of Natural History, Anthropological Series*, Vol. 22, 1933.

Tarahumara

Bennett, W. C., and R. M. Zingg. *The Tarahumara*. Chicago: University of Chicago Press, 1935.

Tarasco

Beals, R. L. *Cheran: a Sierra Tarascan Village*. Washington: U.S. Government Printing Office, 1946.

Thonga*

Junod, H. A. *The Life of a South African Tribe*. London: The Macmillan Company, 1927.

Tiv*

Akiga. *Akiga's Story*. London: Oxford University Press, 1939.
Bowen, E. S. *Return to Laughter*. London: Victor Gollancz, 1954.
Downes, R. M. *The Tiv Tribe*. Kaduna: The Government Printer, 1933.

Trobriands*

Malinowski, B. *The Sexual Life of Savages in Northwest Melanesia*. New York: Horace Liveright, 1929.

————. *Argonauts of the Western Pacific.* London: George Routledge, 1922.

Truk

Fischer, J. L. Personal communication.
Gladwin, T., and S. B. Sarason. "Truk: Man in Paradise." *Viking Fund Publications in Anthropology,* No. 20, 1953.
Goodenough, W. F. *Property, Kin and Community on Truk.* New Haven: Yale University Press, 1951.

Tungus

Shirokogoroff, S. M. *Social Organization of the Northern Tungus.* Shanghai: The Commercial Press, 1929.

Ulithi

Lessa, W. A. "The Ethnography of Ulithi Atoll." Doctoral thesis, University of California at Los Angeles, 1950.

Warrau

Steward, J. H. *Handbook of South American Indians,* Vol. 3. Washington: U.S. Government Printing Office, 1947.

Witoto

Ford, C. S. "A Comparative Study of Human Reproduction." *Yale University Publications in Anthropology,* No. 32, 1945.

Wogeo

Hogbin, H. I. "A New Guinea Childhood: From Weaning until the Eighth Year in Wogeo." *Oceania,* Vol. 21, 1946.

Zapotec

Nader, L. Personal communication.
Radin, P. "An Historical Legend of the Zapotecs." *Ibero-Americana,* Vol. 9, 1935.
————. "Zapotec Texts: Dialect of Juchitan-Tehuano." *International Journal of American Linguistics,* Vol. 12, No. 3, 1946.

GENERAL
BIBLIOGRAPHY

Anthony, A. S. "A Cross-Cultural Study of Factors Relating to Male Initiation Rites and Genital Operations." Doctoral Thesis, Harvard University, 1955.

Armitage, P. "Tests for Linear Trends in Proportions and Frequencies." *Biometrics,* 11 (1955), 376–386.

Ayres, B. C. "A Cross-Cultural Study of Factors Relating to Pregnancy Taboos." Doctoral Thesis, Radcliffe College, 1954.

Bacon, M., H. Barry, and I. L. Child. Unpublished ratings of socialization practices (mimeographed 1954). Department of Psychology, Yale University.

Balint, A. *The Early Years of Life.* New York: Basic Books, 1954.

Bennett, W. C., and R. M. Zingg. *The Tarahumara.* Chicago: University of Chicago Press, 1935.

Berndt, R. M., and C. H. Berndt. "A Preliminary Report of Field Work in the Ooldea Region, Western South Australia." *Oceania,* 13 and 14 (1942 and 1943).

Blackwood, B. M. *Both Sides of Buka Passage.* Oxford: Clarendon Press, 1935.

Bowen, E. S. *Return to Laughter.* London: Victor Gollancz, 1954.

Burrows, E. S. "The People of Ifaluk," unpublished manuscript, 1948. Coordinated Investigation of Micronesian Anthropology, Pacific Science Board, National Research Council, Washington, D.C.

Covarrubias, M. *Island of Bali.* New York: Alfred A. Knopf, 1937.

Dollard, J., and N. E. Miller. *Personality and Psychotherapy*. New York: McGraw-Hill, 1950.

Edwards, A. L. *Statistical Methods for the Behavioral Sciences*. New York: Holt, Rinehart, Winston, 1954.

Eggan, F. *Social Anthropology of North American Tribes*. Chicago: University of Chicago Press, 1937.

Evans-Pritchard, E. E. *Witchcraft, Oracles and Magic among the Azande*. Oxford: Clarendon Press, 1937.

———. "Social Character of Bride-Wealth, with Special Reference to the Azande." *Man*, Vol. 34, 1934.

Fenichel, O. *The Psychoanalytic Theory of Neurosis*. New York: W. W. Norton, 1945.

Finney, D. J. "The Fisher-Yates Test of Significance in 2×2 Contingency Tables." *Biometrics*, 35 (June, 1948).

Fischer, J. L., and J. W. M. Whiting. "Cross-cultural Ratings of Totemism with Food Taboos" (mimeographed). Laboratory of Human Development, Harvard University.

Ford, C. S. "A Comparative Study of Human Reproduction," *Yale University Publications in Anthropology*, No. 32 (1945).

——— and F. A. Beach. *Patterns of Sexual Behavior*. New York: Harper & Brothers, 1951.

Fortes, M. *The Web of Kinship among the Tallensi*. London: Oxford University Press, 1949.

Frazer, J. G. *The Golden Bough*. New York: Macmillan, 1951.

Freud, S. *New Introductory Lectures on Psychoanalysis*. New York: W. W. Norton, 1933.

———. *The Problem of Anxiety*. New York: W. W. Norton, 1936.

———. *Totem and Taboo*. New York: W. W. Norton, 1950.

———. "Analysis of a Phobia of a Five-Year-Old Boy." *Collected Papers*, Vol. II, pp. 149–289. London: The Hogarth Press, 1956.

———. "Formulations Regarding the Two Principles in Mental Functioning." *Ibid.*, pp. 13–21.

———. "The Primary and Secondary Processes—Repression." *The Interpretation of Dreams*, pp. 588–609. New York: Basic Books, 1958.

Goldenweiser, A. "The Origin of Totemism." *American Anthropologist*, 14 (1912), 600–607.

Gorer, G. *Himalayan Village*. London: Michael Joseph, 1938.

Green, B. F. "Attitude Measurement," in Gardner Lindzey (ed.), *Handbook of Social Psychology*, Vol. I, pp. 335–369. Reading, Mass.: Addison-Wesley, 1954.

Greenberg, J. H. "Historical Linguistics and Unwritten Languages," in

A. L. Kroeber (ed.) *Anthropology Today,* pp. 265–286. Chicago: University of Chicago Press, 1953.

Grinnell, G. B. *The Cheyenne Indians.* New Haven: Yale University Press, 1923.

Halverson, H. M. "Genital and Sphincter Behavior in the Male Infant," *Pedagogical Seminar and Journal of Genetic Psychology,* 56 (1938), 95–135.

Heath, D. B. "Sexual Division of Labor and Cross-Cultural Research," *Social Forces,* 37 (1958), 77–79.

Henry, J., and Z. Henry. "Doll Play of Pilaga Indian Children," *Research Monographs,* No. 4. American Orthopsychiatric Association, 1944.

Hogbin, H. I. "Education at Ontong Java, Solomon Islands." *American Anthropologist,* Vol. 33, 1931.

———. "The Sexual Life of the Natives of Ontong Java." *Journal of the Polynesian Society,* Vol. 40, 1931.

———. "The Social Organization of Ontong Java." *Oceania,* Vol. 1, 1930–31.

Hoijer, H. "Chiricahua and Mescalero Apache Texts," *University of Chicago Publications in Anthropology. Linguistics Series,* 8 (1938).

Horney, K. *The Neurotic Personality of Our Time.* New York: W. W. Norton, 1937.

Kinsey, A. C., W. B. Pomeroy, and C. E. Martin. *Sexual Behavior in the Human Male.* Philadelphia: W. B. Saunders, 1948.

Klein, M. *Contributions to Psycho-Analysis: 1921–1945.* London: The Hogarth Press, 1948.

Kluckhohn, C. "Some Aspects of Navaho Infancy and Childhood," in G. Roheim (ed.), *Pychoanalysis and the Social Sciences,* Vol. I, pp. 37–86. New York: International Universities Press, 1944.

———. "Navaho Witchcraft," *Papers of the Peabody Museum of American Archeology and Ethnology,* 22 (1944), Harvard University.

Lessa, W. A., and E. Z. Vogt. *Reader in Comparative Religion.* Evanston, Ill.: Row, Peterson, 1958.

McNemar, Q. *Psychological Statistics.* New York: John Wiley, 1949.

Mullahy, P. *Oedipus, Myth and Complex.* New York: Hermitage House, 1952.

Munroe, R. L. *Schools of Psychoanalytic Thought.* New York: The Dryden Press, 1955.

Murdock, G. P. *Social Structure.* New York: Macmillan, 1949.

———. "World Ethnographic Sample," *American Anthropologist,* 59 (1957).

Murdock G. P., and J. W. M. Whiting. "Cultural Determination of Parental Attitudes: The Relationship between the Social Structure,

Particularly Family Structure, and Parental Behavior," in M. J. E. Senn (ed.), *Problems of Infancy and Childhood*. New York: Josiah Macy Foundation, 1951.

Neihardt, J. G. *When the Tree Flowered*. New York: Macmillan, 1951.

Nimenaju, C. "The Eastern Timbira," tr. and ed. by R. H. Lowie, *University of California Publications in American Archeology and Ethnology*, 16 (1946).

Opler, M. E. *An Apache Life Way*. Chicago: University of Chicago Press, 1941.

Radcliffe-Brown, A. R. "On Joking Relationships," *Africa* 13 (1940), 195–210.

Ramsey, G. V. "The Sexual Development of Boys," *American Journal of Psychology*, 56 (1943), 217–234.

Rapaport, D. *Organization and Pathology of Thought*. New York: Columbia University Press, 1951.

Roheim, G. *The Eternal Ones of the Dream: A Psychoanalytic Interpretation of Australian Myth and Ritual*. New York: International Universities Press, 1945.

————. "Introduction: Psychoanalysis and Anthropology," in G. Roheim (ed.), *Psychoanalysis and the Social Sciences*, Vol. I, pp. 9–33. New York: International Universities Press, 1947.

————. "The Oedipus Complex, Magic and Culture," *ibid.*, Vol. II (1950), pp. 173–229.

————. *Psychoanalysis and Anthropology*. New York: International Universities Press, 1950.

Sachs, W. *Psychoanalysis*. London: Cassell & Co., 1934.

Schroetter, K. "Experimental Dreams," in D. Rapaport (ed.), *Organization and Pathology of Thought*. New York: Columbia University Press, 1951. pp. 234–248.

Spitz, R. A., and K. M. Wolf. "Autoeroticism—Some Empirical Findings and Hypotheses on Three of Its Manifestations in the First Year of Life," in A. Freud, et al. (eds.), *The Psychoanalytic Study of the Child*, 3 and 4: 85–120. New York: International Universities Press, 1949.

Thompson, C. *Psychoanalysis: Evolution and Development*. New York: Hermitage House, 1951.

Thompson, L. "Southern Lau, Fiji: An Ethnography," *Bernice P. Bishop Museum Bulletin* No. 162. 1940.

Whiting, B. "Paiute Sorcery," *Viking Fund Publications in Anthropology*, No. 15 (1950).

Whiting, J. W. M. "The Cross Cultural Method," in G. Lindzey (ed.), *Handbook of Social Psychology*, 1: 523–531. Reading, Mass.: Addison-Wesley, 1954.

Whiting, W. J. M., and I. L. Child. *Child Training and Personality*. New Haven: Yale University Press, 1953.

———— and R. G. D'Andrade. Unpublished ratings. Laboratory of Human Development, Harvard University.

———— and R. Kluckhohn. Unpublished ratings of duration of the post partum sex taboo. Laboratory of Human Development, Harvard University.

————, R. Kluckhohn, and A. Anthony. "The Function of Male Initiation Ceremonies at Puberty," in E. E. Maccoby, T. M. Newcomb, and E. L. Hartley (eds.), *Readings in Social Psychology*, 3rd ed. New York: Holt, Rinehart, Winston, 1958.

————, R. Kluckhohn, and A. Anthony. Unpublished ratings of initiation ceremonies. Laboratory of Human Development, Harvard University.

Wilson, M. "Nyakusa Kinship," in A. R. Radcliffe-Brown and D. Forde (eds.), *African Systems of Kinship and Marriage*. London: Oxford University Press, 1950.

NAME INDEX

Aginsky, B. W., 219
Anthony, A., 55, 75, 152, 154, 159, 183
Arpad, 161–163
Ayres, B. C., 54, 201

Bacon, M., 55, 86, 100
Barry, H., 55, 86, 100
Beach, F. A., 55, 228

Child, I. L., 11, 12, 22, 55, 86, 100, 104, 167, 171n, 201

D'Andrade, R. G., 5, 7, 8, 10n, 55, 124, 148, 213, 244
Driver, H., 219
Drucker, P., 219
DuBoise, C., 219

Essene, F., 219

Fenichel, O., 16, 17, 100
Ferenczi, S., 161
Fischer, J. L., 55, 161
Ford, C. S., 55, 80n, 120, 228
Frake, C., 219
Frazer, J. G., 86
Freud, S., 16–17, 24, 92, 152, 160

Hans, 161
Harley, J. K., 57
Heath, D. B., 121
Henry, J., 22, 26, 34–35
Henry, Z., 22, 26, 34–35
Horner, G., 212, 219

Kinsey, A. C., 19, 24, 28
Klein, M., 30, 38
Kluckhohn, C., 20, 21, 81, 219
Kluckhohn, R., 3, 3n, 55, 67, 75, 152, 154, 183, 213, 246

267

McCall, D., 219
Martin, C. E., 19, 24, 28
Murdock, G. P., 5, 7, 8, 55, 69, 121,
    137, 147, 193, 195

Pomeroy, W. B., 19, 24, 28

Ramsey, G. V., 24
Roheim, G., 47, 85, 129

Schroetter, K., 42
Spitz, R., 35, 36, 37

Voegelin, C., 220

Whiting, J. W. M., 3, 3n, 5, 7, 8,
    10n, 11, 22, 55, 67, 75, 86, 100,
    104, 148, 152, 154, 161, 167,
    171n, 183, 201, 213, 245, 246
Wolf, K., 35, 36, 37

SUBJECT INDEX

Aggression training, severity of, 55, 104, 105, 112
Araucanian kin-avoidance, 125
Avoidance, burden of, 114
  and phobia, 94, 130–131, 151

Balinese menstrual taboos, 87–88
Breasts as sexual stimuli, 56, 67, 81, 83–84, 227–229
  coder agreement, 228
  coders, 228
  coding rules for, 227–228
  ratings of, 229

California sample, 138–140, 145, 219–221
Cases, 49–50
Castration anxiety, 33, 46, 47, 183
  causes, 86, 97–98, 104–112, 119, 183
  composite predicter of, 56, 112–113, 115

Castration anxiety (*cont.*)
  father and, 104–112
  and menstrual taboos, 18, 85, 91–96, 119
  as Oedipal fear characteristic of males, 92–93
  and overt preoccupation with castration, 118
  as unmeasured intervening variable, 113
Change of residence for adolescent boys, 13, 55, 78, 79, 84
Cheating, precautions against, 69–70
Cheyenne brother-sister avoidance, 125–126
Children's sexuality, 18, 19–45
  characterized, 24–26, 28–29, 33
  masturbation, 35–37
  punishment for masturbation, 55, 100, 102

Children's sexuality (*cont.*)
punishment for sexual activity, 100
range of sexual stimuli, 24–26
sex play, 19
sexual acting out, 22
Chiricahua Apache kin-avoidance, 128
Coder agreement, 52–53, 210, 217–218
Coders, 52, 53
Coding, 51–53, 57, 70
Coding rules, 51–53, 70, 206–210, 214–217
Contingency coefficients, 172, 173
Correlation matrix, 172–173
Correlations, 70–71, 183
network of, 1, 2, 15
Culture areas, 69
and nonindependence of cases, 193–198
Customs, underlying cross-cultural variables, 51

Dependency, avoidance therapy, 55, 171n
explanations for illness, 55, 171n
initial indulgence of, 10–11, 55
Descent, rules of, 56, 122, 147–148
unilineal kin groups, 147–148
Diluted marriage variables, 2, 7, 40n
correlates of, 8–13
holding constant, 175–181
and mother-child closeness, 8–13
possible causes of, 7–8
Division of labor by sex, 55
Dreams, hypnotically induced, 42–44

Eastern Timbira, 128
Ethnographers, data-collection methods of, 63–65
Ethnographies, 56–58–66
European menstrual taboos, 86–87
Extra-marital liaisons prohibited, 80n

Father's obedience demands and disciplinary role, 56, 108, 110, 111, 112, 230–233
coder agreement, 233
coders, 233
coding rules for, 230–232
evaluation of ratings, 233
ratings of, 233
Fear of others, 55, 170–171
correlated with post partum sex taboo, 170, 171
Folklore, castration-suggestive incidents in, 55, 113–118
coder agreement, 241
coders, 241
coding rules, 234–240
effects of castration anxiety on, 114
father-son conflict in, 55, 159, 239–240
predictions concerning, 116
sample, 234
scores on variables, 241–243
sexual intercourse usually punished in, 54, 55, 80, 201, 203, 204, 205, 240, 243

Hypothesis-testing, cause and effect, 73, 74
conclusions drawn from data, 70–76
logical sequence of, 74–75

Hypothesis-testing (*cont.*)
"meanings" imputed to variables, 74

Initiation ceremonies for adolescent boys, 2, 3n, 13, 51, 55, 151, 152–159, 183
defined and described, 152–156
and genital operations, 152–153
marginal cases, 153
sample for, 156n
test of the hypothesis concerning, 156–157
Initiation ceremonies for girls, 159

Joking relationships, 56, 144

Kin-avoidances, 2, 13–14, 47, 53, 58–62, 67, 74, 124–150, 183
bonus findings, 137–146
burden of, 128
coder agreement, 217–218
coders, 213
coding rules, 214–217
between cross-sex persons, 143–145, 149
customs, 27
defined and described, 124–129
distribution among kin and generation relationships, 143
duration of, 226
evaluation of ratings, 225–226
focal, with extensions, 128, 137–143, 149
functionalist explanations for, 146–147
Guttman scale, 146, 218–226
hypothesis testing, 134–136
"meaning" of, 124
measurement of, 132–133, 213–226

Kin-avoidances (*cont.*)
patterning of, 56
persons rarely avoided, 141–144
predictions concerning, 132
and propinquity, 147–149
rarity of reported absences, 217–219
relationships, 127–128
sample for, 213
and social structure, 146–149
syndrome, 128, 144, 149
Kwakiutl menstrual taboos, 88

Linguistic groupings and nonindependence of cases, 193, 195

Maternal seduction, 97–98
Measurement, error in, 66
step-by-step, 56–57
Menstrual pads, 56, 120–121
Menstrual taboos, 2, 14, 18, 46, 47, 51, 74, 85–123, 159, 203
and castration anxiety, 18, 91–96, 119
coder agreement, 210
coders, 210
coding and rating of, 86, 89, 206–212
coding rules, 206–210
conclusions from hypothesis-testing, 119
as a consequent variable, 86
and danger to men, 96–97
described, 86–88
disgust for feces, 120
Guttman scale, 86, 89–90, 210–212
hypothesis concerning, 56
hypothesis-testing, 56–57
possible causes for, 119–123

Menstrual taboos (*cont.*)
   predictions concerning, 86
   and sex anxiety, 94–95
   societies' scores on, 90, 211
   summary of evidence on, 118
   widely distributed, 88
Mother-child households, 2, 6, 8–
   13, 55, 175–181
   and polygyny, 7
   ratings of, 7, 244–245

Navaho, 21
No information, cases of, 63, 67
Nuclear family households, 121,
   122
Nursing, duration of (age of weaning), 12–13, 22, 55, 98
   sexual pleasure during, 20, 21,
   34
Nurturance, diffusion of, 55, 99–
   101

Obedience, pressure for, 55, 108
   severity of punishment for disobedience, 55, 106, 108, 109
Oedipal rivalry, 103–112, 154, 155,
   156, 158–159, 161, 169, 183
Oedipal sex attraction, 45–46, 47,
   78, 132, 154, 158, 183
   arousal of, 34–42
   defined, 38–39, 41–42
Oedipus complex, 152, 161
   defined, 16–18
   effects of, 2, 17, 18, 42–47
Oedipus complex hypothesis, 1, 3n,
   17, 48, 84, 124, 151, 158, 182
   assumptions added to, 183
   evidence bearing on, 48, 183–185
   girls ignored in, 41
   testing of, 182

P values, 71–74, 76, 189
Phobia, phobia and institutionalized avoidance, 94, 130–131
   phobic attitude toward incest,
   47, 183
Physical punishment, 55, 104, 106,
   112
Pilaga, 22, 26–28, 34–35
Polygny, 2, 5, 8–13, 55, 121, 122,
   175–181
   proposed consequences of, 6
   ratings of, 5, 6, 241–245
Post partum sex taboo, 2, 3, 3n, 8–
   13, 35, 40, 51, 55, 67, 74, 77–
   84, 97–98, 99, 112, 132, 134–
   136, 147, 151, 156, 157, 159,
   183, 198–199, 203
   distribution of, 3
   duration of, 3
   as hypothesized antecedent variable, 174, 175, 176, 178, 179,
   180, 181
   proposed consequences of, 4, 17–
   18
   ratings of, 3, 4, 241–243
   reasons for, 5, 8
Pregnancy sex taboo, 35, 54, 80,
   200, 201, 204, 205
Premarital intercourse prohibited,
   54, 55, 80, 200, 203, 204, 205

Reported absences, rarity of, 63
Research method, 49–76
   antecedent and consequent variables, 2, 13–15, 46, 47, 74, 86,
   113, 174–185
   prediction, 74–76, 84, 86, 113n,
   132, 151, 183
   replication, 70

Research method (*cont.*)

Residence, rules of, 55, 122, 147–148

    exogamous communities, 147–148

Samples, choice of, 66–69, 70, 72, 76, 156n, 201

    civilized societies excluded from, 68, 76

    for kin-avoidances, 213

    nonindependence of cases, 69, 189–199

    primitive societies in, 49–50

    size of, 71–72

Scales, 53, 54, 56, 70

    composite indices, 54, 67, 112, 200–205

    Guttman, 53, 54, 57, 86, 90–91, 133, 146, 210–212, 218–226

Sex anxiety, 2, 14, 17, 42, 46, 54, 151

    composite index of, 80–81, 82, 84, 112, 200–205

    correlation matrix, 202–204

    face validity, 203

    sample selection, 201

    societies' scores on, 81, 203–205

Sex training, severity of, 45, 51, 54, 55, 77–78, 80, 84, 102, 103, 112, 200, 201, 204, 205

Sexual avoidance therapy, 54, 55, 81, 200, 201, 204, 205

Sexual explanations for illness, 54, 55, 80, 200, 201, 204, 205

Sleeping arrangements, mother-infant, 9

    propinquity of, 55, 148–149

Sorcery, 2, 14, 51, 152, 164–169

    as burden on social intercourse, 166

    coding of, 167

    defined and described, 165–166

    as explanation for misfortune, 165–167

    "fear of humans," 55

    interpretation of, 166–167

    and paranoia, 166

Thonga initiations, 155–156

Toilet training, severity of, 120

Totemism, 2, 14, 151, 152, 159–164

    correlated with post partum sex taboo, 164, 165

    defined and described, 159–161

    with food taboos, 55, 160–161

    Freud's interpretation of, 161–164

Unconscious fantasy, 17–18, 29, 32–33, 38, 46

    castration anxiety as, 119

    concerning sex, 42, 44–46

    primary process, 29

Variables, 50–51

    antecedent and consequent, 2, 13–15, 46, 47, 74, 86, 113

    societies' scores on, 51, 53, 54, 81

    types of, 64–66

Women, contribution to subsistence economy, 121

    status of, 122